Technology, Open Learning and Distance Education

Major changes are needed in the post-secondary and workplace training systems to meet the need for a higher skilled workforce, and for lifelong learning in an increasingly complex society. Recent technological developments provide an opportunity for radical change through the application of open and distance learning. Those countries that harness the power of telecommunications and computing to the education and training needs of the workplace will be the economic leaders of the 21st century.

However, there are still justifiable concerns about the quality and cost-effectiveness of technological applications to teaching and learning. This book provides a guide for policy-makers, education and training planners, senior educational administrators, teachers and trainers regarding the selection and use of modern technologies for open and flexible learning. It suggests a practical decision-making framework, the ACTIONS model:

Access: how accessible is a particular technology for learners?
Costs: what is the cost structure of each technology?
Teaching functions: what are the best teaching applications for this technology?
Interactivity and user-friendliness: how easy is it to use?
Organisational issues: what changes in organisation need to be made?
Novelty: how new is this technology?
Speed: how quickly can courses be mounted with this technology?

Using this framework, Tony Bates analyses the strengths and weaknesses of each technology, and offers the first comprehensive, comparative cost analysis of each. Finally, he provides a vision of technology-based open learning for the 21st century.

Tony Bates is Executive Director for Research, Strategic Planning and Information Technology at the Open Learning Agency in British Columbia. Prior to this he was Professor of Educational Media Research at the Open University, UK, where he was one of the founding members of staff. He is the author of four books and many papers and has worked as a consultant in over 30 countries.

Routledge studies in distance education
Series editor: Desmond Keegan

Theoretical Principles of Distance Education
Edited by Desmond Keegan

Distance Education: New Perspectives
Edited by Keith Harry, Magnus John and Desmond Keegan

Collaboration in Distance Education
Edited by Louise Moran and Ian Mugridge

Otto Peters on Distance Education
Edited by Desmond Keegan

Theory and Practice in Distance Education
Börje Holmberg

Technology, Open Learning and Distance Education

A. W. (Tony) Bates

London and New York

First published 1995
by Routledge
11 New Fetter Lane, London EC4P 4EE

Simultaneously published in the USA and Canada
by Routledge
29 West 35th Street, New York, NY 10001

Reprinted in 1997 (twice), 1999

Routledge is an imprint of the Taylor & Francis Group

Typeset in Times by J&L Composition Ltd, Filey, North Yorkshire

Printed and bound in Great Britain by
TJ International Ltd, Padstow, Cornwall

British Library Cataloguing in Publication Data
A catalogue record for this book is available from the British Library

Library of Congress Cataloguing in Publication Data
A catalogue record for this book is available

ISBN 0–415–11682–1 (hbk)
ISBN 0–415–12799–8 (pbk)

Contents

Illustrations

FIGURES

TABLES

Acknowledgements

This book should be dedicated to those who don't back up their computer work. Three days before emigrating to Canada in 1989, we were moving out of our house. I brought down my computer and placed it with my briefcase in the front hallway. In the briefcase was my passport and immigrant visa, plus a computer disk containing much of the data I intended to use in this book. The removal men left the front door open, someone walked in from the street and stole both my briefcase and my computer. For several hours afterwards, I gave a compelling imitation of a headless chicken.

I did get a new passport and visa, and eventually full Canadian citizenship, but never saw the briefcase or computer again. Fortunately, a colleague, Paul Lefrère, had earlier asked to use some of the data and without my knowing had copied the whole disk. Several months later, I got my data back when he realised what had happened! So the first acknowledgement is to Paul.

The second acknowledgement is to Lord Perry of Walton, who gave me a job 25 years ago as a junior researcher at the British Open University when it was first established, and no one really knew what it was going to be. It was the start of a remarkably rewarding 20 years, which brings me to acknowledge the many inspiring academic and BBC colleagues who made it all happen, and especially those who worked in the Audio-Visual Media Research Group. Most of all, though, I want to acknowledge Walter Perry's pragmatism and determination; he more than anyone created a unique institution that has revolutionised higher education.

I also want to acknowledge the influence of Glen Farrell, the President of the Open Learning Agency in British Columbia, partly for making it possible for me to move to Canada, but most of all for his vision and its influence on me. The good bits of the last chapter are really his. I am also indebted to other colleagues at OLA who are pioneering exciting new approaches to open learning, and who have provided many ideas and much stimulus for this book. Terry Evans, John Tiffin, Terry Hedegaard and Desmond Keegan each read the first draft, and I am grateful for their valuable and helpful comments. Helen Fairlie provided invaluable support and encouragement when I most needed it.

In addition, I would like to thank the Commonweatlh of Learning for the use of some of the material I prepared for them on selecting technology. Some other parts of this book are not too different from what I have published previously in articles or chapters in other books or journals, and I would like to thank the publishers and editors for their cooperation. My thanks also go to those authors and their publishers who gave permission for quotations and their blessing (but not necessarily their endorsement) for my paraphrases of their work. I do recommend you read the originals.

Lastly, my wife, Pat, deserves special thanks. Without her, this book would have been completed at least a couple of years sooner; however, life would not have been so much fun!

1 Executive summary

What have we learned about technology, open learning and decision-making?

STARTING AT THE BACK

This book is aimed at the rapidly increasing number of people in educational institutions, government departments, training organisations, and businesses who are seeking to find innovative and more cost-effective means to provide quality education and training to their students or clients, and who are considering the use of technology-based open learning and distance education to meet those needs.

Because this book is aimed at decision-makers, it starts with my main conclusions, to enable you to decide whether this is the kind of book you want to read. (This should also appeal to people like my wife who likes to read the last page of a detective story to find out who did it, before reading the rest of the book – instructional designers call this an 'advanced organiser'.)

However, one word of warning. The appropriate choice and use of technologies will depend on the particular context in which they are used. What the book attempts to do is to provide a *methodology* by which decision-makers can reach their own conclusions. Thus if you were to apply the methodology to your own context, you may well come to different conclusions from mine, which is why I strongly recommend you to read the other chapters as well! So if you want to avoid being influenced by my conclusions, skip this chapter and come back to it after Chapter 10.

CRITERIA FOR DECISION-MAKING

I suggest that decision-making should be based on an analysis of questions that each institution needs to ask, grouped under the following critieria:

A Access: how accessible is a particular technology for learners? How flexible is it for a particular target group?

C Costs: what is the cost structure of each technology? What is the unit cost per learner?

T Teaching and learning: what kinds of learning are needed? What instructional approaches will best meet these needs? What are the best technologies for supporting this teaching and learning?

I   Interactivity and user-friendliness: what kind of interaction does this technology enable? How easy is it to use?

O   Organisational issues: what are the organisational requirements, and the barriers to be removed, before this technology can be used successfully? What changes in organisation need to be made?

N   Novelty: how new is this technology?

S   Speed: how quickly can courses be mounted with this technology? How quickly can materials be changed?

Access

Access is usually the most important criterion for deciding on the appropriateness of a technology for open or distance learning.

Delivery to the home is usually the best way to widen access. Most people can learn at home. In terms of home access, print, audio cassettes, video cassettes, and the telephone are the most appropriate technologies in most developed countries.

Access depends on the particular priority target groups to be reached. Increasingly in open and distance learning, the 'market' is fragmenting into different types of target group: for instance, independent distance learners studying primarily at home, those in the workforce needing training, those who are combining part-time study with work, those who are studying full-time, but only partly on-campus, or those who are combining one or more of these situations. For an increasing number of people, learning at the workplace is becoming more and more important. For particular target groups, learning at local centres or 'satellite' campuses may also be viable. The appropriate technology mix then depends on the nature of the target group and their location.

Even within these different 'markets', learners are not a homogeneous mass, but vary a great deal more in terms of educational background, income, age and learning experience. This diversity of the student body is growing fast. It will become increasingly important for educational organisations to be able to deliver their teaching in a variety of techno-logical formats, depending on the needs of the individual, the teaching context, and the target groups to be reached.

In distance teaching, adequate inter-personal student support, in terms of contact with both 'human' counsellors and tutors, and with other students, is critical. This often leads to great importance being placed on local study or learning centres. Also, the establishment of local learning centres enables more sophisticated two-way equipment to be used than could be used for purely home-based students.

However, a number of issues arise from the placing of equipment in local centres. Quite difficult policy decisions need to be made about the relative importance of course delivery through local centres or at home, and the extent to which students should be obliged to attend local centres. Access depends on the willingness and ability of the target group to get to local centres regularly. For instance, some learners will never attend because the local centre is not open at the times that are convenient for them, or because it is too far away, and/or because they feel they can use their time better by studying at home. Making attendance compulsory at a local centre can reduce substantially the openness of distance education. There is a tendency then to make use of technology at a centre optional rather than essential.

It is a mistake though to make some technologies 'optional', in the sense that students can pass examinations or do assignments without using a particular technology, just because some potential students will not have access to that technology. Experience suggests that course designers will avoid delivering 'essential' material via any technology which is 'optional'; and those who do have access to the technology soon recognise that they can pass the course without studying the optional material, so even they stop using that particular technology.

Lastly, although a technology may be widely available in people's homes, it may still not be very accessible. There is a requirement with broadcasting for instance to be at a set place and at a set time. Even a combination of two transmissions at different peak times will never reach more than 80 per cent of enrolled students on a course. When transmissions are at inconvenient times, less than half the students will actually see the programme on transmission.

Institutions and course designers are often caught between ensuring access to all, and using more powerful teaching technologies. Distance teaching institutions often want to make use of newer technologies, but are held back by the need to reach minority groups, the working poor, or otherwise disadvantaged learners who do not have access to a wide range of technologies.

Costs

Cost is also a strong discriminator between technologies. It is necessary to distinguish between one-way technologies, which do not include the very substantial additional costs of tutorial support systems, and two-way technologies, in which tutorial-style interaction is usually incorporated. Also, it is important to distinguish between the cost of technologies for courses with low student numbers, and those with large student numbers. Lastly, each institution needs to analyse its own cost structures, as local context and differing assumptions about costs will influence the outcome of such an analysis.

Nevertheless, Figures 1.1 and 1.2 (derived from Table 1.1 on p. 7)

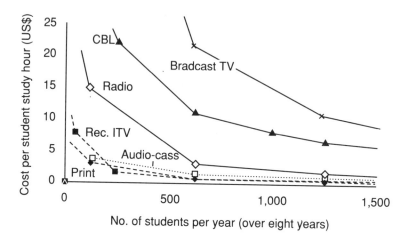

Figure 1.1 Comparative costs of onc-way technologies
Source: Derived from Table 1.1
Note: Rec. ITV = pre-recorded instructional television; costs are for 10 courses per annum

indicate that there are some clear cost differences between technologies in open and distance learning.

Print, and pre-recorded instructional television (lectures), appear to be the lowest cost one-way technologies. A combination of print and audio cassettes appears cost-effective for large courses (500 or more), at less than US$2 per student study hour. Radio really needs to get up to 1,000 students or more to be comparable in cost to most of the other one-way technologies. Broadcast TV made by educational broadcasting organisations is clearly the most expensive technology for courses with 2,000 students or less, but starts to become competitive in cost for very large numbers of students per course. Re-programmed computer-based learning is also expensive.

It must be remembered that additional costs will be necessary for all these one-way technologies to cover tutorial activities or to provide student feedback and inter-personal interaction through other technologies.

Looking at two-way technologies (Figure 1.2), computer conferencing is a low-cost medium. Pre-recorded instructional television (see Figure 1.1) is very much cheaper than live, interactive lectures. Live interactive broadcasts and video conferencing are very expensive technologies, at all levels of output, and at all levels of student numbers. Even BBC-produced television broadcasts become cheaper per student study hour than interactive television and video conferencing, for more than 750 students per course.

Thus the following technologies are relatively low cost for the following course sizes:

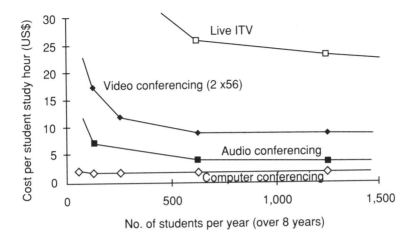

Figure 1.2 Comparative costs of two-way technologies
Source: Derived from Table 1.1

Small (below 250 p.a.)	*Medium* (250–625 p.a.)	*Large* (More than 1,000 p.a.)
Print	Print	Print
Audio cassettes	Audio cassettes	Audio cassettes
Pre-recorded ITV	Pre-recorded ITV	Pre-recorded ITV
Computer conferencing		Radio
(Less than $2 per student contact hour)	(Less than $1.50 per student contact hour)	(Less than $1.50 per student contact hour)

A combination of pre-recorded instructional television, or print and audio cassettes, *and* computer conferencing is much cheaper than video conferencing or live interactive televised lectures or computer-based learning, and provides the necessary tutorial aspect.

A number of general points can be made about the balance of costs for different technologies:

● the major cost of using technologies for distance teaching is in production and hence recurrent, rather than capital: for instance, the yearly recurrent cost often exceeds the total start-up capital cost. In general, the recurrent costs of producing good quality technology-based materials tend to be underestimated;
● audio cassettes and radio have low fixed *and* low variable costs;
● face-to-face teaching, computer-mediated communication and tutor-mediated telecourses have low fixed costs but high variable costs, i.e. costs increase with student numbers;

- good quality broadcast television has high fixed costs and zero variable costs;
- pre-programmed computer-based learning (CBL) and multimedia have high fixed and high variable costs, if work-stations are to be provided;
- since production is the main cost, and hence fixed for any course, for most one-way technologies currently used in autonomous distance teaching institutions, *fixed costs usually far exceed variable costs*. This means that the economies of scale apply to one-way technologies: the more students, the more cost-effective these technologies become;
- two-way technologies, such as audio and computer conferencing, reduce fixed costs, but have high variable costs. Thus, while suitable for courses with relatively low student numbers, they will be increasingly expensive for courses with large student numbers. Even these technologies, though, usually need more than 100 students per course per annum to offset the fixed costs;
- transmission costs are insignificant compared with production costs for most technologies. It is important then to consider *all* costs when deciding on technologies.

It can be seen then that even for the newer, interactive technologies, student numbers are critical. Also, the long-term view needs to be taken: how will the costs work out over a number of years? Lastly, what may look like a low cost for one institution using two-way technologies may be more expensive when added across institutions, compared with one-way technologies used on a mass scale by a single institution.

Table 1.1, which provides the data for Figures 1.1 and 1.2, pulls together the costs for the various technologies for different volumes of activity and student numbers.

Great care needs to be taken in drawing conclusions from this table. Many of the examples are based on hypothetical assumptions. Even where data have been drawn from actual cases, major differences in the data would be achieved by changing some of the assumptions. In particular, differences need to be substantial before they can be considered as having possible value. The main aim of this table is not to determine the cheapest technology, but to show how costs differ, dependent on numbers of students (cost structures).

Teaching and learning

Teaching and learning issues are less strong as discriminators than access or costs, partly because of the flexibility of different media and technologies, and the ability of teachers and learners to make the best of any given situation. Nevertheless, from an analysis of the ways different media or technologies convey or transmit knowledge, several key features emerge.

Table 1.1 Summary of costs (per student study hour)

Technology	No. of students per annum				
	50 *US$*	*125* *US$*	*250* *US$*	*625* *US$*	*1,250* *US$*
One-way technologies					
Print (UKOU)		2.61		0.63	0.37
Audio cassettes (UKOU)		3.51		1.30	1.02
Pre-recorded ITV (hypothetical)					
25 courses	7.71	3.09	1.54	0.61	0.31
20 courses	7.35	2.79	1.47	0.58	0.28
10 courses	7.95	3.18	1.59	0.63	0.31
1 course	18.76	7.50	3.39	1.50	0.75
Radio (UKOU)		14.88		2.97	1.48
Ed. Broadcast TV (UKOU)		109.87		21.97	10.99
Computer-based learning (Stahmer and Green, 1993)					
low-end	59.25	18.75	11.25	6.75	4.50
medium level	99.75	41.25	22.50	11.25	6.75
high-end	322.50	130.50	66.75	28.50	15.75
Two-way technologies					
Audio conferencing (OLA)		7.12		4.11	3.67
Live, interactive lectures (hypothetical)		67.24	50.14	34.36	29.00
Video conferencing (Bates, 1994)					
2 × 56	51.75	17.35	11.98	9.07	9.07
384	56.74	22.17	16.78	14.19	14.19
Computer conferencing (hypothetical)					
Dual-mode					
Institution	1.45	1.12	1.09	0.99	0.93
Student	0.69	0.69	0.69	0.69	0.69
Combined	2.25	1.81	1.80	1.69	1.68

Presentational features

First of all media differ in their presentational features. Some media are more restricted than others with respect to their presentational features. Thus print can handle large quantities of text, diagrams, and pictures. It can also handle colour, but at a high cost. Radio, audio cassettes, and audio conferencing are restricted to sound only; computer conferencing is limited mainly to textual communication at the moment. Most computer-based learning materials at the time of writing are limited with regard to sound and full motion movement, although that is rapidly improving with multi-media. Television is the most complete medium in terms of its presentational qualities, although it is not a good medium for handling large quantities of text.

These presentational qualities have a direct relationship to teaching tasks. For instance, print can precisely represent facts, abstract ideas, rules and principles, and detailed, lengthy or complex arguments. It is a very dense medium, and consequently is still the great storehouse of knowledge. Radio can be used for lectures and studio discussions, but is not good for handling detail or dense amounts of information.

Each medium also varies in the way it represents the world. Thus both television and radio can use drama or documentaries, while computer and audio conferencing allow people to create or build their own interpretations of knowledge through discussion.

In particular, media differ in their ability to handle concrete or abstract knowledge. Abstract knowledge is handled primarily through language. While all media can handle language, either in written or spoken form, media vary in their ability to represent concrete knowledge.

These representational possibilities of media are particularly important for non-academic learners, who often require concrete examples or demonstration rather than abstract theory. Television can demonstrate experiments, and represent complex social situations, but it is not good at providing large quantities of abstract information. However, when television explicitly links concepts and principles to concrete examples, it becomes a powerful teaching medium.

These are only some of the instructional differences between media, but they do indicate the importance of course designers identifying clearly not only the content of a course, but also how best to present knowledge in a particular subject area, and what kinds of learning (comprehension, analysis, application of principles to actual cases, problem-solving, inter-personal skills, mechanical skills, attitude change, etc.) are required. This means that a good understanding of what is required to teach a particular subject needs to be combined with good knowledge of the pedagogic strengths and weaknesses of different media. Thus the selection of media is not just a technical issue, nor one that is purely academic.

Basically, every medium has its strengths and weaknesses in terms of its presentational qualities, but from an instructional point of view, some are clearly stronger than others. In particular, 'high-quality' television, i.e. television that exploits its unique presentational qualities (as distinct from its use as a channel of communication), and multimedia are very strong, and radio, audio conferencing, computer conferencing, live interactive television, (i.e. relayed lectures) and compressed video conferencing are all relatively weak, in presentational terms.

Developing skills

Another area where there appear to be differences between technologies (although this is an area where much more research is needed) is in their ability to develop different types of skills, as distinct from presenting knowledge or content. Thus computer conferencing can develop skills of academic discourse, knowledge building and creative writing, while television, when used carefully, can develop skills of analysis and evaluation.

Technologies that combine strong presentational qualities with strong student control over the technology are particularly good for developing skills. Thus audio and video cassettes and multimedia are strong, and radio and live televised lectures are poor, for skills development.

So even in the more difficult area of pedagogical or instructional differences, there do appear to be important differences between technologies. There appear to be profound pedagogical differences between technologies, from which it follows that they should be used carefully to exploit their strengths and avoid their weaknesses, rather than being used for just relaying a 'popular' mode of delivery, such as an entertainment-style broadcast or a televised lecture.

Unfortunately, though, it is common for educators and media specialists to carry over modes of design associated with an 'old' technology to a newer technology, even though the new technology may have inherent design advantages (or disadvantages) over the old technology. Thus professors often use television to relay lectures, rather than exploit television's presentational characteristics. There is therefore a need to reconsider the design of teaching and learning activities when technology is being used.

Interactivity and user-friendliness

Interaction

Some technologies allow for simultaneous or 'real-time' communication (synchronous), others for communication that can be stored and accessed when the teacher or learner is ready (asynchronous). Some technologies are one-way communication media; others are two-way. Some are permanent; others are transient. All these control features of technology impact on interactivity and user-friendliness.

Some one-way technologies facilitate interaction with learning materials and provide feedback on student responses better than others. Interaction is at its most controlled in computer-based learning, where learners can be tested, corrected, or given remedial activities by the computer. The attraction of computer-controlled video discs or 'multimedia' computer learning is that these technologies combine the potentially strong interactivity of computers with the powerful presentational qualities of television. However, even these technologies have great difficulty in handling teaching contexts where individual interpretation or the development of argument is needed.

Audio and video cassettes can be designed to increase learner interaction with the teaching materials, and do allow for more open-ended and interpretative responses than computer-controlled learning, but still need supplementing with some form of two-way interaction between learners and a teacher or tutor.

Most two-way teaching technologies involve live or spontaneous contributions from the teacher. Where presentations are in real time ('live'), the time and opportunity for student communication is strictly controlled. Audio and video conferencing require the physical presence of a student at both a fixed time and often a fixed place other than the home. Furthermore, when the teaching is in 'real time', and ephemeral, the student is heavily dependent on understanding the presentation and discussions as they happen, and on taking good notes, or on a good memory. Computer conferencing has a unique advantage of being asynchronous, thus allowing for more convenient access to two-way communication.

Two-way communications media are valuable tools for distance educators, and will become increasingly so; nevertheless, they are not always appropriate for all the jobs that need to be done. One-way communication technologies can, with careful design, provide a high level of interaction for students, and so still have an important role to play. There is then a need both for high quality pre-prepared, permanent material, and for two-way communication between students and tutors.

Learner control

Two-way communication under the students' control allows students to interact easily not only with tutors, but also with other students. Until recently, the telephone has been the only means of doing this for students at a distance, and costs have been high. Computer-mediated communication now enables two-way communication at a distance, at asynchronous times, at relatively low cost, both between students, and between students, regional tutors or even central academic staff. Computer-based communications have revolutionary implications for distance education, providing the means to free students from the centralised control of pre-prepared and constricted curricula.

The extent to which any particular medium encourages interaction or active learning depends to some extent on the way it is designed, but is also determined to some extent by the nature of the medium. What is clear is that the design of multimedia distance learning materials which encourage active learning requires considerable instructional as well as subject or production expertise.

Organisational issues

If technologies are to be exploited effectively in open and distance learning, it is clear that organisational structures have to change. The newer, more flexible two-way communications technologies are less expensive to install than the one-way technologies of print and broadcasting. As a consequence, dual-mode and previously conventional institutions are increasingly moving into distance learning with these technologies. One reason why these two-way technologies are becoming popular in conventional teaching institutions is because they require very little change in the behaviour of the teaching staff from their normal face-to-face teaching.

In comparison with the production costs of large, autonomous distance teaching institutions designed around mainly one-way communications technologies, a university or college can make use of the newer two-way communications technologies such as video conferencing to reduce the production costs of open and distance learning, by making the teacher almost instantaneously available, without the need for a great deal of preparation.

However, one of the great contributions of distance teaching institutions has been to raise the quality of instructional design, resulting in extremely well designed learning materials. This is a result of a great deal of preparation time and team work. High quality teaching materials are particularly important where students have a variety of educational backgrounds and experience of study, and are especially important where entry to courses is open to all.

However, in few cases have either campus-based or autonomous distance teaching institutions significantly re-structured their internal organisation or resource allocation process to exploit fully the possibilities of the newer two-way technologies. With the exception of computer conferencing, the impact of these new technologies has been restricted usually to off-campus or 'remote' campus students. Costs of technology have been treated as a necessary additional expense to accommodate extra students.

This does not make a great deal of impact on average student costs or internal efficiency; indeed, unit costs are likely to increase rather than decrease. Few conventional institutions have sought to re-structure their teaching completely, to integrate the benefits of technology for both internal and external students. For instance, if teachers were organised in teams and given release time to create high quality learning materials, in the form of print and video cassettes, supported by asynchronous tutoring through computer conferencing, both on-campus and distance students could equally benefit. Teaching staff would be freed from lecturing and group seminars on a regular basis, and could give more time to individual or group tutoring on-line.

Thus it is critical to re-examine the whole organisational structure when introducing new technologies (sometimes called 're-engineering the organisation').

Novelty

While novelty should be the least important of all the criteria, in practice it is often easier to attract external funding for the use of new technologies.

Also, suppliers of equipment and services will often offer attractive subsidies or 'free offers' for new products and services.

There are real dangers though in being driven by funding specifically linked to the use of new technologies. The first is the question of sustainability. If the technology is not cost-effective, an institution will find it difficult to continue with the technology when external funding or subsidies cease. Secondly, external funding for new technologies tends to be limited to capital investment in the technology, or subsidy of transmission costs, both of which are usually minor compared with the costs of course production and educational support during presentation of the course.

Novelty then is very much a two-edged sword.

Speed

In a society subject to such rapid change, it is essential to be able to change and revise content very quickly. One of the advantages of all the two-way technologies, plus radio, is their ability to bring students the latest information on research, social events, new developments in science and technology, and government policy changes.

In comparison, because of the long lead production times, or the high cost of changing material once made, broadcast television, computer-based learning and pre-programmed multimedia all rate poorly on this criterion.

POLONIUS' ADVICE TO HAMLET

Before summarising the differences between different distance teaching technologies, I suggest twelve golden rules for using technology in education and training which apply whatever technologies are being used.

Good teaching matters

Clear objectives, good structuring of learning materials, relevance to learners' needs, etc., apply to the use of any technology for teaching, and if these principles are ignored, then the teaching will fail, even if the unique characteristics of the medium are stylishly exploited. Good teaching may overcome a poor choice in the use of technology, but technology will never save bad teaching; usually it makes it worse.

Each medium has its own aesthetic

Professional production and design is important. Each medium has a different range of production skills necessary to exploit its unique features; this means that 'quality' production counts – a computer-assisted learning programme that does not fully utilise the special design features of computer-based learning (e.g. fails to use interaction, graphics, or remedial aspects) will not work, even if in theory the computer was the most appropriate medium for the particular task.

Educational technologies are flexible

Technologies are generally flexible and hence interchangeable in education and training, i.e. what can be achieved educationally through one technology can usually be achieved through any other technology, given sufficient imagination, time and resources. Thus the absence or non-availability of a particular technology does not necessarily prevent learning goals from being achieved.

Each technology can be used in a wide variety of ways. Consequently, differences *within* a technology or medium (for instance, between two television programmes, one a televised lecture and the other a documentary) may be greater than *between* media (for instance, between a face-to-face lecture and a lecture on a radio programme). Nevertheless, intrinsic differences between technologies have been identified which have implications for teaching and learning, and knowledge of these differences should guide technology selection.

There is no 'super-technology'

All technologies have their strengths and weaknesses (yes, even multimedia). They therefore need to be combined.

Make all four media available to teachers and learners

In most open and distance learning, learners are not a homogeneous mass, but vary a great deal in terms of educational backgound, age, experience, and preferred learning style. Decision-makers should therefore try to ensure that all four media (print, audio, television, computers) are available for teaching purposes, in one technological form or another. This will give variety to a course, not only providing an individual learner with different ways of approaching the same material, but accommodating different learning styles.

Balance variety with economy

The greater the number of technologies used, the more complex the design process, and the greater the chance of redundancy and wasted expenditure; the aim therefore should be to use a limited range of technologies in any given context, but covering all the main media.

Interaction is essential

High quality interaction with learning materials, and interaction between teachers and other learners, is essential for effective learning. Inter-personal interaction can be provided as effectively at a distance, through the use of appropriate technologies, as through face-to-face contact.

Student numbers are critical

The total number of learners to be served over the life of a course is a critical factor in technology selection. Some technologies are much more economical than others with large numbers; with other technologies, costs increase proportionately with student numbers. Take the long view; what may appear cheap in the first year may be more expensive over eight years – and vice versa.

New technologies are not necessarily better than old ones

There is no law that says new technologies will automatically be better for teaching than old ones. Judgement about new technologies should be made on educational and operational criteria, not by date stamp. Many of the lessons learned from the application of older technologies will still apply to any newer technology.

Teachers need training to use technologies effectively

Teachers and instructors need training not just in the choice and use of appropriate technologies, but more fundamentally in how people learn, and in instructional design. Lack of appropriate training is the biggest barrier to the use of technology in education.

Teamwork is essential

No one can know everything there is to know about the educational use and design of every technology now avaliable, and be a subject expert. Subject experts, media specialists and instructional designers are essential on every team.

Technology is not the issue

The issue is: *how* and *what* do I want students to learn? And where? The effectiveness of technology-based open learning is now a non-issue (see Moore and Thompson, 1990); concentrate on designing the learning experience, and not on testing the technology. There is more than enough technology around now to allow you to teach in whatever way you choose.

Evidence to support these rules will be found in the more detailed comparison of technologies below.

COMPARING TECHNOLOGIES

Given the wide range of technologies now available for open and distance learning, what lessons have we learned? Are, as Clark (1983) suggests, all technologies 'neutral'? Or are there significant educational and operational differences between them?

My answer is an unequivocal 'yes': there are significant instructional and operational differences between different technologies.

Table 1.2 provides my own assessment of the strengths and weaknesses of different technologies. When you have read this book, you should be in a position to make your own assessment, which will probably differ from mine, because your context and values are also likely to be different.

DOWN WITH LECTURES AND INCREMENTALISM!

A fundamental issue that is addressed in this book is whether to use technology to replicate 'traditional' instructional methods, or to use technology to change teaching methods to improve the quality of teaching and learning.

There is a predominant view, certainly amongst faculty in North American universities and colleges, that the traditional form of group face-to-face instruction is still the preferred and most effective form of education, and that the closer distance education can directly 'mimic' or imitate this, the more effective distance education will be. Also, where autonomous distance teaching institutions have introduced newer interactive technologies, they have merely added them to the high-cost, front-end development of print and television.

It is my view that neither of these approaches is adequate. It is increasingly difficult to defend the current system of teaching, as it applies to what is now mass post-secondary education. The 'old' methods of small classes and a direct and frequent person-to-person contact between teacher and young student worked well with an elite and restricted entry to higher education. Those days are long gone. Society is faced with a struggle for economic survival, where the future of developed countries depends on large numbers of people being educated to a high level, not just in late adolescence, but throughout their lives.

Also, the one-way transmission model of mass distance education practised by the autonomous distance teaching institutions needs to be modified. There is no longer a single mass market for adult continuing education, but an increasingly wider variety of needs, and increasingly smaller and unique target groups. This means more individualised approaches to open learning.

Even more importantly, the model of transmission of information from teacher to student practised by both conventional institutions and the large, autonomous distance teaching universities is no longer sufficient in a

Table 1.2 Summary of strengths and weaknesses of different technologies for open and distance learning

Media	Access	Costs Student nos		Teaching		Learning materials	Interactivity Social	Organisation	Speed
		Large	Small	Presen-tation	Skills				
One-way media									
Print	Good	Good	Average	Average	Average	Average	Poor	Poor	Poor
Radio	Good	Good	Poor	Poor	Poor	Poor	Poor	Average	Good
Audio cassette	Good	Good	Average	Average	Good	Good	Poor	Good	Average
Educational broadcast TV	Average	Poor	Poor	Good	Average	Poor	Poor	Poor	Poor
Pre-recorded ITV	Poor	Good	Poor	Average	Average	Average	Average	Average	Poor
Video cassettes	Good	Average	Poor	Good	Good	Good	Poor	Average	Poor
Computer-based learning	Average	Poor	Poor	Average	Average	Good	Poor	Poor	Poor
Multimedia	Poor	Poor	Poor	Good	Good	Good	Poor	Poor	Poor
Two-way media									
Audio conferencing	Good	Poor	Good	Poor	Average	Poor	Good	Good	Good
Live interactive TV	Poor	Poor	Poor	Poor	Poor	Poor	Average	Average	Good
Video conferencing	Poor	Poor	Average	Poor	Average	Average	Average	Average	Good
CMC	Average	Average	Good	Poor	Good	Average	Good	Good	Good

society where knowledge is changing rapidly, and the skills needed both at work and in our social lives are becoming increasingly complex. People need to know how to communicate effectively, work in teams, search out and analyse new knowledge, participate actively in society, and generate as well as assimilate knowledge.

In particular, the predominance of the lecture-based classroom model in post-secondary education needs to be challenged. The ancient Greeks did not learn this way. Plato argued for dialogue rather than instruction. Indeed, the 'lecture', so prevalent in post-secondary education these days, is itself a technological artefact. The word 'lecture' comes from the Latin verb 'to read'. Because books in mediaeval times were painstakingly and beautifully written by hand by the monks, only one copy usually existed in each university. The one copy was so precious that the university professor literally read from the book to his students. Also, instruction was controlled by the church; therefore control over access to knowledge was essential, to prevent unorthodoxy. It is no accident that the invention of printing influenced not only the rise of Protestantism, but also the development of schools.

The Industrial Revolution, with its need to educate large numbers of people for commercial life, led to mass education, and the large group method of teaching was the most economical way to provide this. However, while twentieth-century technology has revolutionised communications, leading to the information society, our educational institutions are still pickled in the aspic of the Industrial Revolution.

Technology does provide an opportunity to teach differently, in a way that can meet the fundamental needs of a new and rapidly changing society. The evidence is now overwhelming that technology can both improve the quality of education and enable new target groups to be reached, at less cost than by using conventional methods.

This, however, requires new approaches to teaching and learning, that exploit the unique features of different technologies in order to meet the widely different needs of many types of learners. These approaches must be based on the considerable amount of knowledge now available about how people learn and how to design effective learning environments, as well as on a good understanding of the educational strengths and limitations of different technologies.

Some possible approaches are described in the rest of the book, but basically there is a need to invent or re-discover methods of teaching and learning that match the use of technology to the needs of learners in the twenty-first century. What cannot be justified is continuing with a system of teaching which, while it may have served an elite well in the past, is very expensive and ineffective, in that it does not facilitate the vast majority of people to learn and think creatively and independently throughout their lives.

If you are interested in such issues then read on!

ORGANISATION OF THE BOOK

Most of the chapters in this book are organised in pairs around a particular medium, depending on whether they use one-way or two-way technologies for delivery. Broadcast TV is discussed in Chapter 4, and instructional and two-way television in Chapter 5. Print is discussed in Chapter 6, one-way audio in Chapter 7, two-way audio in Chapter 8, computer-based learning and multimedia in Chapter 9, and computer-mediated communication in Chapter 10.

In order to make competent decisions about which technologies to use, there must be a clear vision of how learning and teaching should take place. These issues are addressed specifically in Chapters 3 and 11, but also run through the discussions of each of the technologies covered in this book.

Even a clear vision of how we want learning to take place though is not sufficient for decision-making about the use of technology. Other factors, such as access and cost, also need to be considered. Decision-makers need a framework for decision-making, based on a set of guidelines, criteria or questions to be answered, if they are to avoid being driven by the personal prejudices of key individuals, or by the notion of the newest being the best. In this book, I have developed and applied such a set of criteria or questions to be asked for each of the technologies now available. This approach is outlined more fully in Chapter 3, and applied systematically to different technologies in Chapters 4–10.

The value of technology in open and distance learning

It is my view that technology could and should be used a great deal more in education and training than it is, but I do not see it as a panacea. The value of technology is its ability to reach learners not well served by conventional educational institutions, to meet better the newly emerging educational needs of an information society, and to improve the quality of learning. Indeed, I argue that the intelligent application of technology to education and training will be critical to economic well-being, particularly in Europe, North America and other 'older' developed countries. Its value will be greater when applied to the existing workforce, rather than to younger people in full-time education. These issues are discussed in some detail in Chapter 11.

I hope that this book then will offer at least one step towards providing a more sophisticated and better informed approach to decision-making regarding the use of technology in open and distance learning – indeed in education and training in general.

2 Technology, decision-making and open and distance learning

TWO STORIES

In 1985 I attended my one and only mega-conference, to which the organisers had hoped to attract over 10,000 participants. It was called 'The World Congress on Technology and Teaching', and was held in that most beautiful of cities, Vancouver, on the west coast of Canada.

One of the major reasons for attending was to find out the latest developments in the use of video discs in education. At one of the workshops on this topic, the presenters had great difficulty in getting the equipment to work. Having given several presentations myself of computer-controlled video disc technology, I had some sympathy for them. Like good Burgundy, it doesn't travel well.

However, in the embarrassing interlude while the technical people were trying to get the computer to interact with the video disc, one of the presenters asked if there were any questions. A Canadian elementary school teacher asked how much the equipment cost, and how much it cost to produce the disc that we were waiting to see.

'About $100,000 to produce the disc, and about $5,000 for the equipment', came the reply, followed by gasps and some laughter. 'Well', persisted the teacher, 'how do you expect schools to be able to afford such technology?' 'Easy,' came the reply. 'The biggest cost in education in the USA is teachers. Replace the teachers, and you can afford the technology.'

At this point, several of the audience got up and walked out, one commenting, 'If you think education is just about sitting a child down in front of a piece of machinery, you clearly don't know what you're talking about.'

Still in British Columbia, eight years later, 295 local area managers of Crown corporations and utilities are gathered together in groups of 10 to 15, in 13 different locations across the province. They are participating in a satellite-delivered video conference, which is being led by one of North America's leading specialists in managing diversity and multi-culturalism in the workplace.

The one-day workshop consists of a formal presentation, drama segments, and a panel session from a studio in Vancouver, local discussion groups led by facilitators at each of the local sites, and reporting and two-way question and answer sessions, between the local sites and the people in the central studio, using telephone audio conferencing.

This workshop was more than two and a half times cheaper than the usual method of training (sending managers to Vancouver for a one-day workshop), and 13 per cent cheaper, and five weeks quicker, than sending a local specialist 'on the road' to each site. Almost all the participants rated the video conference experience as comparable to or better than other forms of training they had received (Conklin, 1993). The employers were so satisfied that they decided to run a whole series of training events in similar fashion.

TECHNOLOGY AND DECISION-MAKING

These two stories illustrate a recurrent theme throughout this book: that technology is neither good nor bad in itself, but it is the way that it is used that matters. We need to understand the relative strengths and weaknesses of different technologies, and the requirements for their effective use in widening access or meeting the needs of learners in a flexible or open manner.

This is particularly important given the rapid development in technology, and particularly communications technology. Hardly a conference on education goes by without a major section being devoted to technological change. Technology indeed provides educators and governments with the capacity to transform radically our whole education system, and nowhere is this more true than in the area of open and distance learning.

However, the focus tends to be more on the actual technology itself, the information highway, the hardware, and the potential for change. It is certainly important to understand the technology, but even more important is the need to understand its strengths and weaknesses in terms of its actual applications. Also important is an understanding of the system and operational requirements for the successful use of technology in education and training.

Thus while it is hoped that this book will also appeal to experienced distance education practitioners, its main targets are key decision-makers in education and training, such as a Dean of Humanities in a university, faced with pressure from the Division of Continuing Education to make courses available to local communities through compressed video conferencing, and from the Vice-Chancellor to take more students for less cost; or a State Commissioner for Higher Education, who has received a request from the state university for $8 million to enhance and update its instructional television facility, but who feels that this is not the right technology to be investing in at this time; or politicians and civil servants, who are

looking at ways to meet the growing demand for access to higher education. and want to improve the quality of education and training, for
economic development reasons, but who are faced with pressure from
the Treasury to reduce expenditure in their ministry. Will technology-
based open learning provide an answer to this conundrum? Lastly, the
book is aimed at managers in the business community who are trying to
up-grade the skills of their workforce, while at the same time keeping their
training costs under control.

The book then is not so much about technology-based curriculum design,
as about decision-making regarding technology systems for teaching and
learning, including human, economic and organisational factors. After
reading this book, you should be much more confident about how to go
about selecting and using different technologies in relation to your educational goals and local circumstances. It should provide a set of questions or
criteria to protect yourself and your organisation from the temptations of
the vendors of the latest breakthrough in technology, without missing the
chance to adopt appropriate new technologies as they come along. It should
also help you understand some of the barriers to the adoption of technologies for teaching and learning, and what needs to be done to remove
those barriers. Perhaps even more importantly, it should lead you to
develop strategies for dealing with rapid technological change, and even
help you to create a clear view or vision as to how you would like to
structure and organise teaching and learning in the future, so that it leads to
the quality of education and training that you would like to achieve.

One of the basic premises of this book is that newer technologies such as
computers and video conferencing are not necessarily better (or worse) for
teaching or learning than older technologies such as print or broadcast
television; they are just different, and we need to understand the differences and the appropriate circumstances for technology applications if we
are to use technology for effective teaching and learning. The choice of
technology should be driven by the needs of the learners and the context in
which we are working, not by its novelty.

Another premise is that lessons learned in the past from research into
some of the older technologies are often still relevant for the newer
technologies. Whenever a new technology emerges in education (and
there is a new one almost every year), it becomes the latest 'wave', the
technology that will revolutionise teaching. People in general ignore what
has been learned in previous contexts. In most cases, though, many of the
lessons learned from previous applications of technology are just as
relevant for the new technology application, yet the same mistakes are
made. They often ignore for instance the need to re-organise and
re-structure teaching to exploit fully the technology.

Indeed, lessons learned from research by the English psychologist Philip
Vernon as long ago as 1950 on the intelligibility of radio talks would still
apply to many lectures delivered today by video conference. This means

that in some cases, the research quoted in this book may be more than 10 years old, because research in this field tends to abandon older technologies and move to the latest development (even though those older technologies, such as print, remain the major delivery medium for most distance education). Thus the use of research in this book is driven not so much by its date-stamp as by its usefulness for decision-making.

This book draws heavily on research and experience in two institutions, the British Open University, where I worked for 20 years conducting research into the use of technology for teaching, and from the Open Learning Agency in Canada, where I have worked for the last five years as a manager responsible for planning, research and information technology. There are obvious dangers in drawing generalisations from research and experience from just two institutions (although the two are about as different as you could get). Nevertheless, the book concentrates on lessons from these experiences which, from visits to other institutions, regular reviews of the literature, and from discussions with colleagues elsewhere, I truly believe have much wider relevance, and which are often supported by research from other institutions.

A third major premise is that there is a direct link between the use of technology and different ideologies of teaching and learning. The effectiveness of a technology cannot be judged without making some basic assumptions about what constitutes effective teaching and learning. Therefore some space is taken in the early part of the book to discuss some of the basic differences in approach to education and training, and how these relate to the use of different technologies.

Lastly, it is easy to be seduced by the excitement of the latest technology, but technologies do not roll out evenly and all at once. Even in more advanced industrial countries, there will still be some target groups who will have access only to print, television, and possibly the telephone, and in developing countries, many of the newer technologies will be beyond the reach of most of the target group for many years to come. For these reasons then, I have deliberately given roughly equal attention to each distance education technology, irrespective of its age or youth.

Nevertheless, despite – or rather because of – what we have learned from the past, I do believe that more recent developments in technology have the potential to revolutionise the education and training system, and the last chapter, especially, looks to the future. In particular, it is my view that technology developments will mean the end of distance education as a discreet educational activity.

Distance education is one of the few areas of education where technology has been central to the teaching task, for over 25 years. A feature of distance education institutions is that they are deliberately designed and structured to exploit the cost and educational benefits of technology.

Distance education and open learning therefore have provided a valuable test-bed for understanding the potential and limitations of a wide range of technologies in education. At the same time, one of the main conclusions reached in this book is that while distance education has historically been at the leading edge in applying technology to education, recent techno- logical advances are making the distinction between conventional and distance education more and more meaningless. Technology will dramatically impact on *all* educational institutions, and change their nature.

This book therefore is of relevance not just to distance educators, but to all who are concerned about the future of education and training. Nevertheless, its focus is on open and distance learning.

DISTANCE EDUCATION

It has been argued (Nipper, 1989; Kaufman, 1989) that there are three generations of distance education. The first generation is characterised by the predominant use of a single technology, and lack of direct student interaction with the teacher originating the instruction. Correspondence education is a typical form of first generation distance education.

Second generation distance education is characterised by a deliberately integrated multiple-media approach, with learning materials specifically designed for study at a distance, but with two-way communication still mediated by a third person (a tutor, rather than the originator of the teaching material). Autonomous distance teaching universities are examples of second generation distance education.

Third generation distance education is based on two-way communica- tions media which allow for direct interaction between the teacher who originates the instruction and the remote student – and often *between* remote students, either individually or as groups. Third generation tech- nologies result in a much more equal distribution of communication between student and teacher (and also between students).

Kaufman (1989) characterises the three generations as a progressive increase (from first to third generation) in learner control, opportunities for dialogue, and emphasis on thinking skills rather than mere comprehen- sion. More significantly, third generation distance learning is leading to new types of educational organisation.

Correspondence education

Although St Paul's epistle to the Corinthians could be considered an early form of distance education, distance education in the modern sense really began in the nineteenth century, with the establishment of commercial correspondence colleges, made possible by the development of a reliable and speedy postal service. For many years people from overseas were able to sit London University's examinations without ever living in Britain, many studying primarily through correspondence education. Long before the Second World War, campus-based universities in North America and the Dominions were offering off-campus extension services to adults living and working away from the university. In general, though, despite some notable achievements by individual students, correspondence education did not have a high reputation, being characterised by high drop-out and low examination pass rates.

Autonomous distance education institutions

The establishment in 1969 of the British Open University marked a turning point in the development of distance education, in two ways. Not only was it the first institution designed solely and specifically for distance education at degree level, but it was also designed as a multimedia teaching institution, combining print, broadcasting, and face-to-face tuition in an integrated manner. Its annual operating budget is approximately £100 million (US$150 million), and it produces 9 per cent of all the undergraduates in Britain each year, at a cost of 5 per cent of the national university operating budget, reflecting the high investment/high output potential of technologically-based teaching.

The Open University's provision of higher adult education, at a distance, through the use of technology, has led to an organisational structure quite different from that of conventional universities. It is thus an excellent example of the structural changes in organisation that are needed for the systematic large-scale application of technology to education.

Since the creation of the Open University, over 25 similar autonomous university institutions dedicated solely to distance education have been established in different countries throughout the world. These are institutions that operate across whole countries, states or provinces. They are enabled by government to award their own accreditation, in the form of degrees, diplomas or certificates. They use a variety of media, and usually have large numbers of students. However, large, autonomous distance teaching institutions are by no means the only or even major form of distance education.

Dual-mode institutions

These are conventional teaching institutions, with on-campus students, who also offer some of their courses at a distance. Usually, the off-campus students sit the same examinations as the on-campus students. Courses may be primarily print-based, usually with some additional media support, such as audio cassettes or telephone tutoring, delivered to students at home; or primarily lectures delivered to satellite campuses by an increasingly wide range of 'broadcast' technologies. Often the numbers of distance students per course are relatively small, compared with the autonomous institutions dedicated to open and distance learning.

Collaborative arrangements

In some educational jurisdictions, open and distance learning are centrally co-ordinated, not just to avoid duplication between institutions, but to build on the resources already existing in the conventional education system.

In a collaborative system, dual-mode universities and colleges, together with a separate open learning institution, offer an integrated programme of studies through open and distance learning, so that students are able to take courses from any of the participating institutions, with full credit transfer between institutions. As well as course integration and collaboration, institutions may also share common production and/or distribution facilities, including electronic highways.

In the USA, state regulations frequently conflict with one another, making co-operation among institutions more difficult. Nevertheless, the Western Interstate Commission of Higher Education is a collaboration between 15 states in the Western USA. One of its creations is the Western Co-operative for Educational Communications, which has been very successful in obtaining Federal funds for educational telecommunications projects. The National Technological University in the USA is another such example, linking together 45 different universities for the purposes of nation-wide post-graduate distance courses in engineering and management, via satellite.

In British Columbia, Canada, a separate institution within the overall system, the Open Learning Agency, provides co-ordination and also offers courses itself via open and distance learning. Although structured somewhat differently, and based at Monash University, the Open Learning Agency of Australia provides a similar co-ordinating role.

International consortia

Open and distance learning is not limited by geographical boundaries. Very small states find it difficult to offer a full range of educational opportunities within national boundaries. Open and distance learning allow small or isolated states to share teaching and facilities, and to use communications technologies to cross large distances. Two examples of where a number of different countries have co-operated in this way are the University of the West Indies and the University of the South Pacific.

Workplace training

Perhaps the most interesting development in the last five years has been the increased interest shown by commerce and industry in distance teaching and open learning methods.

Vocational training is undergoing radical change. For the last 50 years, there have been three main methods of vocational training: on-the-job 'apprenticeship' (essentially learning at work with a master craftsman); public sector classroom teaching (either as day-release or evening classes); and company-organised, in-house training (seminars/courses). These three methods are all primarily based on personal contact between teacher and taught, and are hence time and place dependent. They are all also costly. Such methods are also inflexible. They do not easily adapt to rapid change in either content or methods. In the last few years, though, we have seen the large-scale and effective introduction of open learning and distance teaching methods to vocational training. There are several reasons for this.

First is the changing nature of work. Because of rapid developments in technology, the idea of being trained as a youth for the same job for life – as, for example, through the apprenticeship system – is becoming less and less tenable. Most people are likely to change careers at least two or three times. Within a particular job, the need for continuing training is rapidly increasing.

Job mobility is increasing, especially across national frontiers. An employee of a large company in Europe can increasingly expect to move around Europe, or at least within his or her own country; this makes the provision of continuing education difficult through traditional means, if at one time you are in Frankfurt, a year later in Toulouse, and the next back in the United Kingdom.

Lastly, because training is costly, efforts are being made to find more cost-effective ways to train. Open learning centres, where employees can 'drop-in' for training during breaks, or after work, or during slack periods at work; or distance learning, where employees can learn either at home, or at their desk or workplace, both suggest greater flexibility and lower costs.

The growth of distance education

In the last 20 years, 'second generation' open and distance learning has spread to many countries, and become an important part of most modern educational systems. Although initially concentrated at the post-secondary level, open learning and distance education projects now exist at school and at career, technical and vocational levels, and in the private sector, in the form of work-based training, as well as in the public sector. There are now examples of thriving open and distance education initiatives operating across all subject areas, at all academic levels, and in every continent.

Distance education illustrates well the relationship between the use of technology and the need to re-organise to maximise its benefits. It also illustrates the capacity to reach new target groups, and to expand the range of educational provision, through the use of technology, when properly organised and structured.

OPEN LEARNING AND DISTANCE EDUCATION

Although the two terms are often used to mean the same thing, there are differences.

- *Open learning* is primarily a goal, or an educational policy: the provision of learning in a flexible manner, built around the geographical, social and time constraints of individual learners, rather than those of an educational institution.
- *Distance education* is one means to that end: it is one way by which learners can study in a flexible manner, by studying at a distance from the originator of the teaching material; students can study at their own time, at the place of their choice (home, work or learning centre), and without face-to-face contact with the teacher.

Open learning may include distance education, or it may depend on other flexible forms of learning, including a mix of independent study and face-to-face teaching. It may also include other concepts, such as open access without prior requisite qualifications. Both open-ness and distance education are never found in their purest forms. No teaching system is completely open, and few students ever study in complete isolation. Thus there are degrees of open-ness and 'distance' – indeed, distance is more likely to be psychological or social, rather than geographical, in most cases.

Although open learning and distance education can mean different things, the one thing they both have in common is an attempt to provide alternative means of high quality education and training for those who either cannot go to conventional, campus-based institutions, or do not want to.

There are several quite different reasons why governments, the private sector and individual students have given strong support to open and distance learning:

- *Lifelong learning and economic development.* Open and distance learning provide the flexibility needed for mature adults to continue their education or training while still working or with family responsibilities. Some governments and employers have recognised the importance of life-long learning and distance education both for increased economic productivity and competitiveness, and for social and cultural reasons.
- *Social equity and access.* Many adults are unable to enter or complete higher education on leaving the school system for academic, personal or social reasons. Open and distance learning gives a second chance to such people, by removing the barriers of access to higher education.
- *Cost effectiveness.* In many countries, demand for places in the conventional education system far exceeds the supply. Under the right circumstances, open and distance learning systems can provide quality

education and training to large numbers at lower unit costs than conventional education systems.

- *Geography.* In geographically remote or sparsely populated areas, it is not economically possible to provide a full range of educational and training opportunities through conventional institutions. Open and distance education enable learning and training to be delivered more effectively and economically in such communities.

This is a very brief introduction to open and distance learning (see Verduin and Clark, 1991, for a more detailed treatment). However, open and distance learning – or at least the provision of education and training in more flexible ways than regular, full-time attendance at a single campus-based institution – is growing rapidly. Technology is an essential component of most (but not all) open learning initiatives. Open learning is also blurring the distinction between campus-based and distance teaching institutions.

THE TECHNOLOGICAL EXPLOSION

The increasing development and diversification of open and distance learning has been paralleled by an even more rapid explosion in the range of technologies now available to education.

For over 3,000 years, from Homer, Moses and Socrates onwards, the teacher, in direct, personal contact with the learner, has been the primary means of communicating knowledge. Indeed, this remained the primary form of educational communication until the fourteenth century, when the invention of the printing press allowed for the first time the large-scale dissemination of knowledge through books.

Printed books however did not replace the teacher. A consequence of the improved availability of printed matter was that many more of those engaged in government, commerce, medicine, law and even agriculture had to be literate to cope with the explosion of ideas and knowledge that followed. So teachers retained their importance in the educational process, since they were required to help large numbers of children develop the skills of reading and writing, to such a scale that it became necessary to found schools and colleges to allow greater numbers to be educated in an economical manner. Thus not only did the invention of books require more teachers, it also led to a radical re-organisation of teaching and an opening of access to education.

The Industrial Revolution by and large reinforced these developments, without really changing the basic organisation of education. To meet the needs of growing industrial and imperial nations, school and college education expanded rapidly and the curriculum was broadened, but the Industrial Revolution curiously made little impact on the technology of education. The introduction of the postal service did stimulate the start of correspondence education, and the telephone was later to be used to some extent for distance education, but on balance the technology of teaching remained almost the same from the fifteenth century well into the twentieth century.

Then came the wireless. In a remarkably prescient publication in the *Radio Times* of 13 June 1924, the newly appointed first Director of Education at the BBC, J. C. Stobart, speculated about the possibility of a 'broadcasting university'. The first adult education talk, broadcast on 6 October 1924, was actually about fleas. It was entitled 'Insects in Relation to Man' (Robinson, 1982). The first schools radio programme was broadcast by the BBC in 1926. By 1981, the BBC was broadcasting over 450 radio programmes a year in the continuing education area.

Sixteen mm. film became used extensively in schools from the 1930s onwards, to become eventually replaced to a large extent by television. In Britain, it was the new commercial television service that began schools television on a regular scale in 1957, followed shortly by the BBC, thirty years after the introduction of schools radio. Educational television for adults was introduced by both the BBC and the British commercial television companies in 1963. By 1981, the British television organisations were broadcasting well over a thousand schools and a thousand adult education television programmes a year. By the 1980s, broadcasting was well established as a major form of educational 'publishing'.

Until the late 1970s, then, the rate of change, while accelerating, had nevertheless been reasonably sedate, as can be seen from Table 2.1.

Table 2.1 The development of new technologies in teaching up to 1980

Development	Years in operation
Teacher	3,000
Book	500
Postal service	150
Radio	60
Film	50
Television	20

Table 2.2 (p. 30) though shows the rapid expansion of the number of new technologies introduced into education in one institution or another since 1980. Beneath this pile of technology are the poor teachers, administrators and learners. It is not surprising that there is often confusion, fear and hostility to the use of technology in education and training.

Media and technology

It is useful to make a distinction between media and technology. The term *medium* is used in this book to describe a generic form of communication

Table 2.2 The development of new technologies in teaching since 1980

Type of technology
Audio cassettes
Video cassettes
Telephone teaching
Computer-based learning
Cable TV
Satellite TV
Computer-based audio-graphics systems
Viewdata
Teletext
Video discs
Computer-controlled interactive video
Video conferencing
Electronic mail
Computer conferencing
Internet
Computer-based multimedia
Remote interactive data-bases
Virtual reality

Table 2.3 The relationship between media, technology and distance education applications of technology

Media	Technologies	Distance education applications
Text (including graphics)	Print	Course units; supplementary materials; correspondence tutoring
	Computers	Data-bases; electronic publishing
Audio	Cassettes; radio	Programmes
	Telephone	Telephone tutoring; audio conferences.
Television	Broadcasting; video cassettes; video discs; cable; satellite; fibre-optics; ITFS; microwave; video conferencing	Programmes; lectures; video conferences
Computing	Computers; telephone, satellite; fibre-optics; ISDN; CD-ROM; CD-I	Computer-aided learning (CAI, CBT); e-mail; computer conferences; audio-graphics; databases; multimedia

associated with particular ways of representing knowledge. Each medium not only has its own unique way of presenting knowledge, but also of organising it, often reflected in particular preferred formats or styles of presentation. A single medium such as television may be carried by several different delivery *technologies* (satellite, cable, video cassette, etc.).

In education, the five most important media are:

- direct human contact (face-to-face);
- text (including still graphics);
- audio;
- television;
- computing.

While certain technologies are closely associated with each medium, a variety of different technologies may be used to deliver these media, as Table 2.3 indicates.

It is arguable whether computing is a medium or a technology, although we shall see that there are quite sharp functional differences between the computing learning environment and those of other media. Certainly the distinctions between media and technologies will become less meaningful as they become integrated into single machines or transmission systems. Nevertheless, there are still significant differences in the bandwidth required for different media (uncompressed television requires 1,000 times the bandwidth capacity of an audio telephone call), and in the educational applications associated not just with different media, but also with different technologies within a single medium.

Table 2.4 One-way and two-way technology applications in distance education

Media	One-way technology applications	Two-way technology applications
Text	Course units; supplementary materials	Correspondence tutoring
Audio	Cassette programmes; radio programmes	Telephone tutoring; audio conferencing
Television	Broadcast programmes; cassette programmes	Interactive television (TV out; telephone in); video conferencing
Computing	CAL, CAI, CBT; data-bases; multimedia	E-mail; interactive data-bases; computer conferencing

One-way and two-way technologies

A second major distinction is between technologies that are primarily one-way, and those that are primarily two-way, in that they allow for inter-personal communication. Table 2.4 summarises the distinctions.

The significance of two-way technologies is that they allow for interaction between learners and instructors or tutors, and perhaps even more significantly, for interaction between distance learners themselves.

Given then the range and variety of media and technology, it is essential to develop a framework for deciding on the choice and use of technology in education and training.

3 Selecting technologies
Sorting out the differences

BUILDING A FRAMEWORK FOR DECISION-MAKING

The need for a decision-making framework

Because of a lack of generally agreed criteria for media and technology selection in education and training, crucial technology decisions have tended to be made primarily for commercial, administrative or political reasons: the availability of spare broadcasting capacity; an offer from suppliers of free or cheap equipment or services; the comfort level of academics with technologies that replicate the lecture format; or the enthusiasm of a key decision-maker for a particular technology. When a new technology has been introduced, it has more likely been added on to existing services, rather than to replace more costly or less effective teaching approaches.

Consequently, three decision-making scenarios are common. The first is basically to do nothing. The reasons for using technology are not clear, or there is a well-judged recognition of ignorance. Doing nothing is safer.

The second is 'sympathetic anarchy': an organisation leaves it to individual, enthusiastic teachers or trainers to use whatever media they can lay their hands on. This usually ends up with cupboards full of unused equipment, as individual enthusiasts run out of either money or support within the system, or move on to other jobs.

The third is 'monomedia mania': a government, company or institution decides to invest heavily in a single technology for all teaching or training throughout its system. This can lead to leap-frogging between competitive institutions, as new technologies develop. Thus one bank may decide to install video cassettes for staff training in every branch. A little later, another bank, with similar training requirements, will install computer-based learning in every branch. Not to be outdone, a third bank comes along and installs video discs. 'Monomedia mania' is usually driven by the decision to go for the latest or most sophisticated technology available at the time of the decision. No comparative analysis though is done on the appropriateness of older or more established technologies.

Strategic and tactical decision-making

Another limitation has been the confusion between strategic and tactical decision-making. There are two quite different levels of decision-making involved in selecting and using media and technologies in open and distance education. The first is the decision to set up a system of teaching based on technological delivery. This might be to create a new open or distance teaching institution, or to use technology to extend the reach of an existing campus-based institution. The decision to use instructional television as a main teaching medium for instance will require capital investment, and recurrent expenditure in the form of regular, specialist staff. Once production equipment is purchased, transmission facilities leased, and professional and technical staff hired, the monster must be fed, i.e. the facilities need to be used. Establishing a general facility for technological delivery is a strategic decision.

The second level of decision-making is concerned with the most appropriate use of the media and technologies already available to an organisation. Many institutions now use a range of different technologics. What is the best mix of these technologies for a particular course? What is the best way to combine print, audio and television on a course? Do all courses need the same amount of television, or would it be better to concentrate television on some courses rather than others? If so, which? These are tactical decisions.

Ideally, strategic decisions should be driven by the teaching needs of the institution, i.e. by the kinds of decision taken at the tactical level. But it is an iterative process: if television is made available (a strategic decision), a different kind of course can be produced than if it is not, permitting different learning objectives to be achieved (a tactical decision).

Furthermore, the continuing reduction in the costs of technologies, and their increasing accessibility, is making it easier for organisations to enter directly at the tactical level, by picking and choosing different technologies 'off-the-shelf' for particular purposes. This is bringing a number of institutions into distance and open learning for the first time. Without a strategic approach, however, short-term tactical decisions can lead to duplication and waste, as different parts of the organisation start to build a patchwork quilt.

Theoretical models of media selection

There already exist a number of existing models of *media* selection. Romiszowski (1988) provides a good example of a systems approach to instructional design and media selection. Reiser and Gagné (1983) carried out a useful analysis of 10 models of media selection, and identified a number of common characteristics of such theoretical models.

There are several problems though with applying these models to the use of technology in open and distance learning. Firstly, they are mainly designed for use in a classroom or face-to-face environment. Secondly, because these models concentrate primarily on matching a particular medium to a particular instructional event, the teaching or learning process is fragmented into basic elements of activity (e.g. understanding the symbols on a map), against which a particular medium is selected. It is an algorithmic, reductionist approach to decision-making, requiring many different media for even a small amount of teaching. Since these models rarely deal with non-instructional, practical issues, such as costs and organisational requirements, it is impossible to make strategic decisions about which technologies to choose, using these models.

For these and other reasons, technology decision-making has rarely been based upon theories of media selection in open and distance learning, although there is usually an otherwise fairly systematic approach to course design and development. Instead, technology decisions have been taken 'intuitively' by senior decision-makers, professors and professional media producers, based on personal experience.

Even with just a few technologies to choose from, though, there are obvious difficulties with a purely intuitive approach. If there is no clear rationale for the selection and use of particular technologies, there is likely to be inconsistency and confusion between the various stakeholders (subject experts, media professionals, and, critically, learners) regarding the design and function of the different technologies within a course. With a rapidly expanding number of technologies now available, and many new organisations entering the area of open and distance learning for the first time, a new approach to decision-making is needed in this area.

An alternative framework

A model for technology selection and application is needed which has the following characteristics:

- it will work in a wide variety of contexts;
- it allows decisions to be taken at both a strategic, or institution-wide, level, and at a tactical, or instructional, level;
- it gives equal attention to instructional and operational issues;
- it will identify critical differences between different technologies, thus enabling an appropriate mix of technologies to be chosen for any given context;
- it will accommodate new developments in technology.

The factors I believe to be important for selecting and using technology in open and distance learning were stated in the **ACTIONS** framework in Chapter 1 (pp. 1–2). This framework comprises a set of questions that need to be answered, irrespective of the type of institution or distance teaching programme, to enable appropriate decisions to be made regarding the choice and application of different technologies; in other words, these questions need to be asked in any context; the answers, though, will depend on the context.

ACCESS

No matter what the quality of the teaching material, it will not teach if learners do not receive it. The first question to ask then is:

● Who are the priority target groups to be served?

Answers might be: learners denied access to conventional institutions, equity groups, the unemployed, the working poor, or workers needing up-grading or more advanced education and training.
    The second question to be asked is:

● What is the most appropriate location for these open and distance learners?

There are several possible answers to this, depending on the nature of the target group:

● at home;
● in a local centre dedicated to open learning;
● at a local public education institution, with shared facilities for campus-based and distance students;
● at work – which could be either at an individual work-station, or in a company learning centre.

If an institution's policy is open access to anyone who wants to take its courses, the availability of equipment already in the *home* (usually purchased for entertainment purposes) becomes of paramount importance. Open access, home-based learning will be limited in many countries to relatively few technologies.
    Sometimes, it may be possible for the distance education institution to provide equipment or facilities at relatively low cost to students in their homes. For instance, a home experiment kit, such as chemical apparatus, may be supplied to a student. The kit is returned after the course is completed, then reissued to other students on the following year's course, thus spreading the initial capital cost over several years' students.
    One option is to make technology available through *local study centres*. These can be of two kinds: those established specifically and mainly for the use of open and distance learners; and those which may be located in existing colleges or schools, where facilities or at least rooms are shared between distance and open learners and campus-based students.
    The *workplace* is becoming an increasingly important location for open and distance learning. Often employers have technology that is not available in the home. For instance, if a distributed computer system already

exists for stock control, ordering or financial management, it may be possible to use it also for training purposes. Some employers now are establishing local site-based training centres, which may be no more than a room with equipment dedicated for training purposes, where employees can drop in for training.

As well as location, another factor that impacts on access is flexibility. For instance, a local learning centre set up in such a way that students can drop in at any time may be more convenient or accessible for some students than home delivered television courses, if the broadcasts are at an inconvenient time.

Access to and availability of equipment is likely to be the most powerful discriminator for assessing the appropriateness of a particular technology for distance learners; if learners cannot get the teaching, then other factors, such as design and interactivity, become irrelevant.

COSTS

The value of cost-benefit analysis

A cynic once defined an economist as someone who knows the cost of everything and the value of nothing. Like most jokes, there is a serious point in it. It is very dangerous just to look at costs without also examining the benefits. Nevertheless a proper understanding and analysis of costs is essential for making sensible decisions about the use of technology in education. The main questions to be asked regarding costs are as follows:

- What will be the average cost per student study hour for a particular technology for a given number of students over the expected life of courses to be delivered/supported by that technology?
- What will the costs be for necessary additional services or technologies?

In order to answer these questions, it is necessary to understand and analyse the cost structures of different technologies.

Capital and operating costs

Technologies such as television and computing may require high initial capital expenditure – purchase of a mainframe computer or television studio and equipment. Operating or recurrent costs are those that have to be found each year to run the system. This would include the staff required to operate the capital equipment (e.g. TV production staff), the money spent on production or purchase of teaching materials, and the cost of delivering it. This distinction is common to both conventional and distance teaching institutions, and is reflected in financial and resource allocation practices (capital and operating are usually quite separate budgets and have to be accessed independently).

However, this is where the resemblance ends. In conventional education, capital is used to cover fixed assets, such as buildings and equipment, which last many years. Operating budgets are used for teaching and administrative costs; the teaching is 'renewed' each year. In distance education, though, learning materials may take over two years to develop, may cost over $1 million to produce, and may be used for eight to ten years or more. On the other hand, three years may be the replacement time for desk-top microcomputer equipment. Thus distance education course materials, paid for out of operating budgets, may last longer than the equipment used to produce them, paid for out of capital. Logically, the development of learning materials should be seen as a capital, not an operating, expenditure. However, in practice they are always treated as an operating cost.

Fixed and variable costs

Even more important is the difference between fixed and variable costs. Fixed costs do not change with output, while variable costs do. In conventional education, teachers are a variable cost, if the service is run on a set teacher–pupil ratio; the more pupils, the more teachers required. Since teachers account for about two-thirds of the costs of school education, the majority of costs in conventional education are variable, i.e. dependent on student numbers.

The opposite is true for some technologies used in distance education. The BBC department that produced programmes for the British Open University (BBC/OUP) claimed at one time that 80 per cent of its costs with regard to audio–visual production were fixed, and 20 per cent variable. In other words, only 20 per cent of its costs were directly related to the number of programmes it made. Thus a general feature of most single-mode distance teaching institutions is that in relation to conventional institutions, a much higher proportion of their costs are fixed.

When fixed costs are a high proportion of total costs, it is necessary to keep output running as near to the maximum as possible in order to keep average costs down. This is just the same as the need to run a factory production line at maximum capacity in order to keep down the cost of each unit produced. Thus volume of activity is an important cost variable.

However, fixed costs are only fixed within certain parameters or boundaries. A substantial increase or decrease in the number of courses in production will seriously impact on fixed costs. Thus there are usually step functions with regard to fixed costs, a point in terms of output where fixed costs suddenly increase or decrease (the need for an additional studio or mainframe computer, for instance).

Technologies vary not only in total costs, but in the proportion of costs that are fixed and variable. This breakdown between fixed and variable costs becomes essential in determining the numbers of students necessary to justify the use of a particular technology.

Production and delivery costs

In conventional education, the cost of each course tends to be roughly the same each year. There is also little difference between the production and presentation of a course. The teacher both prepares the teaching and delivers it. Teachers also repeat the teaching to a new group of students each year. The first year may take more preparation, but in subsequent years, adjustments or changes to the course are equally likely. Thus in conventional education the cost of designing and presenting a course is unlikely to change substantially from year to year, nor is it meaningful to separate the design costs from the presentation costs.

In single mode distance teaching institutions, though, there are major differences between the costs of designing and delivering a course each year. It can take two years, and a team of over 30 people, to produce a full-credit course in a distance teaching institution. These design and production costs for one course (36 weeks) may well exceed US$1 million, and will be independent of the number of students or of the number of years for which the course runs (the course life). Thus, once a programme is made, or a text designed, it then becomes a fixed cost.

Some technologies have much higher average production costs than others for developing or producing one hour of study material. Table 3.1 (adapted from Sparkes, 1984), reflects the ratio of preparation and production costs associated with various media in producing one hour of teaching material.

This table is based on Sparkes' experience, and needs to be empirically verified. However, the general point still holds: there are considerable differences between technologies in their fixed production costs.

The cost of delivering a course each year though is variable, since delivery costs will depend on student numbers. The main delivery costs

Table 3.1 Production costs (including overheads) for one hour of teaching material

Medium	Production cost
Face-to-face lecture	1 unit
Audio cassette/radio/teleconference	2 units
Televised lecture	2–5 units
Computer-mediated communication	2–5 units
Print	2–10 units
High-quality TV programme	20–50 units
Pre-programmed computer-based learning	20–50 units
Computer-controlled video disc (from scratch)	50–100 units

will be payment of part-time tutors (if there is a set student–tutor ratio), the printing and delivery of textual materials, copying and delivering audio or video cassettes, and/or telephone costs.

Technologies differ considerably also in their delivery costs. The variable cost for delivering a radio programme is zero: it costs the same to transmit whether listened to by one or one million listeners. Audio cassettes on the other hand vary according to the number of cassettes that need to be sent: if students are to receive cassettes at home as part of the package, the delivery costs vary in direct proportion to the number of students.

These differences in fixed and variable costs reflect the cost *structures* of different technologies.

It should also be noted that there are two different parameters or dimensions for fixed and variable costs, with regard to technologies. The first is associated with courses or materials, the second with students. For instance, the overheads of buildings, permanent staff, etc. of a television production centre are fixed, and the number of programmes produced variable, determined by the number of courses and the requirement for television. However, once a programme is produced, its production cost is fixed for a specific course, although its distribution costs (if on cassette) will be variable, dependent on the number of students and the course life.

We shall see that it is essential to break down the costs of each technology in these ways in order to compare their relative costs for teaching.

Average cost

Wagner (1982) defines the average cost function as: 'the total cost function divided by the units of output produced'. He states that in education, the number of students is usually taken as the output measurement. In comparing the costs of different technologies for teaching, though, some other measure is needed, which brings us straight into the major problem of cost analysis: what is the output of a single educational technology?

Learning gains would certainly count, if the influence of one technology could be distinguished from that of all the other technologies used, and accurately measured. In practice, though, it is usually extremely difficult to isolate the learning gains of an individual technology in what is usually a mixed-media teaching situation. There are too many other factors – differences in students' use of technology and previous knowledge, the importance and roles given to a particular technology in course design, the influence of learning from other media on the impact of a particular technology, and so on – to identify with confidence the learning gains due to that technology. While studies have been done to isolate the impact of a particular television programme, for instance, the cost of doing such studies on a comprehensive scale across all technologies is considerable. For this reason, more crude but easily measured criteria tend to be used.

One commonly favoured by international agencies such as the World Bank is the dollar cost per student contact hour. This can be represented as follows:

$$\$ = \frac{t}{h \times n}$$

where: $\$$ = the cost per student contact hour

t = the total costs of materials (text or programme, etc), including overheads, production, and delivery

h = the average number of hours spent studying those materials per student

n = the number of students studying the material over the life of the course

For instance, Grundin (1983) calculated that the average cost for broadcast television on British Open University post-foundation courses was US$50 per student contact hour (at 1982 prices). Thus the institution spent $50 for one hour of studying television for each student.

Marginal costs

As Wagner points out, average costs are useful when estimating the costs before a project begins, or for evaluating the cost-benefits of a whole system; they are though less useful for fine-tuning a system once operational. What decision-makers within an organisation often need to know is the effect of increasing or reducing activities associated with a particular technology. For instance, what is the cost of adding an extra television programme, given all the investment already made in the system, or of adding an extra student to an existing course? These are known as marginal costs.

Variables impacting on costs

In summary, the costs of any given technology are influenced by the following variables:

- fixed costs, irrespective of levels of production or utilisation (overheads);
- the costs of production and delivery;
- the amount of material/teaching produced (volume);
- the number of students or learners;
- the length of time the teaching material is available for use. Some teaching materials based on 'live' teaching can be used only once; recorded materials can be used as long as the materials are relevant.

In most cases in this book, an eight-year life has been assumed for any particular course. Shortening the life of a course to five years, though, could dramatically affect the cost advantages of a particular technology.

Costs and decision-making

There are several ways in which costs can be expressed. Each of these costs has its value, depending on the purpose.

1 Total costs over the whole life of a course, for different numbers of students taking that course: of interest to those deciding whether or not to establish a technology, or to those working within a fixed overall budget. For instance, although adopting a particular technology may reduce the cost per student, or allow for a rapid expansion in student numbers, it could require an increase in total expenditure beyond the means of the funder. Total costs will depend not only on the number of students per course, but also the volume of activity, e.g. the number of hours of programmes produced each year.
2 The marginal cost of increasing the volume of teaching by one unit: of interest to a manager of a service, wishing to maximise investment in production resource. Relatively small cuts in funding can in certain circumstances have a dramatic effect on such unit costs, if fixed costs make up a high proportion of a unit's cost.
3 The marginal cost of adding an additional student to a course: of interest to any organisation wishing to match student fees to delivery costs, or where delivery costs exceed student fees (since extra students will increase total costs).
4 The average cost per student study hour i.e. the cost per student hour of contact with the technology.

In this book, points (1) and (4) will mainly be used, for several reasons. Absolute cost comparisons between different technologies are very difficult to make. Costs for very similar uses of the same technology can vary enormously between institutions. There may be very few institutions within the same country using the same technology in similar ways. Comparisons then tend to be international, with all the problems of currency conversion. Also, actual data in these areas in a form that is comparable are difficult to find. Data may have been collected at different times, and therefore affected by inflation.

However, what is not affected by these variations between institutions and different times of data collection are the cost structures, i.e. the relationship between volume of teaching, numbers of students and the costs of production and distribution. This can be reflected using cost curves, showing how costs vary along these dimensions. This can be of value to decision makers within an organisation, as they can then use a common methodology to calculate local costs for different technologies, then use cost curves to see at what points, in terms of volume and student numbers, technologies become more or less economical than others.

Total costs of a course over eight years will be used in this book, because this shows most clearly the differences in cost structures between different technologies. However, because the total cost of most technologies is related to volume of activity, costs have been calculated for as near as possible to 50, 100 and 150 hours of learning material produced per year.

Cost per student study hour, i.e. the average cost per hour of study contact with the technology for every student taking the course will also be used, because this is the measure that best takes into account both volume of activity, and number of students, and thus provides the best comparison between costs of different technologies.

It is very important to be aware that the cost data and cost curves used in this book are meant to be illustrative rather than definitive for any particular application. In some cases they are based on actual data collected specifically for cost analysis. In others, they are based on hypothetical data, but influenced by real applications and experience. The lack of empirical data and comprehensive cost studies on many of the newer technologies highlights the need for more research on costs.

Most of the tables and curves in this book are based on summary data. The full data and calculations are available in the form of a spreadsheet data-base (Excel 4.0).

TEACHING AND LEARNING

Many might feel that teaching and learning considerations should be the first criterion to be considered. If the technology is not effective educationally, then no matter how cheap, or how convenient it may be for access, it should not be used. However, it is much easier to discriminate between technology on the basis of access or cost, than it is on teaching effectiveness, for reasons that will become apparent.

There are three critical questions that need to be asked about teaching functions:

- What kinds of learning need to be developed?
- What instructional strategies will be employed to enable the learning needed?
- what are the unique educational characteristics of each technology, and how well do these match the learning and teaching requirements?

I will briefly discuss the first two questions, to illustrate some of the issues involved in answering them. The third question will be discussed through an analysis of each technology in the following chapters.

Different kinds of learning

Embedded within any decision about the use of technology in education and training, there are bound to be assumptions about the learning process. These assumptions, while often implicit, are nevertheless likely to be reflected in one or other of the major theories of learning. It is worth saying something briefly about these theories of learning, since the choice and use of technology should be driven by a coherent and conscious view of how people learn.

Behaviourism

The design of teaching machines, and subsequently the majority of computer-based training, has been strongly influenced by the theories of behaviourists such as Skinner (1968). The essential feature of behaviourism is that it denies or ignores the role of conscious strategies or self-will in learning. Learning takes place through the impact of the external environment, which rewards or punishes 'trial-and-error' behaviour. Learners seek rewards or avoid punishment. The teacher's job is to manage the learners' environment to create the most appropriate learning outcomes.

Cognitive theories

While behaviourism has its value for certain kinds of learning (e.g. rote memory, correcting deviant or psychopathic behaviour, learning certain motor skills), most cognitive psychologists (i.e. psychologists who study thinking and learning) believe that behaviourism is inadequate for explaining a great deal of intellectual activity. Nevertheless, there is a large body of cognitive psychology which follows in the behaviourist tradition of looking for explanations of learning and thinking in terms of physical rules which ignore consciousness or self-will. Although the approach is much more sophisticated than simple behaviourism, the majority of research into artificial intelligence follows this behaviourist tradition. This has led to the development of machine-based intelligent tutoring systems, which use computer programmes to embody teaching strategies. Self (1989) summarises this approach as follows:

> The ITS [intelligent tutoring system] philosophy derives from a commonsense theory of knowledge, which holds that items of knowledge exist in an objective sense in the external world and that we can acquire knowledge from the world, via our senses or teachers, or from ITSs.
>
> (Self, 1989, pp. 4–5)

Self considers this approach also to be inadequate in itself. He argues that 'all knowledge, even in natural sciences, is conjectural. Knowledge grows only through criticism'.

There are in fact many cognitive psychologists who emphasise the importance for learning of conscious intellectual strategies. Bruner (1966) for instance, argues that learning is an active process in which a learner infers principles and rules, and tests them out. Bruner also argues that a subject area is defined not only by its content or topics, but also by the methods used to define and validate knowledge within that subject area, and these methods vary between different subject areas (such as science and humanities, for instance).

Piaget (1970) argued that before children can comprehend concepts or manipulate symbols such as words, they have to experience directly or physically the actions or events which are represented by abstract concepts or symbols. Piaget is not alone amongst psychologists in pointing out the importance of direct experience and the manipulation of objects for laying the foundations of logical thinking.

For those who accept these characteristics of learning and thinking, it will be important, when considering the choice of appropriate technologies, to assess the extent to which a particular technology enables learners to develop and test their own inferences and to explore for themselves the underlying structure and assumptions of a subject. Also, to what extent does the technology enable feedback and criticism to be provided for learner-generated inferences and hypotheses? There is also the underlying question of the extent to which media and technology can substitute for direct, physical experience (see Olson and Bruner, 1974, for an excellent discussion of this issue).

Humanistic psychology

Humanistic psychologists, such as Carl Rogers, are at the opposite end of the spectrum from behaviourism. They argue that each person acts in accordance with his or her own conscious perception of the world, and hence each person is unique, and free to choose his or her own actions. Rogers (1969) states that 'every individual exists in a continually changing world of experience in which he is the centre'. The external world is interpreted within the context of that private world. Rogers, then, like Bruner, believes that knowledge is constructed by each individual interpreting and testing the meaning of external events in terms of the relevance to that individual's past experience.

For Rogers, though, this is critically a social process; inferences are primarily tested through feedback from and social contact with other people. Rogers then rejects the notion that learning is mainly about the absorption of information. Learning requires interpersonal communication between a learner and a 'facilitator' with whom the learner can personally and genuinely relate.

What has caused so much interest for open and distance educators is the potential of some of the newer technologies for developing an inter-personal relationship at a distance, as distinct from a person–machine relationship.

Taking a position regarding learning theories

The need to make a conscious choice of learning theory is a profoundly practical issue with respect to the selection of technologies for teaching. Can artificial intelligence, for example, represent the development of creative processes due to the unique experiences of individual people? Can machine-based education represent the diversity of and differences between the experiences of individuals, and how those experiences lead to original or new thoughts or insights? If not, what will be the educational consequences of relying heavily on machine-based education? These questions cannot be answered solely in objective or scientific terms; they require value judgements to be made about what kinds of education and training we want.

Knowledge and skills

When preparing for decisions about technology use, it is also useful to make a distinction between knowledge and skills. Olson and Bruner (1974) argue that learning involves two distinct aspects: firstly, acquiring knowledge of facts, principles, ideas, concepts, events, relationships, rules and laws; and secondly, using or working on that knowledge to develop skills.

The representation of knowledge/content

Media differ in the extent to which they can represent different kinds of knowledge, because they vary in the symbol systems that they use to encode information (text, sound, still pictures, moving images, etc.). Different media are capable of combining different symbol systems. Books can represent knowledge through text and still pictures, but not through sound or moving pictures. In this respect, computers in the past have been similar to books, although now they can also incorporate sound and moving pictures (i.e. multimedia). Television and film in the past have been the richest media, symbolically. They were the only media which could encompass text, still and moving pictures, natural language, natural movement, music and other sounds, and full colour. Of all the technologies they are still the most able to represent closely 'real' experience in all its facets, although it is only a matter of time before computer-based technology surpasses television and film in this respect.

Differences between media in the way they combine symbol systems influence the way in which different media can represent knowledge. Thus there is a difference between a written description, a televised recording, and a computer simulation of the same experiment. Different symbol systems are being used, conveying different kinds of information about the same experiment. This is significant for media selection, because different subject areas (e.g. art, history, science, mathematics) have different requirements for the representation of knowledge, or, rather, they place differing emphases on the importance of different ways of representing knowledge.

Media also differ in the way they structure knowledge. Books, the telephone, radio, audio cassettes and face-to-face tuition all tend to present knowledge linearly or sequentially. While parallel activities can be represented through these media (e.g. different chapters dealing with different events occurring simultaneously) these activities still have to be presented sequentially through these media. Computers are more able to present or simulate the inter-relationship of multiple variables simultaneously occurring, but only within closely defined limits. Computers can also handle branching or alternative routes through information, but again within closely defined limits.

Subject matter varies enormously in the way in which information needs to be structured. Subject areas (e.g. natural sciences, history, etc.) structure knowledge in particular ways determined by the internal logic of the subject matter. This structure may be very tight or logical, requiring particular sequences or relationships between different concepts, or very open or loose, requiring learners to deal with highly complex material in an open-ended or intuitive way. Even within a single curriculum area, subject matter may vary in terms of its required structure (e.g. social theories and statistics, within sociology).

Some media are better than others for certain kinds of representation of particular significance to teaching. In particular, media differ in their ability to handle concrete or abstract knowledge. Abstract knowledge is handled primarily through language. While all media can handle language, either in written or spoken form, media vary in their ability to represent concrete knowledge (examples, demonstrations, etc.).

If media then do vary both in the way they present information symbolically and in the way they can conveniently handle the structures required within different subject areas, one needs to select the media which best match the required mode of presentation and the dominant structure of the subject matter. Two consequences of this are the need for a different balance of media between different subject areas, and for subject experts to be deeply involved in decisions about the choice and use of media, at least at a tactical level.

Skills

Technologies also differ in the extent to which they can help develop different skills. Gagné (1985) drew attention to different levels or kinds of learning, as also did Bloom *et al.* (1956).

Table 3.2 Distinction between content and intellectual skills

Content	Intellectual skills
Facts	Comprehension
Ideas	Analysis
Principles	Application
Opinions	Synthesis
Relationships (e.g. A causes B)	Restructuring and modifying
Criteria	Evaluation
Problems	Problem-solving

Source: A. W. Bates, 1981

Comprehension is likely to be the minimal level of learning objective for most education courses. Some researchers (e.g. Marton and Säljö, 1976) make a distinction between surface and deep comprehension. At the highest level comes the application of what one has comprehended to new situations. Here it becomes necessary to develop skills of analysis, evaluation, and problem-solving. We shall see that there appears to be a relationship between the type of skills that need to be developed and the choice of media and technology. In analysing each technology, I shall attempt to identify the relationship between that technology and the development of certain specific skills.

Different kinds of teaching

To date, there have been basically two dominant instructional models or paradigms in open and distance learning:

- the remote classroom
- front-end systems design.

The remote classroom model is a straight transfer of the dominant paradigms of face-to-face teaching to the distance teaching context, such as a televised lecture, or an audio conference seminar. Thus while the technology enables the method of delivery to be different, the teaching strategy is more or less the same as in a face-to-face context.

The second dominant paradigm was developed specifically for distance teaching. It is based on a systems approach to course design, with heavy investment at the initial design stage, and with varying degrees of post-design 'fine tuning', through the use of third-party tutors.

In general, a wider range of people with specialist skills are involved in the design, production and delivery of distance teaching materials than in classroom teaching. Distance teaching has been described as an industrial process (Peters, 1983), because of the division of labour, and the nature of the process of developing and delivering teaching materials.

Figure 3.1 summarises this process, indicating the stages of development,

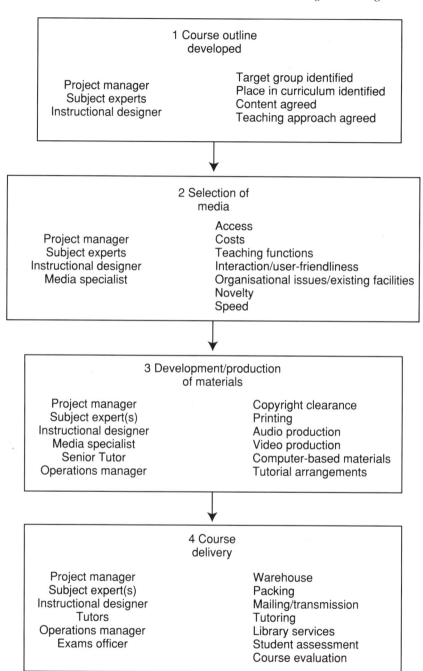

Figure 3.1 The course development process

the people involved, and the nature of the tasks to be accomplished. Figure 3.1 does not include all activities and specialists, and there are considerable variations in practice and terminology from institution to institution. With the move towards some of the more interactive technologies, the model becomes less accurate. Nevertheless, it is useful in indicating the nature of the process, and in particular for locating selection of media and technologies within the process.

This model has the following characteristics that distinguish it from the classroom model:

- heavy reliance on theories of instructional design, with strong emphasis on building in student activities, feedback and carefully structured and coherent content;
- content and methods are determined and monitored through a team process; content is prepared in draft form for amendment and approval by the team;
- both content and skills are defined in terms of specified learning objectives, closely linked to student assessment;
- technology is an essential part of the design and delivery of a course; technology choice is made by the team, on the basis of the learning tasks to be completed, and the technologies available (determined on an institutional basis);
- different kinds of learning tasks are carefully defined, and assigned to specific technologies or learning modes, e.g. comprehension of scientific theory via print; demonstration of experiments and experimental design by television; manipulative skills and experimental design by home experiment kits and laboratory-based summer schools; student support and assessment by remote tutors, who are not directly involved in the design of the course;
- detailed course planning (in terms of tasks to be completed and deadlines for tasks) and detailed specification of course content;
- lack of adaptation to the needs of individual learners; all learners receive the same materials; individual modification is left to the remote tutor;
- slow development time: it may take two years or more from initial design to delivery of a course.

This model applies particularly to courses making heavy use of one-way technologies, such as print, broadcast television, and audio cassettes. There is a strong emphasis on quality control before teaching starts, through assessment of draft materials by external academic peers.

The course team model has helped establish the credibility of the autonomous distance teaching universities. The material is publicly available, and in most cases is recognised externally to be of very high academic quality, and reflects advanced and effective instructional strategies. It has brought a high degree of professionalism to the teaching of content and skills.

It is, though, expensive to create, lacks flexibility, in that it cannot be easily changed or up-dated, and it requires a wide range of highly skilled people. The approach has been heavily criticised by, for example, Harris (1987), for being authoritarian in content specification, and pre-determining the structure and arrangement of content (doing all the work for the student), making it difficult for students to negotiate, re-configure or transform the learning experience to their own needs.

On the other hand, the remote classroom model is more casual, less open to analysis and criticism, and hence may have problems with the quality or effectiveness of the instructional process. It is certainly more heavily dependent on the ability and conscientiousness of individual teachers, and is therefore more likely to be variable. Students have greater freedom in interpreting what it is important to learn and structuring their learning to their own needs, but may have difficulties with assessment if they have not correctly identified the intellectual skills and content areas expected of them by the teachers.

In terms of the use of technology, there is likely to be less preparation or skill in choosing or using technology in the remote classroom model, because the level of professional media support is deliberately reduced, partly for cost reasons, but also partly for reasons of control.

Remote classroom teachers are more likely to replicate their face-to-face classroom teaching approaches when using technology. This may prevent them from exploiting the unique teaching characteristics of the technology, although many learn to adjust their teaching technique to the different context of remote learners. We shall see though that this tends to be more like fine tuning than a new approach to teaching.

With the introduction of some of the newer two-way technologies, in particular computer-mediated communication, a number of new distance teaching models become possible, such as knowledge building and resource-based mentoring. These will be discussed in later chapters.

Before ending this discussion on the relationship between teaching, learning and the use of technology in open and distance learning, I want to discuss in some detail the issue of interactivity, because this is a critical aspect of learning through technology.

INTERACTION, USER-FRIENDLINESS AND CONTROL

One important aspect of the use of technology in education and training is the 'interface' between people and machines, namely the way learners or teachers are able to interact with or through a particular technology. There are three different elements of the person–machine interface: the need for active learning, the need for easy-to-use or 'transparent' technologies, and the need for teacher and student control over teaching and learning activities.

Interactivity

Most theories of learning suggest that for learning to be effective it needs to be active; in other words the learner must respond in some way to the learning material. It is not enough merely to listen, view or read; learners have to do something with the learning material. Thus they may need to demonstrate (if only to themselves) that they have understood, or they may need to modify their prior knowledge to accommodate new information, or they may need to analyse new information in the light of their existing knowledge.

Feedback is considered an important component of interaction. Feedback provides learners with knowledge of results that indicate whether they have learned correctly, or it can take the form of a response from another person indicating how well the learner has learned.

Technologies differ considerably in the ways in which they encourage interaction. Many arguments about the value of technology in distance education, and the extent to which it can or should replace face-to-face or human interaction, are often based on confusion and misunderstanding about the contexts in which interaction takes place.

In effect there are two rather different contexts for interaction: the first is an individual, isolated activity, which is the interaction of a learner with the learning material, be it text, television or computer programme; the second is a social activity, which is the interaction between two or more people about the learning material. Both kinds of interaction are important in learning.

The loneliness of the long-distance learner

Particularly in higher education, high value is often placed on academic discourse, i.e. developing student skills of analysis, constructing and defending an argument, assembling evidence in support of an argument, and critiquing the work of scholars and fellow learners. Many professors consider the skills of academic discourse are best learned through small group discussions, led by an experienced academic (Plato's 'Socratic Method'). In reality, though, this kind of small-group, face-to-face interaction is quite rare in post-secondary education today.

The fact is that for both conventional and distance education students, by far the largest part of their studying is done alone, interacting with text books or other learning media. The difference is that for distance learners, this fact is acknowledged by the designers of the teaching materials, who often take steps to build opportunities for interaction into the learning materials. The aim is to simulate a face-to-face conversation between teacher and student. Holmberg (1983) has argued that:

> the character of good distance teaching resembles that of a guided conversation aiming at learning . . . the distance-study course and the

non-contiguous communication typical of distance education are seen as the instruments of a conversation-like interaction between the student on the one hand and the tutor counsellor . . . on the other.

(Holmberg, 1983)

This simulated guided conversation is conducted through the interaction of learner and teaching materials, and is not dependent on (although may be enhanced by) the intervention of a human tutor. The simulated conversation is achieved through the design of the teaching materials (embedded questions and feedback, etc.). This is interaction between the learner and the learning materials.

Learning as a social activity

Social interaction may be of three types in open and distance learning:

- interaction between the learner and the originator of the teaching material;
- interaction between the learner and a tutor, who mediates between the original material and the learner, by providing guidance or assessment;
- interaction between the learner and other learners.

The first kind of interaction has been relatively rare in distance education, but it is becoming more common with the use of interactive technologies. The second has been the most common, but has in the past been mainly done through correspondence via the mail service, or by telephone contact. Interaction with other students is possibly the most important for many learners, but it has tended to be neglected in distance education, except where students have been able to attend local centres or summer schools.

Note that in all three types, interaction can take place without face-to-face contact; in other words, even inter-personal interaction can be at a distance, via the mail service or through technologies such as the telephone or computer-based electronic mail. In the area of social interaction, then, we need to differentiate between interaction which is remote or face-to-face, and also interaction that is in real time or asynchronous. In other words, social interaction is not necessarily time or place dependent, or even instructor-dependent if a mediating tutor or peer groups are used.

A perceived weakness of the older technologies, such as print and broadcast television and radio, is that they are one-way technologies, good for delivering large quantities of information to large numbers of students, but not good for interaction between student and teacher.

One reason why many distance educators are increasingly interested in some of the newer technologies such as audio-graphics, audio, video and computer networking is their potential for two-way communication, thereby allowing the student to interact directly and flexibly with the teacher or other students, even if at a distance.

The quality of interaction

It is very simplistic to think that a technology like computing is auto-matically more interactive than one like television, because computers force a learner response, while television is a passive medium. The quality of the interaction and feedback is critical. Much of the most useful interaction between a learner and the learning material is covert – perhaps best described as thinking. A well-written book or stimulating television programme may well encourage a high level of interaction in the learner, without any apparent overt actions. Similarly, learners can easily find ways to beat a computer, not by thoughtfully responding to its questions, but by second-guessing the pattern of pre-determined, multiple-choice answers, or by random guessing until the correct answer is found.

Feedback can be very simple, merely providing correct answers to straightforward questions; or it can be much more complex, suggesting a variety of alternative responses, and ways to evaluate among them.

One way of evaluating a technology's capacity for feedback is to examine the extent to which it provides flexibility for dealing with the learner's response to activities. Does it provide merely 'yes/no' information as to whether the learner has responded correctly; does it provide remedial activities, e.g. further information or reading, if the answer is not rated correct or adequate; or does it engage the learner in some form of discussion or dialogue about the quality of the learner's response? For instance, does it allow the learner to develop or test an argument or a pattern of thinking as a result of interaction with a tutor or learning material? How does it handle an original response not anticipated by the instructor or learning material? It is this latter quality of feedback which is more easily handled by the intervention of a teacher or tutor, and is less easily provided by machines.

It is important to separate the quality of the interaction from the technol-ogy through which it occurs. Some forms of interaction, such as academic discourse, are hard, but not impossible, to replicate through technologies such as print or computer-based learning. Other two-way technologies have the capability of handling high-quality inter-personal interaction, even if done at a distance. However, the mere attendance at a face-to-face seminar, or participation in a computer conference, does not of itself guarantee high quality interaction. Good design or good teaching is critical. Nevertheless, experience suggests that high-quality interaction is more easily achieved with some technologies, while with others, it has proved quite difficult to achieve such interaction. The differences between technologies in their capacity for interaction will be explored further in the following chapters.

User-friendliness

In general, technologies which are easy to use will be used more than those that are difficult. While this is hardly an earth-shattering revelation, it is often a factor overlooked by enthusiasts for the latest advanced technology. Virtual reality may be of tremendous educational potential, but if designers find the whole process of creating high-quality programme material difficult, or if learners cannot control adequately the learning environment, the technology will quickly fall into disfavour. Furthermore, there is clearly a disadvantage in using a particular technology if it takes students several weeks to learn how to use it, before they can start on the course content.

Reliability is another critical factor. If the technology breaks down or 'crashes', it can severely disrupt the learning process. While the reliability of educational technologies is improving, too often the technology breaks down, or inordinate effort is needed to make it work reliably.

Learner control

Technologies also differ considerably in the control they allow learners.

Perhaps the most important control distinction is between transient and permanent media. Broadcast television, face-to-face lectures, cable television, telephone tutoring, and radio are all transient media. The learner must be at a particular place at a particular time, and unless a recording is made, there is no chance to repeat the experience, nor to review it a second time.

Video cassettes, books, computer-assisted learning, video discs and audio cassettes on the other hand all provide learners with permanent learning materials. The material can be used many times by the learner, allowing for mastery of the content through repetition and review. Furthermore, the material can be accessed at times and, for some media, at places which are convenient to the learner – such as at home in the evening.

Another factor which helps learners to organise their study is portability. Some media – such as books – can be taken wherever the learner goes. Other media – such as computer-controlled video discs or broadcast television – are far less portable.

Interaction and user-friendliness are therefore strong discriminators between different technologies, and these issues will be discussed in more detail against each technology in the following chapters.

The need for better understanding of the teaching and learning process

I have only touched on what is a very complex and controversial area. One of the great difficulties in media and technology selection and use is the lack of a generally agreed, empirically grounded educational theory that defines unambiguously the role of different media and technologies in the teaching and learning process. I strongly believe the main barrier to greater use of technology in post-secondary education is not so much fear of or resistance to the technology itself, but the lack of knowledge or understanding regarding the teaching and learning process. Without this, it is very difficult to identify appropriate roles for different technologies.

Laurillard (1993) has made an important contribution in this area. She analysed the nature of teaching and learning in a university context. She states:

> Academic knowledge is not like other kinds of everyday knowledge. Teaching is essentially a rhetorical activity, seeking to persuade students to change the way they experience the world . . . . The learning process must be constituted as a dialogue between teacher and student, operating at the level of descriptions of actions in the world, recognizing the second-order character of academic knowledge.
>
> (Laurillard, 1993, pp. 28, 94)

In particular, she argues that university teaching needs to be:

- *discursive*: teaching needs to be conversational, in the sense that an environment must be created where student and teacher can communicate agreed goals and conceptions to each other, and generate and receive feedback;
- *interactive*: the student must take actions to demonstrate learning, and the teacher must respond to those actions, by providing feedback;
- *adaptive*: the teacher must use information about the student's understanding of concepts to determine appropriate future learning activities for the student;
- *reflective*: the teacher needs to encourage students to reflect on the feedback in relation to the instructional goals.

Having determined the desired goals of university teaching, Laurillard then analyses different educational technologies, to see to what extent they are functionally capable of matching these four characteristics. Her conclusion is that while each of the technologies she analyses can meet some of the above requirements, only computer-based tutorial programmes can meet all, and then only within a highly constrained student–teacher dialogue.

It should be understood that her analysis here is not so much of technologies as tools for use by 'real' (if remote) teachers, but as substitutes for direct student–teacher interaction, which I do not believe to be necessary or appropriate, even in distance education. I also have some criticisms of her analysis of individual technologies in terms of their ability to meet the four essential characteristics of teaching. Also, the ideal teaching environment that she is trying to replicate is the one-to-one tutorial, which in itself is open to argument. What is important about Laurillard's work though is that it is a rigorous attempt to define 'good teaching' in a particular context, and then to analyse the suitability of different technologies in those terms.

Despite the lack of agreed theory, then, it is nevertheless important that decision-makers at each institution should go through the exercise of reaching agreement on what kinds of learning, or approaches to learning, are desirable before committing to particular teaching strategies, let alone a particular technology. The professional input of instructional and/or curriculum designers, as well as subject experts, is essential for this kind of exercise. However, if this exercise is done successfully, it should result in new models of instruction that exploit the full potential of the new technologies, rather than merely replicating the remote classroom or the front-end system design models.

ORGANISATIONAL ISSUES

Successful technology applications usually require more than just the purchase and installation of equipment, hiring of technical staff, and the training of teaching staff. Successful implementation also requires some major structural or organisational changes within an institution. In addition, there are often powerful external factors influencing the decision to use a particular technology, such as government initiatives or high-profile marketing of services by the commercial sector. These can be seen either as distorting factors, or opportunities. The important questions then that need to be asked in this area are:

- What opportunities or threats exist in the external environment that may influence the choice of particular technologies?
- What are the internal organisational requirements, and the barriers to be removed, before this technology can be used successfully?

External factors

The existing technological infrastructure within a country is a major factor in influencing media selection. If there is already a broadcast network in place, and it is underused, it is much easier to introduce television for distance education purposes. The transmission of programmes for the distance teaching institution then becomes a marginal cost on an already established system.

Most distance learning rides on the back of technologies already established for entertainment or business purposes; although there have been a number of technologies or networks specially created for education, they have in general not been possible to sustain, for economic or political reasons.

Government initiatives, such as the development of a state-wide education and training network, or commercial vendors of services such as video conferencing or fibre-optic networks, will also generate potential technology-based projects. The critical point is that institutions need to be proactive rather than reactive to such initiatives. It is essential then to develop a clear vision of the role of technology within an organisation, so that when particular initiatives come along, there is a framework for project evaluation (see Bates, 1995). Too often organisations find themselves involved with short-term technology-based projects, which, while successful in themselves, cannot be sustained because of lack of continuing (external) funding or a clear idea of where such projects fit into the long-term plans of an institution.

Internal restructuring

Innovation often depends on 'champions for change' at a high level: a president, dean or course team member who is willing to fight for the introduction of new technology and approaches. The reverse is also true: inappropriate decisions often stem from champions of a particular technology, who may not have the necessary experience or knowledge of other technologies. However, institutional commitment at a senior level, together with the resource allocations needed to back that commitment, are essential if technology is to be used extensively in an institution.

A major implication of using technology is the need to reorganise and restructure the teaching and technology support services in order to exploit and use the technology efficiently (sometimes called 're-engineering the organisation'). Too often technology is merely added on to an existing structure and way of doing things. Reorganisation and restructuring is disruptive and costly in the short-term, but usually essential for successful implementation of technology-based teaching.

The need to exploit an already existing technological infrastructure within an institution can be a major conservative influence limiting the application of new technologies. Thus if a heavy investment has already been made in a particular technology, with both capital equipment and permanent staff, it is likely that the head of department responsible for production in that area has a senior decision-making role, because of his or her control over a large budget.

However, introducing the use of a new technology may require the shift of funds away from 'traditional' cost centres into new ones. Indeed, unless this is done, it will be hard to justify the use of new technology on cost grounds. This, though, is likely to lead to opposition not just from those who control the budgets of traditional technologies, but from those in the departments who fear for their jobs.

These organisational requirements are extremely difficult to meet, and are often major reasons for the slow implementation of new technology. Thus there is often a bias towards those technologies that can be introduced with the minimum of organisational change, although these may not be the technologies that would have maximum impact on learning.

NOVELTY

This is perhaps the least important criterion, but it is often easier to get funding for new uses of technology. While audio cassettes combined with print materials can be a very low-cost but highly effective teaching medium, they are not sexy. It may be easier to persuade funding agencies to invest in much more costly but spectacular technologies such as computer-controlled video discs or satellite voice and data networks.

Furthermore, the application of a new technology can stimulate change and development in well-established institutions that are becoming a little stale, and this new impetus may be far more important than merely the use of the technology itself.

SPEED

In a society subject to rapid change, courses need to be put on quickly, and easily up-dated. An increasing problem for open and distance learning systems is the time it takes to produce a course, and the length of time a course has to last. Once produced, many courses have to remain unchanged, despite known errors or weaknesses in the material, or changes in the subject matter that make the material out of date, because funds are not available for major changes, or production of new courses is seen as a higher priority.

Again, technologies vary in their capacity for speed of implementation and flexibility in up-dating.

CONCLUSIONS

One should have no illusions that there are simple solutions to selecting and using technology in either conventional or distance education. In fact, decision-making in this area is getting more difficult all the time, with the proliferation of new technologies and new teaching initiatives.

The appropriate use and selection of technology depends very much on local circumstances: context is all-important. Even between countries with similar levels of economic development, decisions will differ according to geography, local technological infrastructures (e.g. availability of broadcast services), and educational structures. Even within a single institution, different decisions will be required between different areas of teaching, dependent on the needs of the target group and the teaching requirements of a course.

Decision-making about technology in open and distance learning is a complex process, requiring consideration of a great number of factors. Decision-making in this area is also about personal choice, driven as much by values and beliefs as by technical considerations. These different factors cannot easily be related to one another quantitatively. In the end, an intuitive decision has to be made, but based on a careful analysis of the situation.

Fortunately, one of the great advantages of the human brain over computers is that the brain is far better than a computer at handling this kind of decision, provided that people have the necessary information and an appropriate framework for analysis and decision-making. From this point, decision-makers can then come to their own conclusions intuitively about the best mix and match of specific technologies to use, taking into account not only the factors enumerated, but also all the local conditions which only they can know fully.

Thus it is important to identify the salient factors (i.e. **A C T I O N S**) that have to be considered when making decisions about particular technologies, and to ensure that systems are set up in such a way that resources can be re-allocated as technologies change. The following chapters analyse each of these salient factors for the main technologies now available for open and distance learning.

4 Television
Educational broadcasting

TELEVISION: PROMISE, DIVERSITY AND MISUNDERSTANDING

Of all the media available to educators, television comes in the most diverse forms, has arguably the greatest potential for teaching and learning, and is probably the least well used.

Diversity

There are many different forms of educational television: for example, educational broadcasting; instructional television; interactive television; tutored video instruction; video conferencing. It can vary between being a one-way or two-way medium. It also varies enormously in production style: for example, relayed lectures, studio discussions, magazine format, documentary, case-study, audio–visual resource, audio–visual data-base. Television varies in organisational structure, and particularly in terms of who controls production and/or delivery: broadcasting organisations, educational institutions, satellite or telecommunications companies, training organisations. Lastly, it varies enormously in the different technologies used (satellite, terrestrial broadcast, cable, video cassettes, etc.).

Every one of these differences has a significant implication for technology selection and educational design. However, while the diversity of television applications makes generalisation difficult, a good deal is known about how to use it successfully in education, even if this knowledge is not often applied.

A complex medium

Perhaps of all the media available for learning, television is the least understood and most under-rated by teachers and learners, and probably the most over-rated by educational policy-makers.

When television is used in education, it is often used very badly, in that its presentational characteristics are grossly under-exploited. Very few institutions use television as part of an integrated mixed-media teaching system. Learners often mistakenly assume that it is an easy medium to learn from, and many teachers do not see television as a serious instructional medium; indeed, many are openly hostile to it, seeing it as trivialising the educational process. On the other hand, decision-makers, and particularly politicians, often underestimate the costs and limitations of television. It costs money to exploit fully its presentational qualities, and television requires a great deal of training and expertise to use well.

Differentiating between types of educational television

It is important to be clear about the different kinds of television available for educational purposes. Programmes produced by broadcasting organisations have a different purpose and target audience from those produced by educational institutions. Because of this diversity, it is helpful to differentiate between *educational broadcasting* (the subject of this chapter), and *instructional television* (the subject of the next chapter).

First, though, it is necessary to describe briefly the different technologies used for television. The broadcast technologies will be described in this chapter and the recorded technologies in the next.

THE TECHNOLOGY

A full analogue colour television signal requires the equivalent of approximately 1,000 telephone lines to transmit at the same speed as a voice-only communication, and thus needs a very wide transmission bandwidth. Analogue television signals are transmitted, or stored and played back from recordings, at 25 frames ('still' pictures) per second in Europe, and 30 frames per second in North America.

Terrestrial transmission

There are a number of different ways in which television can be transmitted. With terrestrial ground transmission, broadcasts are radiated from a ground transmitter, with programmes often relayed between different transmitters to form a network perhaps covering a whole country.

The frequencies within which television (and radio) can be broadcast terrestrially are limited. The International Telecommunication Union (ITU), to which virtually all countries are signatories, allocates frequencies for terrestrial broadcasting to individual governments, who then re-allocate bandwidths to broadcasting organisations, either directly, or through national commissions established by government (e.g., the Home Office in the UK, the Federal Communications Commission in the USA, the CRTC in Canada; these bodies may also allocate other television services, such as cable and satellite frequencies). This means in effect that in many countries, radiated terrestrial transmission is limited in practice to four or five national networks at a maximum, and local services are also restricted.

In compact and densely populated countries, such as in Europe, national radiated terrestrial networks are economically viable, but in countries covering a large geographical area such as the USA, Russia, Brazil or Canada, providing a national network solely through a terrestrial radiated network could be prohibitively expensive.

One particular form of terrestrial transmission system used in the USA is Instructional Television Fixed Service (ITFS). This enables sites in various locations with appropriate reception equipment to receive broadcast signals in frequencies not allocated for public television reception, thus providing a closed-circuit television network for instructional use. However, such transmissions by definition have to be accessed at local centres, which have the equipment and licence to receive, and therefore ITFS is not available for home delivery.

While ITFS allows several local sites to receive a single transmission, point-to-point microwave provides two-way video and audio signals between two sites. Microwave links require clear line-of-site, relatively short distances and, again, special transmit and receive equipment at each end.

Cable services

Cable television is essentially a local distribution facility, with the facility to link into national networks through the relay of satellite signals. There are two main kinds of cable television: co-axial and fibre-optic. Co-axial cabling uses copper wires, but configured differently from telephone wiring, and allows up to 30 or so television channels to be delivered into any one site. Co-axial is still the main system of delivering cable television to homes. Fibre-optic cabling is being installed mainly on 'trunk' routes, although it will increasingly be used for connecting individual sites with large telecommunication requirements, such as tower blocks in downtown city centres.

Satellite

A satellite is like a mirror in the sky, allowing telecommunications signals of various kinds (television, radio, voice, data) to be sent up from the ground (up-linked) then re-transmitted down again.

A satellite is likely to carry several transmitters (called transponders). Each transponder can usually carry the equivalent of one analogue television channel and several radio channels, or over a thousand voice channels, or very large quantities of digitised information, such as words, computer programs, still pictures, or any combination.

Since the footprints of several satellites are likely to overlap, and since there are also terrestrial-based radio, television and microwave signals, it is important that satellites broadcast at frequencies which do not interfere with those of other satellites or of other ground services. This means that there has to be international agreement about the power and the frequencies at which satellites will operate, and where they must be placed in the geo-stationary orbit. They need to be spaced apart (between 6° and 9°) to avoid interference with one another.

Because there is a limit to the number of satellites that can be placed in the geo-stationary orbit at any one time, there also has to be agreement on how many satellites (or rather satellite channels) each country can have. These agreements are also made through the ITU. In many countries, a national telecommunications monopoly controls all access to satellites within that country, and also usually sets the tariffs for accessing satellites. However, the government of the USA has deregulated, allowing a number of organisations to operate satellites.

There are basically three kinds of satellites. First, there are low-powered satellites built primarily to facilitate world-wide telephone and television communications. The second type are regional or domestic satellites. Because the signal is more concentrated, the signal at the point of reception tends to be stronger than that of global communications satellites, and hence domestic satellites can be used with substantially smaller and cheaper ground-stations (about 3 metres in diameter for a receive-only antenna for television). The signals from regional or domestic satellites are usually picked up and then re-transmitted by terrestrial means, although television signals for instance may be received directly by hotels or apartment blocks, or by people living in remote areas.

The third type of satellite is used for direct (or quasi-direct) broadcasting services (DBS). These satellites are much larger and more expensive to build and launch, but are much more powerful and operate at much higher frequencies (in the 12 GHz or Ku-band range). Consequently, analogue television signals can be received on smaller antennas (around 1.4 to 1.6 metres in diameter). These satellites (such as ANIK-E in Canada, AUSSAT in Australia, and ASTRA in Europe) can be used for direct transmission of television broadcasts to individual homes, and to cable head ends. They can also carry extremely large quantities of data and many voice channels on one transponder. ASTRA carries 16 television channels. OLYMPUS, a European Space Agency experimental satellite, broadcast at even higher frequencies, and could transmit a single footprint over half of Europe for high-quality reception on a satellite dish no larger than a dinner plate (0.4 metres diameter).

Digital transmission

While there is a limit to the number of satellites that can be placed in the geo-stationary orbit, digital compression techniques enable a single transponder to carry several television transmissions simultaneously, thus increasing the overall television channel capacity (see the next chapter for a fuller description of digital compression techniques). However, domestic television sets currently require analogue signals. Thus conversion equipment is required, either at the cable head end, or connected directly to an analogue television set.

In Europe, there have been several attempts to introduce digital services (e.g. D-MAC or D2-MAC), but at the time of writing these are still mainly experimental. In the USA, PBS is offering up to 20 educational channels over 5 Ku-band transponders on a single satellite (Telstar 401) from 1994, and the National Technological University has already converted to digital transmission, with four channels on a single transponder.

It is likely that most broadcast services in North America will be originating in digital format by 1996. Initially, these signals will be converted to analogue for domestic television receivers, until these are gradually replaced with all-digital sets. Digital television allows not only the number of channels to be increased significantly, but also for the integration of television with computing and telephone technologies. The significance of this will be discussed further in Chapter 11.

Thus while there is technically a limit to the number of satellites that can be 'parked' in geo-stationary orbit, channel capacity is continually being increased through the use of more powerful satellites, higher frequencies, video compression techniques, and more sophisticated ground reception equipment. From the point of view of education and training, this means that transmission rates are dropping, and the availability of broadcast channels is increasing.

EDUCATIONAL BROADCASTING

Broadcast educational television is found in one form or another in most countries. While its organisation, objectives and operation are extremely diverse (for a full description of broadcasting in education, see Hawkridge and Robinson, 1982, and Bates, 1984), there are certain common general characteristics.

The oldest and most established form of educational television is the programming transmitted by major public broadcasting organisations, such as the BBC in the United Kingdom, the Public Broadcasting System in the United States, and TVOntario in Canada. This kind of educational television is designed for specific if broad target groups, such as pre-school children, pupils in schools, or adults with a curiosity about the world of arts or science. It is an open-access service, available to anyone interested enough to tune in and watch, and usually designed with this general audience in mind.

Educational broadcasting organisations provide a particular kind of programming, characterised by high production standards (and hence large budgets, relative to television materials produced by universities, for instance), exploitation of the presentational characteristics of the medium, and certain prevalent styles and formats, such as documentaries.

ACCESS

Broadcast educational television is one of the more accessible and more heavily used technologies in education.

Homes

In many countries, nearly every home has at least one television set. The programmes though may be delivered through a variety of technologies. From an educational point of view, the distribution system for broadcast television can be critical, particularly if the teaching institution has an open access policy.

Most Western European countries have comprehensive and technically high standard national terrestrial transmission systems for television, with some regional services as well. Thus the British Open University is able to deliver its television programmes into 98 per cent of United Kingdom households, using one of the BBC's two national terrestrial transmission networks (BBC2). Television programmes for the UK Open University 'frequently attract audiences of up to 400,000', which 'suggests that the OU philosophy of "openness of instruction" extends well beyond its cohorts of students formally registered in the undergraduate and CE areas' (Open University, 1988, p.13). Thus for every registered student watching, there will be about 100 'general' viewers.

In North America, educational broadcasting is delivered primarily through local cable stations, and/or direct reception of satellite transmissions. TVOntario, the provincially funded educational television station, has access to two channels dedicated to educational programming (one in English, one in French), and is able to cover the whole of a very large province through a combination of cable and satellite distribution. Similarly, in British Columbia, Knowledge Network, a part of the Open Learning Agency, distributes educational programmes to over 90 per cent of homes over a huge area, through a combination of local cable stations linked by satellite, and direct broadcast satellite transmission to more remote homes, using the Canadian Anik-E satellite. Audience research figures indicate that in any one week, approximately 400,000 will have seen at least one Knowledge Network programme (from a population base of around 3.5 million). Some countries in Europe, such as Belgium, are heavily cabled (80 per cent of homes). Conversely, relatively few homes in Britain, France or West Germany are linked to cable TV, although numbers are increasing rapidly.

The use of satellite transmission for educational programming in Europe is quite recent, and has been fraught with technical difficulties. The European Space Agency offered free transmission time on the experimental OLYMPUS satellite to educational users. It helped create Eurostep, made up of over 100 different member educational institutions from over 20 countries that wanted to broadcast educational programmes across Europe. Transmission started in 1990, and over 1,700 hours of programming were transmitted. Although the two television transponders on OLYMPUS each covered a very wide European footprint, the broadcast standard was the experimental D2-MAC, requiring special reception equipment, and little is known about who actually received the programmes.

Unfortunately, in January 1991, OLYMPUS was hit by space debris from a previously 'dead' satellite, resulting in a loss of power, and on 29 May 1991, an operating error occurred which resulted in the satellite spinning out of control, and no longer responding to ground control commands. Remarkably, ESA was able to recover control of the satellite, and move it back into geo-stationary orbit on 13 August 1991. Eurostep resumed a shortened transmission schedule in January 1992, but eventually had to transfer its services to a commercial satellite, because of the damage done to OLYMPUS.

Access at local centres

In the United States, a number of states with multiple university and college campuses (e.g. Indiana) have used ITFS to originate and deliver programming between campuses.

Access at work-sites

A number of education and training systems use cable and satellite transmission to deliver instruction into the workplace. Stanford University has for many years offered masters courses in engineering by cable and satellite television to employers in California and beyond.

More recently, the National Technological University, with headquarters in Fort Collins, Colorado, has used satellite transmission to relay post-baccalaureate engineering and management courses from universities across North America to business and other sites. These programmes specialise in bringing either outstanding researchers or the latest research developments to the workplace. NTU is using digital transmission requiring special reception equipment, which ensures that its transmissions are limited to those end users that have paid for the service.

The importance of quality of delivery

Because of bandwidth restrictions, most Western European countries are limited to around four or five national terrestrial-based broadcast television channels. Because of competition between a limited number of channels, minority programming, such as education, has tended to be pushed into off-peak times.

The British Open University has had access to over 35 hours a week on the national BBC television network since its inception. In theory, it should be able to access all students at home in this way. However, as competition from commercial channels increased, the quality of transmission times allocated by the BBC for Open University programmes progressively deteriorated from 1979, so that by 1990 the bulk of the Open University transmission times were either very early in the morning or late at night. Neither period is suitable for working adults wishing to study seriously, and many studies (Bates, 1975; Gallagher, 1977; Grundin, 1978, 1980, 1981, 1983, 1985) showed the adverse effect that poor transmission times have on the proportion of students who watch the programmes. By 1984, barely half of Open University students were watching off-air transmissions. The use of a particular medium must be questioned if it cannot deliver learning materials to most of the target students. Course designers are reluctant to teach essential content or skills through a particular technology if substantial numbers of students are disadvantaged in this way.

Fortunately, the advent of video cassette machines reduced the impact of poorer times on Open University students to some extent, but the average viewing figure (viewing on transmission combined with viewing recordings) was still down to 60 per cent by 1984. Given the cost of television to the university (13 per cent of its budget that year), a 40 per cent loss of viewing on each transmission is extremely inefficient.

As the number of channels available by cable and satellite proliferate, institutions will find it easier to access transmission, but whether all those they target can receive the transmission will depend on whether the local cable station carries the signal, or on the type of satellite reception equipment installed. However, in general, broadcast television is a widely accessible medium, provided it is broadcast at times convenient for the target audiences.

TEACHING AND LEARNING

What is special, if anything, about the role of television in learning? What can it do that can't be done by other methods, such as print or face-to-face tutorials? If television is to be used merely to relay a lecture, for instance, might this not be done more cheaply and effectively by print, or a combination of print and audio cassette, or by audio conferencing? To answer such questions means looking at the unique educational characteristics of television.

General educational characteristics of broadcast television

There are five general reasons that are frequently used to justify the use of educational broadcasting in open and distance learning:

- personalising the teaching;
- improving learning efficiency;
- pacing;
- student recruitment;
- academic credibility.

There has been some research which has tested the validity of these arguments.

Personalising the teaching: yes

The argument is that television allows the student both to identify the individuality of the teacher(s) responsible for the distance teaching material, and to provide a public image and awareness of the university's presence, a sense of belonging and community for the otherwise isolated student. The feedback collected from British Open University students over a number of years indicates clearly that students appreciate seeing the people responsible for the production of the teaching materials on television.

The general reaction of students was to be reasonably tolerant towards nervous or slightly 'unslick' lecturers who made small verbal fumblings or dropped things. One student commented: 'It's important to me to know that the materials are created by human beings who are not always perfect, but do care about what they are doing.' Many lecturers became very proficient with practice. However, in recent years the BBC producers have tended to keep lecturers off camera, and to use broadcasting professionals for the voice-over commentary, concentrating the visual component instead on the phenomena rather than the personality.

Improving learning efficiency: yes

The argument here is that by using some of the unique presentational features of television, understanding can be achieved better than through reading alone. In the next section, evidence will be examined that suggests that television programmes can improve learning efficiency for many students.

Pacing: no

Do regularly scheduled broadcasts keep students working regularly, and break the inertia of beginning to study? The evidence on pacing is less conclusive. A study by Ahrens, Burt and Gallagher (1975) showed clearly that what influenced students' pacing was not the regular television programmes (students were often several weeks behind with their reading when the programmes linked to the reading were transmitted) but the regular monthly assignments, which counted towards their end-of-course grade. The implications of this experience are that it is a combination of factors that keeps students on schedule, and not just regular transmissions of programmes.

Student recruitment: almost certainly

When the British Open University started in 1971, its association with the BBC, and the controversy over using broadcast television for university-level teaching, contributed to publicising the Open University. In its first year, there were over 50,000 applicants for the first 25,000 places. Even in 1994, there were still twice as many applicants as there are places available.

The broadcasts also allow Open University students to sample materials on other courses, assisting students to decide which courses to choose next. Some course teams, while opting for video cassette distribution for teaching purposes, still wish to retain a broadcast slot for the video material for this purpose.

The context in Ontario, Seattle, or Vancouver, where TVOntario, KCTS (PBS), and Knowledge Network are competing with more than 30 different channels, is quite different. Nevertheless, Knowledge Network was rated the second most valued channel in British Columbia in a Gallup Poll survey in 1990.

Academic credibility

One of the factors which clearly led the British Open University to be accepted by the rest of the academic community in Britain, despite initial scepticism, was the academic quality of the television programmes, which were publicly available and easily accessible. Its course materials (both television and printed matter) are now used by many lecturers and students in regular universities.

However, the availability and prominence of the Open University's teaching through public television has been a two-edged sword. The then Conservative education minister, Sir Keith Joseph, strongly objected to a particular social science television programme that he had seen on Marxist economics (on a foundation course that was based on examining similar social phenomena from three different ideological perspectives, including Marxism), and the following year the university's operating budget was reduced by £2.5 million, against the trend of previous and subsequent years. This incident indicates that there is a particular pressure on open learning institutions using public television to ensure that their courses have academic credibility and are free from bias; the corollary is that there is inevitably a pressure towards safe and uncontroversial teaching.

In general, both research and experience suggest that with the possible exception of pacing, the claims for the general benefits of using public television have held true at the British Open University.

Unique teaching resources

As well as the ability of television to deliver learning material to large numbers of students, to sites far removed from the classroom or lecture hall, there are presentational characteristics of television that are important for education.

Television is the richest medium, in that it can combine all the major forms of symbolic representation: words, pictures, movement, sound, and 'real-time' representation of events (computer-based multi-media still cannot do all these things for any sustainable period, without severe loss of picture or sound quality). Television can also of course be used merely to relay a lecture, a talking head with simple graphics. It is important then to distinguish between television which exploits its full range of presentational qualities (which I will describe as high-quality television), and television which is merely another way of delivering the lecture format at a distance (which I will describe as televised lectures).

High-quality television has certain presentational advantages over other media, in that it can represent events and concepts that would be impossible to do for distance learners in a practical way by other means (see Bates, 1984, for a full listing of the unique teaching characteristics of television).

Perhaps the most obvious presentational characteristic is television's ability to bring resources to learners that would not be possible through any other medium, or even through direct experience, such as, for instance, scientific experiments, case-study material of social and technological events, field-visits (particularly in foreign countries), and dynamic presentation of ideas through animation and graphics.

This feature of television is particularly important for learners who cannot get to institutions, or who cannot access resources available in, for instance, larger universities or urban areas. However, even for students in the best equipped and resourced universities, there are often phenomena or experiences that are not easily available to them through campus-based provision.

I will attempt to describe just three of the many unique ways television can be used in distance education.

To demonstrate experiments or experimental situations

There are several reasons why television is particularly useful for experimental work:

- television, through enlargement, editing and split screens, enables students to see experimental work even more clearly than in a well-equipped laboratory;
- editing allows well-conducted experiments to take place, ensuring that students see a 'model' experiment;
- saving on student time: the use of television can cut down the time spent on laboratory work by a factor of up to 10; once an experiment is video recorded, there is no need to set up the experiment again for a different set of students, thus saving the time of both those setting up the experiment, and students themselves;
- there are some experiments that cannot be demonstrated in even well-equipped universities, because they require specialist equipment found in only one or two places: television allows such demonstrations to be available to students in any institution;
- television can reduce the dependency on live animals.

Television of course should not be used to replace students' own experimental work (students can conduct experiments at home, using specially designed home experiment kits, or at summer schools), but television can make the demonstration of experiments and procedures much more efficient.

To provide students with case-study material

Television can be used to record naturally occurring or dramatised events or processes, and can be edited to bring out the principal features of the story or case. This allows events which often occur over a considerable time-span to be condensed into a short period of study time, while at the same time providing all students with a common case or example to work on.

Television case-study material can play a vital role in teaching in social sciences, technology and education courses. Such material can be used to:

- illustrate some of the general principles or ideas introduced elsewhere in the course;
- provide students with the opportunity to apply what they have learned in the course, by analysing, explaining or identifying the phenomena contained in the case-study;
- allow students to draw on their own experience and knowledge to suggest and discuss solutions to problems posed in the case-studies.

To demonstrate processes

This is an extremely broad category, covering use in many different contexts. Television, though, is ideal for showing a sequence of activities that need to be carried out in a certain order, within a certain context. In an

Open University Arts course, a programme demonstrates how craftsmen during the Renaissance used gold leaf to construct portraits in relief. An art historian reconstructs the process, using original tools and materials, exactly as it was carried out in the sixteenth century.

These three examples illustrate the point that television allows the students to access materials which it would be extremely difficult to access in any other way. But how does such material actually influence the learning process?

From the concrete to the abstract

For many students there are often times when words are not enough; they need to be able to see to understand, and television is one way in which this can be done.

A major presentational characteristic of television is its ability to provide an illustration or a concrete example of an abstract principle or generalisation. Examples or illustrations can be given in texts, but the power of the moving picture, combined with the ability to synchronise such pictures with words and sound, creates striking audio–visual images symbolising important concepts or ideas. Paivio (1980) for example argues that we carry around in our heads a library of audio–visual images. These images can be used by the learner like keys to a room. One function of television is to generate appropriate audio–visual images linked to otherwise difficult abstract concepts.

It is extremely valuable to be able to provide students with powerful audio–visual concrete examples, especially, but not exclusively, in higher education, where abstraction and generalisation are important aspects of learning. Abstract ideas are usually stored and communicated in words. However, cognitive psychologists such as Bruner and Piaget have recognised that full understanding and internalisation of abstract concepts is preceded by some form of concrete experience.

It is often difficult to provide this physical experience directly for learners, but television can act as an effective substitute. Some help is often needed to move learners from the concrete to the abstract, or from the specific to the general. Because television can combine and integrate concrete images with words, it can act as a bridge between the concrete operational and formal (more abstract) stages of learning. One of the major limitations of both text and computers is their inability (at least until recently) to synchronise natural voice with full moving pictures, yet the importance of being able to link words and pictures to develop this higher level of abstract thinking cannot be too strongly emphasised.

Gallagher (1977) found that in Open University Mathematics courses, it was the borderline students (i.e. students getting Grade C or D for the course – E and F were fail grades) who tended to rate the programmes as very helpful (50 per cent of C/Ds, compared with only 24 per cent of A/Bs).

While this tendency was most marked in Mathematics courses, it was also found in all other faculties except Arts; the more 'abstract' the courses, the stronger the finding.

I interpret this to suggest that the higher achieving Mathematics students were able to follow the course primarily from the text, i.e. they were already able to work at a high level of abstraction, and hence needed less help from television; but for those struggling with the course, the television programmes were able to provide extra help in understanding concepts, mainly through the use of concrete examples.

Television then can be of particular value to those students on a course who are struggling with difficult concepts. Television seems to be of particular value to 'high risk' students, and can help to keep down drop-out resulting from the difficulty of a course.

Content or skills?

Much of the educational media research conducted in North America has been concerned with measuring to what extent a particular medium leads to comprehension. Are the students able to reproduce accurately and with understanding what they have been taught?

However, in education we are often wanting to do more than that. To what extent can the learner apply what has been taught to new situations? Can the learner evaluate evidence or arguments, on the basis of what he or she has been taught? Can the learner analyse a new situation on the basis of previously taught concepts? Can the student bring new or unanticipated insights to the situation portrayed?

One major criticism of distance learning is that the hard work, the evaluation of what it is important to learn, the analysis of issues to be taught, is done by the teacher, not the student. Knowledge is packaged in texts by the teacher, then studied and churned back by the learner. The structuring of the print material makes it difficult for students to impose their own order or structure on the subject matter, or to re-structure it for themselves.

Television on the other hand lends itself to interpretation, to presenting new situations which have to be analysed or recognised in terms already taught in the texts. Television can encourage students to analyse for themselves real-life situations, and what they themselves might do in similar circumstances (Trenaman, 1967). When used in this way, television can provide an opportunity for students to make their own interpretations, and to develop skills of analysis and application of principles taught elsewhere in the course.

In this sense, television is very different from computer-based learning, which has great difficulties in handling situations where a wide range of different responses and interpretations from students are all legitimate. There are many areas of study, not only in the humanities and social sciences, but also in science and technology, where it is important to develop students' skills in handling open-ended situations, or to encourage students to bring not only their learning from the printed materials, but also relevant life experiences, to analyse situations and suggest possible courses of action.

A particular form of television programme which can encourage skills of analysis and application of knowledge is the documentary-style programme. While documentaries encompass a wide range of production styles and approaches, they tend to have a loose semantic structure (e.g. there is not usually a strong, continuous narrative line), and they tend *not* to build in explicit guidance or interpretation in the sound track. 'Open-ended' documentary-style programmes can be a valuable teaching resource, if used to encourage students to interpret, analyse and problem-solve.

However, far too often the educational purpose behind a documentary-style programme is not articulated or recognised by the teacher using the material or by those who designed the programme, nor, more importantly, do the students themselves understand how they are expected to use such material. In fact, there is strong evidence that these kinds of programmes are often ineffective in developing students' skills of analysis and interpretation, even when this purpose is made explicit.

A number of studies of such programmes were carried out at the British Open University (see Bates and Gallagher, 1977). From the results, they drew up a 'one-third rule'. One third of students watching this kind of programme knew what they were supposed to do with such material in their course, and were able to do so successfully. These students tended to get high grades in the end-of-course examination. Another third knew that this type of programme was not meant to be didactic, and that they were meant to analyse and interpret it, but were unable to do so. The last third of students not only failed to approach the programme in the way intended, but were totally unaware that they were meant to do so. This group of students were highly instrumental in their approach to studying at the Open University. They wanted didactic programmes, and were often furious that they were expected to watch, in the words of one student, 'this irrelevant rubbish'. This group tended to get relatively low grades over the course as a whole.

It is also important to relate the use of different media to assessment of students. If television is used for developing skills or providing knowledge not available elsewhere in the course, but these skills are not assessed in the examination, then students are unlikely to make the effort to learn from television. It will also be impossible in such circumstances to relate learning gains to the technology used. Also, if students, rightly or wrongly, perceive the television programme as optional, and the source of examination success residing in the text-book, for instance, then they will not watch the programmes.

Conclusions

In the end, what do learners get from television? Do they learn just as well as from, say, print or face-to-face lectures?

Media differ in the *kinds* of learning they encourage. Thus in general, print is best for teaching in a condensed way, dealing with abstract principles, where knowledge of detailed facts or principles is important, and where knowledge is clearly defined. Television on the other hand is much better for presenting complex or ambiguous 'real-world' events, for providing concrete examples to illustrate abstract ideas or principles, and for encouraging students to make their own interpretations and to apply to new situations what they have learned in an abstract way.

The extent to which television is successful in doing this depends on how programmes are made. Television is rarely best used as the prime medium for delivering large quantities of information; instead, it is much more valuable for providing deeper understanding and for developing skills of analysis and application of ideas presented through other media, particularly print.

Despite the difficulties and the extra costs incurred, there is no doubt that high-quality television that exploits the unique presentational characteristics of the medium has an important and valuable role to play in learning. A well-designed television component can not only help reduce drop-out and increase comprehension, it can also assist the development of higher-order learning skills. In other words, television can increase the *quality* of learning.

INTERACTION AND USER-FRIENDLINESS

While the presentational qualities of broadcast television make it valuable to learners, its main instructional weakness is its lack of interactivity and its inconvenience. Students often have great difficulty in interacting with television, for a number of reasons.

Prevailing broadcast professional ideologies about what constitutes 'good' television can conflict strongly with educational approaches that would encourage interaction. For instance, to keep viewers watching, broadcast television is continuous, and uses techniques which discourage the interruption of the flow of the programme. By its nature broadcast television cannot be interrupted unless recorded. Even educational or training programmes that are never intended for broadcasting, however, are usually made in a continuous sequence, using broadcast formats such as documentary-style.

This of course is not an inherent characteristic of television that cannot be changed. Some experimentation in designing video materials that encourage overt interaction can be found at the British Open University (see Kirkwood and Crooks, 1990). However, even when such techniques are built into the production of the programme, the difficulty of providing good feedback on learners' responses to the material remains. Indeed, Durbridge (1982) found that learning best occurred from video materials in a group context, where students could test out their interpretations on tutors and/or other students.

Because television is such a familiar medium, it tends to be taken for granted that students will know how to learn from it. This is not the case, particularly where comprehension is not the main purpose. Most students approach television as if it were a lecture, unless the programme is made in such a way as to encourage them to question and analyse what is being presented to them. Students may need a 'bridge' between the concrete and the abstract, through the commentary. Without explicit links, students may not see concrete examples in a television programme as illustrators of ideas or principles learned in the text (Salomon, 1983).

In a situation where television is a regular component of a course, a strategy can be used of gradually moving from highly didactic to more open-ended programmes, with guidance within earlier programmes on how to use or interpret the television material. This strategy was adopted on D102, a re-make of the British Open University's Social Science foundation course. The students rated the programmes on this course much more highly than students on the first foundation course (D100).

Another successful way to help students is to provide a discussion of a television programme on a separate audio cassette. Durbridge (1985) found that integrating audio cassettes and notes with a television programme enabled students to analyse the video material more easily than placing the analysis within the TV programme itself.

Lastly, the education system devotes a great deal of time, resources and energy teaching students to read and write; however, very little is done in schools or colleges to help students learn from television. There are skills needed by learners in order to learn effectively from television, and these can be taught.

Production

It is though perhaps unwise to assume that viewers are passive, if they do not overtly respond during the act of watching a programme. As with a good book, play or film, the programme may stimulate deep thought, imagination or fantasy, raise awareness, provide new information which is easily absorbed, or challenge the values or attitudes of the viewer. This of course depends on the ability or motivation of the viewer, and the quality and purpose of the programme. Not all teaching is didactic, and not all learning is focused on mastery of facts or skills.

However, while educational broadcasts tend to be continuous and non-didactic, in particular to appeal to the general viewer, they do not have to be. It is possible to design even broadcast programmes so that they encourage interaction. This can be done in a variety of ways:

- by 'wrapping' programmes with a prologue (giving viewers 'advance organisers' on what to look for) and/or a conclusion, summarising some of the points or issues raised;
- using 'voice-over' questions, or questions to camera by the narrator/presenter, during the programme;
- interruption of the narrative by teacher/professor in the studio, asking questions, indicating what to look for, summarising points;
- repeating a segment of film, with perhaps an additional comment;
- use of captions/animation/still frame to highlight a concept being illustrated;
- using a still frame (or black screen) to give time for a viewer response to a prompt or question, possibly followed by feedback 'on screen';
- use of a telephone call-in from viewers at the end of a programme, with an expert, or panel of experts, responding to the calls (sometimes called 'interactive' television in North America).

Many of these techniques will seem strange or artificial to producers working primarily in an entertainment medium; the effectiveness of these techniques also depends on fine judgement of the needs and ability of the audience. They do illustrate the point though that educational broadcasts need a style appropriate to the teaching function, and that the style of the programme is an instructional as well as a television production decision.

The less able or less educated the target viewers, or the more instrumental the learner (in the sense of being 'credit-driven', rather than by subject interest), the more viewers are likely to require this 'interventionist' style of programme, if they are to learn from television.

After a lifetime, in some cases, of using television as a relaxing entertainment medium, it is hardly surprising that many adults, as well as children, have great difficulty in learning from television; nor, in most cases, do they even believe it to be a problem. For instance, Open University students often complained that the programmes were 'too easy' or 'irrelevant' (because they were seeking factual information or comprehension) yet they were unable to use the programmes in the ways intended by the course designers and TV producers, which was often for analysis or interpretation.

Thus, despite the various techniques available for increasing interaction, and the ability of skilful producers to stimulate thoughtfulness and emotional involvement in a programme, the continuous and 'seamless' nature of most broadcast television makes it a difficult medium for most learners.

COSTS

Probably no other teaching medium varies so much in its costs, especially regarding production of learning material. Educational broadcasts produced by national broadcasting organisations such as the BBC tend to be very expensive compared with programmes produced by universities for limited distribution on local cable channels or for cassette distribution. Although the Knowledge Network provides a public broadcast service, its productions tend to be between one fifth and one tenth the cost of those of the BBC-Open University. Some BBC-Open University drama productions (co-produced with other broadcasting organisations) have cost over £100,000 (US$150,000) an hour to produce and transmit, when overheads are included; the direct costs of producing and relaying a lecture to a few off-campus sites may be under $300 an hour. Nevertheless, the cost structure of television is clear and consistent.

An example: BBC-Open University productions

The data for broadcast television are drawn from the BBC-Open University Production Centre. This reflects programming that sets out to exploit television's unique presentational characteristics. Data are from the year 1983/84. Grundin (1984) completed a study of the costs of television for that year; in that year BBC-OUP was operating closer to its optimum cost level than in subsequent years. Some of Grundin's figures have been re-worked, to ensure consistency with costing in other parts of this report.

The total cost of the BBC-OUP Centre to the Open University in 1983 was £9.98 million. The BBC estimated that 90 per cent of this sum was spent on television, and the rest on radio. Removing value-added tax and general administrative costs, BBC-OUP in 1983/84 spent £6,281,500 on the production and transmission of television material, equivalent in production to 230 × 25-minute television programmes, and broadcasting a total of 35 hours, 25 minutes per week over a 33-week period. Of the programmes broadcast, 86.5 per cent received two transmissions; the remaining 13.5 per cent received one transmission.

Fixed costs

The BBC-OUP estimated that 85 per cent of its costs were 'fixed' (Open University, 1988, p.15). The remaining 15 per cent 'variable' cost is the money directly related to the volume of production, i.e. the additional money needed for each production, which in 1983/84 was roughly £6,000 (US$9,000) a programme.

The production figure of 230 programme equivalents for BBC-OUP in 1983/84 refers to actual production in terms of the budget available; the BBC claimed that it would have been able to produce 300 programme equivalents with the same studio capacity, but was not allocated the necessary variable production funds (estimated to be £420,000) for the extra 70 programmes.

Production costs

In 1983/84, the variable cost of a BBC-OUP television programme production was about US$9,000 (£6,000) per 25-minute programme. This was the cash a producer had to spend per programme, and covered travel, fees to contributors, copyright clearance incurred in the making of a television programme, graphics, set design, etc. It did not, though, include the cost of the producer/director nor of the studios and their staff, which were treated as overheads or fixed costs.

To calculate the average production cost of an Open University television programme, Grundin divided all production costs, including studio overheads, by the number of programmes produced in a year. This gave a figure of US$36,000 (£24,000) per programme (£5,508,000/230 × 25-minute programmes), or US$86,400 (£57,600) per hour.

Excluded from these costs is the time of the Open University academics involved in the development and production of a programme. This is extremely difficult to calculate, but a rough estimate would be an average of 10–12 days per programme, if one includes programme planning and discussion, script preparation, collecting material, and recording time. A rough figure of US$1,800 (£1,200) in 1983/84 would be a reasonable estimate for academic time per programme, making a total production cost of roughly US$37,700 (£25,147) per programme, or US$90,500 (£60,353) per hour.

Transmission costs

Transmission costs in 1983/84 were £275 per transmission (£773,000/2,809 transmissions), or £660 (roughly US$1,000) per hour for single transmissions, and £1,320 (US$2,000) per hour for repeat transmissions. Note that for transmission, these were direct, marginal costs, since they covered just the extra costs of extending the times of an already established national transmission network.

Total costs: production and transmission

Table 4.1 summarises these costs.

Two calculations have been made in Table 4.1, one for the actual production load in 1983/84 (230 programmes), and one for the maximum load (300 programmes). It could be claimed that if the full production load had been reached, the average costs would have been reduced by about 20 per cent.

It can be seen that volume of activity is critical, when such a high

Table 4.1 Costs of television: BBC-OUP, 1983–1984 (over eight years)

	Actual 230 programmes p.a		Maximum 300 programmes p.a.	
	per prog £	per hour £	per prog £	per hour £
Development/production				
Academic time	1,200	2,880	1,200	2,880
Production (fixed costs)	17,947	43,073	12,360	29,664
Programme budget	6,000	14,400	6,000	14,400
Cost per programme	25,147	60,353	19,560	46,944
(Cost per programme: US$	37,720	90,530	29,340	70,416)
Delivery				
Transmissions (two): 1 yr	550	1,320	550	1,320
Transmissions (two): 8 yrs	4,400	10,560	4,400	10,560
Cost per programme	29,547	70,913	23,960	57,504
(Cost per programme: US$	44,320	106,370	35,940	86,256)

proportion of costs are fixed. A 7 per cent increase in budget would increase output by 30 per cent, from 230 to 300 programmes a year. Unfortunately, the reverse happened. When the BBC-OUP budget was cut by 11.5 per cent over the period 1984–88, output dropped by 46 per cent , from 230 programmes a year to 125, because the fixed costs remained largely untouched.

If production had continued at 1983/84 levels, the total costs over eight years would have been as follows:

Table 4.2 Total costs of broadcast TV: UK OU (over eight years)

Production level	125 programmes 52.08 hrs £	230 programmes 95.83 hrs £	300 programmes 125 hrs £
Fixed	44,064,000	44,064,000	44,064,000
Programme budget	6,000,000	11,040,000	14,400,000
Academic costs	1,200,000	2,208,000	2,880,000
Transmission costs	550,000	1,242,000	1,320,000
Total	51,814,000	58,554,000	62,664,000
(Total US$	77,721,000	87,831,000	93,996,000)

Broadcast TV costs are unaffected by the numbers of students studying, as can be seen from Figure 4.1 (p. 82).

Costs per programme per year, and per student/study hour

Table 4.3 converts Open University production and transmission costs into costs per student and per student study hour, assuming an allocation of 16

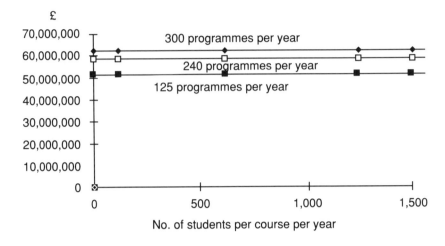

Figure 4.1 Total costs for broadcast TV, BBC-OUP (over eight years)

programmes (one 25-minute programme every two weeks), over a 32-week course, with each programme broadcast twice each year, which is not an untypical allocation for an OU course.

These figures show clearly the importance of economies of scale for television (Figure 4.2, p. 83).

The marginal television cost per student, i.e. the additional cost of adding one extra student, is nil, since neither the cost of production nor transmission is determined by the number of students. Thus the more

Table 4.3 Costs of television per student study hour: UK OU, 1983–1984

	1,000 students (125 students per year × 8) £	5,000 students (625 students per year × 8) £	10,000 students (1,250 students per year × 8) £
Fixed production	287,165	287,165	287,165
Programme budget	96,000	96,000	96,000
Academic costs	19,200	19,200	19,200
Total production	402,365	402,365	402,365
Transmission (over 8 years)	86,000	86,000	86,000
Total	488,365	488,365	488,365
Cost per student	488.36	97.67	48.84
Cost per student/hour	73.25	14.65	7.33
(Cost per student/hour US$	109.87	21.97	10.99)

Note: 16 × 25 minute television programmes, transmitted twice each year: annual production = 230 programmes

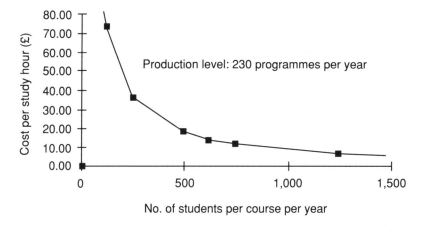

Figure 4.2 Cost per study hour for broadcast TV: UK OU (over eight years)

students per course, the lower the student unit costs for television. They vary from about US$730 (£488) a student, at US$110 (£73) per study hour, for courses with 125 students per year, down to US$75 (£50) per student, at about US$11 (£7.33) per study hour, for a course with 1,250 students a year, assuming an eight-year course life. Delivery accounts for 17 per cent of the cost per student, irrespective of numbers.

What is clear from these figures is the relatively high cost of broadcast television per study hour. If utilisation is taken into account (only 65 per cent of students viewing programmes), then the cost per viewing student increases by over a third. Even with 6,000 students a year (equal to the largest Open University foundation courses) television costs are still over US$2.30 per student study hour (£1.53), at 1983/84 prices.

The impact of using in-house production

To set up an educational television production centre is expensive. The BBC-Open University Production Centre cost £5.5 (US$8.25) million in 1979. The Queensland Government spent A$4 million (US$2.64 million) on equipping a studio for production for technical and further education. It is not necessary though to build or provide one's own facilities. In many countries, there is plenty of spare production capacity; what is often lacking are the funds for making programmes.

The high investment and high fixed operating costs of providing in-house production facilities can be justified only if production levels are kept high, i.e. studios and ancillary facilities are used at least 75 per cent of normal working times for in-house programming. If production levels are less than this, it is almost certain to be cheaper to contract out production to other organisations, thus reducing overheads.

The high fixed costs of maintaining an in-house production capacity leads to managers putting enormous pressure on educators within the organisation to utilise fully the production capacity, *irrespective of the appropriateness of educational use.* The decision to have in-house television production facilities also reduces the flexibility of an organisation to change quickly its use of technology.

The Open Learning Agency has tried to deal with this issue in several ways. It buys in 80 per cent of its educational programmes from other producers (such as TVOntario and the BBC) for its Knowledge Network. It also encourages educational institutions within the province to produce their own programmes, for transmission on Knowledge Network. It also does not maintain a fully staffed production facility, but contracts in crews and producers as and when needed.

The relative cost of BBC-OUP productions

The BBC-OUP costs in 1983/84 were not out of line with educational programmes produced by other broadcasting organisations, such as BBC and ITV Schools Broadcasts in the UK, TVOntario in Canada, and the Corporation for Public Broadcasting in the USA. Also, technological advances in recent years, such as light-weight video cameras, fully computerised video editing, improvements in camera lenses requiring lower levels of lighting, etc., have not only reduced dramatically the cost of equipment required for television production, but also have reduced the previously high levels of staffing needed, thus allowing for still quite sophisticated production for considerably less cost. Nevertheless, location shooting, computerised graphics and other special effects often needed and used in educational broadcasts are still expensive.

Thus, the standards required of broadcast-quality educational television mean that television production costs are still relatively high.

Summary

The following general principles can be stated:

- a full in-house production studio system requires high levels of production to maximise fixed costs;
- once an in-house production system is established, the marginal cost of producing each extra programme is relatively small;
- conversely, in a full in-house production studio system, a small reduction in overall resources will lead to large reductions in output, unless fixed costs are slashed;
- transmission (delivery) costs are less than 20 per cent of production costs, even over eight years;
- substantial numbers of students (more than 5,000) per course per year

are needed to bring the cost per student study hour down to £1 (US$1.50) or less.

Although actual costs will be lower for organisations using less expensive production facilities than the BBC-OUP, nevertheless their cost structures, i.e. the ratio between different types of costs (production, transmission, etc.) and the shape of their cost curves, will be very similar.

ORGANISATIONAL ISSUES

Collaboration and partnership

Broadcasting organisations tend to have an ideology or a professionalism that is often markedly different from that of educational institutions. This is both an organisational strength and weakness. Trained and experienced television producers are able to think visually, and have learned ways to attract and hold an audience. Teachers, on the other hand, especially in higher education, often have difficulties in thinking 'visually' or in concrete terms, or have settled into approaches to teaching that are not appropriate for a broadcast television format (e.g. lecturing). Furthermore, broadcast television works best when there is active follow-up or integration with learners' other studies or with other media. Thus, a team approach is often needed, with a teacher and producer working together to exploit the medium.

In Canada, Knowledge Network has always offered open access on its transmission facilities to all educational and training organisations within the province; 50 per cent of its transmissions are still 'reserved' or available for this purpose. It also has a Planning Council drawn from the educational and voluntary sectors, that not only provides guidance and strategic directions for programming, but also allocates funds for production or programme acquisition.

The Open Learning Agency is also a lead partner in the development of the Western (Canadian) Universities Telecourse Consortium. This is a partnership of nine universities and educational broadcasting organisations, which is sharing the development and transmission costs of first and second year university telecourses. Students in any particular province will be able to take any of these courses, irrespective of origin, and partner institutions will accept these courses for credit.

Copyright

Copyright is a major issue in educational broadcasting. Copyright covers not only the production of original material (for instance, graphics produced by the organisation transmitting the programme), but also the inclusion of material produced elsewhere (by, for instance, a film company) and included within the programme. These secondary rights have to be bought by the educational broadcaster. The fewer the number of people likely to view, or the more restricted the context, the lower the cost of buying copyright clearance for secondary rights is likely to be. Thus educational broadcasters tend to buy rights for limited numbers of show-ings (e.g. a maximum of eight, thus allowing either two transmissions a year over four years, or one transmission a year for eight years). The copyright 'deal' may include or exclude off-air recording or distribution of material on video cassettes. If the deal does include off-air recording and/or video cassette distribution, this can considerably increase the cost of copyright clearance.

Copyright clearance is a major cost for educational broadcasting organ-isations. As well as the payment of fees, specialist staff have to be employed. The process is labour-intensive, and very time-consuming. However, educational broadcasters are scrupulous in clearing and tracking rights; they have to be, as infringement of copyright on their part is easily identified and proved.

NOVELTY AND SPEED

Broadcast educational television is neither novel nor speedy. It has been around for about 30 years, and in comparison to the newer developments of satellite television and 'narrowcasting', is not seen as terribly exciting by decision-makers, a perception re-inforced by the belief that it is an expensive medium.

Nor is it fast; while news or current affairs programmes can be developed at great speed, educational broadcasting tends to be much slower. Pro-grammes can take anything from six weeks to six months from conception to transmission. They are also expensive to change. Thus programmes at the British Open University are often broadcast for eight years.

Nevertheless, good material can be relatively timeless; a computerised animation of a mathematical function, a film of aboriginal dance rituals, or a production of Macbeth are not time-dependent, and can be used many times in many contexts (provided copyright is cleared).

CONCLUSIONS

Broadcast television is one of the most accessible media for education. In the past, broadcast television has been limited to major broadcasting organisations, but increasing de-regulation, and access to cable and satel-lite channels, is making it easier for educational organisations or systems to access and use broadcast television.

The major strength of high-quality television is its unique teaching characteristics. Broadcast television has its own way of stimulating think-ing and interaction which, while 'covert', can still be powerful. Broadcast styles, however, tend to be influenced by a desire to catch the much larger 'eavesdropping' audience. This tends to militate against instructional approaches that encourage active learning or integration of the programme with other learning materials.

However, for learning to take place, programmes have to be carefully designed, following sound instructional as well as 'good' television production principles. Learners need help, within the programmes, especially when the programmes are not didactic, but used for development of higher-order learning skills. In other words, educational television needs to develop its own styles and formats somewhere between formal lectures and open-ended documentaries.

The main disadvantage of high-quality broadcast TV is the high initial cost of production. This requires substantial investment, and can be justified only if used by large numbers of students. However, it is important not to look too narrowly at costs. There are increasing opportunities for cost recovery, and even profits, from the production of high-quality television material. As the number of points of distribution increase – satellite and cable channels, video cassette distribution, video discs, CD-I and multimedia – demand for good quality original programme material will increase. Re-sale of material will become increasingly important, and needs to be factored into production costs.

In order to ensure that the context in which television is used is appropriate, collaboration and partnerships between educational and broadcasting organisations are important, but are not always easy to achieve. Co-production and shared use of materials across different educational jurisdictions reduce the high costs of original production, but increase the complexity and difficulty of production and distribution.

Lastly, when television is used to exploit its unique teaching characteristics, the material is likely to be time-independent and valuable in a variety of contexts.

High-quality broadcast television then is a complex medium, with both strong advantages and disadvantages. Its potential and use in any given context needs to be carefully examined; when used well, though, it can be one of the most powerful instructional media.

5 Instructional television

NEW – AND BETTER?

Television as a medium has been subject to considerable change since the mid-1980s. Increasingly, the development of low-cost and more user-friendly production equipment, and easier access to transmission and distribution facilities such as satellite and cable channels, video cassettes, video discs and video conferencing, have encouraged many educational institutions to use television for teaching. Also new organisations have developed, built around new delivery methods for television.

However, programmes produced by educational institutions are usually different in character from those produced by educational broadcasters. Production budgets are usually much lower, programmes tend to be based on a 'classroom' format, and hence there are often attempts to introduce two-way interaction between those creating the programmes and those receiving them. Also instructional television is more likely to be directed to a restricted market of 'registered' students or learners (narrowcasting), while educational broadcasting is directed at anyone who may be interested in watching, whether for credit or not.

THE TECHNOLOGY

Instructional television may be distributed by 'narrowcast' broadcasting, video conferencing, video cassettes, or video discs.

'Narrowcast' broadcasting

Instructional television is more likely to be distributed through 'narrowcasting', i.e. ITFS, satellite, cable, video cassette or video disc distribution, than through national terrestrial broadcast television networks, mainly because it is difficult for individual institutions to get access to limited national terrestrial broadcast channels for relatively small numbers of viewers.

Video conferencing

One of the fastest growing technologies in distance education in North America and Australia is video conferencing. Video conferencing enables people at different locations to have two-way video communication, i.e. at each site, participants can see and hear people at all the other sites connected.

The importance of bandwidth

In order to understand the technological issues in video conferencing, a basic understanding of transmission technology is necessary. The more information that has to be transmitted, the more capacity or bandwidth is required. One analogy is to think of messages as tiny collections of sand, or 'bits' of information. If a lot of information has to be sent quickly, a wide 'pipe' is required. The same amount of information can be sent through a thinner 'pipe' more slowly. Thus, telecommunications capacity is a combination of bandwidth and speed of transmission.

The bandwidth required depends on the application. Thus, data, such as letters or numbers, which singly do not carry a great deal of information, can be sent using a narrow bandwidth and at relatively slow speeds. Sounds, such as speech on the phone, contain more information than a printed word, and have to be carried at the same speed as normal speech for conversation to be possible; thus, voice needs both a wider channel and a faster speed of transmission than text. A photograph or image can also be digitised, and carries more information than a page of text; if the pictures move (as in television, at 25 to 30 frames a second), a great deal of information has to be sent quickly, particularly if pictures are synchronised with sounds, such as speech and music. Colour requires a great deal more bandwidth than black and white images. The greater the amount of information, and the faster it needs to be sent, the greater the bandwidth required.

Transmission capacity is measured in the number of 'bits' of information transmitted per second: the *baud rate*. Telephone lines carry voice messages at roughly 2,400 bps (bits per second); a full-motion analogue colour television signal requires a transmission speed of about 90 million bps. Even though telephone lines can carry several calls simultaneously, the bandwidth required for one-way full-motion analogue colour television transmission is over 1,500 times that required to carry a single voice telephone conversation.

Video compression

A video image, such as a television picture or a computer animation, can be created from two different forms of 'coding': analogue signals and digital signals. Until recently, most television signals have been in analogue form; for an analogue picture to be created, stored or transmitted, all the equipment must be standardised in an analogue format. On the other hand, most computer signals are in digital form.

An analogue television signal takes up a great deal of bandwidth. Since costs are related to both bandwidth and distance, wide bandwidth signals are much more expensive to transmit than narrow bandwidth signals. Thus, engineers are constantly seeking ways to reduce the amount of information to be transmitted down a given bandwidth.

It is now possible to originate television signals in digital form, or convert analogue signals to digital signals, and vice-versa, by using encoding and decoding equipment (known as codecs). Thus, for a digital television signal to be received on a standard analogue domestic television set, somewhere between origin and reception the signal must be converted. Both analogue and digital signals can be carried by any medium, such as satellite, fibre-optics, or even telephone cable, provided that the transmission and reception equipment uses the same format, or that there are codecs for conversion.

One way to reduce the bandwidth required for transmission, and hence costs, is to 'compress' the video image; that is, to digitise the signal and then to remove as much extraneous or redundant data as possible. Although a full-motion analogue television picture changes 30 times per second in North America (25 times per second in Europe), not all of the picture changes in each frame. For instance, with a 'talking head' against a still background, probably less than 10 percent of the picture changes from frame to frame. Once the basic picture is captured, all that needs to be transmitted per frame are the changes. It follows that the more movement, and the faster the changes, the more difficult it becomes to compress without losing quality. Similarly pictures transmitted at narrow baud rates tend to be jerky and have problems with lip synchronisation.

Compression technology is changing rapidly; engineers are developing more and more powerful algorithms for converting from analogue to digital, allowing increasingly more data to be compressed without noticeable differences in the quality of the picture. At the time of writing, several levels of compressed video are beginning to be adopted, depending on the application:

- *Video on desk-top computers*: 56 kbps (one telephone line). This allows video to be integrated into a small 'window' on the computer screen; it can also be used for video conferencing, but because of the jerky movements, it tends to be more appropriate for a single talking head, and/or transmission of still or relatively simple animated graphics. As compression techniques improve, and as computers become more powerful, this speed may well become the standard for video phones and desk-top video conferencing, i.e. allowing individuals to video conference without leaving their office.

- *Group video conferencing*: currently, transmission at around 112–124 kbs ('switched 56kbs' or ISDN) provides adequate sound and picture quality for meetings/instruction for small groups at each site. This usually requires two telephone lines.
- *Movement/good picture resolution*: if the instruction depends on good quality picture resolution, or the transmission of movement (e.g. on video cassette), transmission at 384 kbs or higher is necessary.

The appropriate bandwidth/baud rate for transmission will depend on the applications; the higher the quality of image and the more movement to be transmitted, the greater the transmission requirements, and hence the higher the cost of both transmission and site equipment.

If more than two sites are to be linked together simultaneously, the transmissions need to go through a special exchange or 'bridge'; there are usually additional costs associated with this. At the time of writing, there are few video conferencing bridges available on an operational basis; consequently all sites may have long-distance links to the nearest bridge, even though the sites may be only a few miles apart.

There is, therefore, an increasing variety of ways in which to deliver video conferencing. The most appropriate choice of system will depend partly on the physical configuration of sites to be connected, the applications that are required, the amount of traffic to be carried, and the distances between sites. There are also still some problems of standardisation between different video conferencing hardware systems.

Video cassettes

Television material can be recorded on and replayed from electro-magnetic tape. Video cassette machines can record and playback, enabling both 'time-shift' recording and playback from broadcast television, and also replay of pre-recorded educational programmes. Video cassettes can be copied and distributed via the mail. Video cassettes have now more or less standardised on one format for domestic and educational playback purposes ($\frac{1}{2}$" VHS), although there are still difficulties internationally when moving between different television standards (NTSC, PAL, SECAM).

Video cassettes store images in a linear, analogue form. This means that to access information in the middle of a cassette, the machine has to wind through the cassette to reach the desired point. Even with fast wind mechanisms, it can take up to a minute to locate the right segment. Furthermore, searching usually requires an element of trial and error.

There are several technological advantages of video cassettes: the widespread availability of the technology, the ability to record as well as replay, the low cost of the recording format (video tape), and standardisation of format.

Video discs

Video discs operate differently from video cassettes. Optical video discs work by a laser beam 'reading' or detecting tiny pits below the surface of the plastic coating. A single frame can be stored in one rotation of the disc.

Furthermore, images can be accessed randomly, rather than linearly. The laser 'head' that reads the disc moves in a straight line between the centre and the perimeter of the disc, and the disc rotates quickly. This means that any image on an optical video disc can be accessed within a couple of seconds or less. Furthermore, each 'frame' has its own digital code number, allowing any single frame to be accessed almost immediately. Each single frame can be held steady and for as long as desired, since there is no physical contact with the disc and the 'reading' medium, a light beam. Picture quality is higher than that on cassettes or broadcasts.

Video discs can store over 50,000 separate images or still frame pictures in full colour; full video motion can be achieved by playing frames at 25 or 30 per second, depending on whether the equipment is on the PAL or NTSC television standard. As well as video images, video discs can also store sounds on several different audio tracks, and huge quantities of text, in the form of digital data. However, the television pictures are stored in analogue form.

Production of video discs requires recording on high-quality video tape, which is then sent away for the discs to be pressed. While programmes made for broadcasting or video cassette distribution can be transferred straight over to video disc without further editing, this will not exploit the control characteristics of video discs; producing for educational video disc replay can be a complex and highly specialised job. The complexity increases considerably when production exploits the linking of a computer with the video disc.

There are also several competing video disc systems that are incompatible, i.e. discs made for one system will not play on another. While the number of discs suitable for educational purposes is growing slowly, there is still a lack of appropriate learning material on video disc.

The cost of a video disc player is similar to that of a video cassette recorder. However, video disc players are nowhere near so widespread in use as VCRs.

ACCESS

Home

There is widespread availability of video cassette machines in homes in Western Europe, North America, Australia, New Zealand, Japan and several other South-East Asian countries. In most of these countries more than 70 per cent of all homes have video cassette recorders. Video cassettes for home use have virtually standardised on a single system (VHS).

Video cassettes are a good example of the difficulties caused when not all potential students have access to a particular technology. Despite apparent instructional and cost advantages of video cassette distribution over broadcasting, there was considerable reluctance to use video cassette distribution or production methods at the British Open University, until home penetration reached 80 per cent, on the grounds that this would discriminate against those without a video cassette recorder, and thus restrict access to those on low incomes. (In fact, from 1985, apart from the unemployed, those with low incomes were *more* likely to have had a video cassette machine than those with higher incomes; low income and working class families are often the first to adopt new technologies in the home; university professors are often the last!).

Even though the replay technology is more or less the same price as video cassettes, video disc players are available in very few homes, even in more advanced developed countries. For instance, in 1992, less than 1 per cent of Canadian homes had a video disc player (Statistics Canada, 1993). While an increasing number of homes (33 per cent in Canada in 1992) have audio compact disc players, these are unsuitable for playing back video or for connection to computers. Thus video discs and CD-ROMs tend to be used more in educational institutions or training establishments.

Video conferencing to date requires high-cost specialist equipment and will not be used in the home until video phones and desk-top, computer-based video conferencing become widespread.

Local centres

Several distance teaching institutions have placed equipment in local centres, particularly when a substantial proportion of students have suitable equipment at home, but others do not. Video conferencing, requiring as it does special equipment and communications facilities, lends itself to local centre use. It is particularly useful when an institution has to spread its teaching across more than one campus. However, there are serious difficulties in using local study centres to provide alternative access for students who do not have particular technologies at home.

In 1982, the British Open University, worried about the loss of viewing due to a deterioration in transmission times, and aware of the growth in home access to video recorders, introduced a back-up system for broadcast television programmes. This followed the introduction several years earlier of a popular scheme for audio cassette back-up for radio broadcasts, for use in homes. A central copying facility was set up, to make available video cassette recordings of selected television broadcasts, and 311 VCR machines were located in local centres. Students applied to the university's headquarters for a copy of programmes in the scheme, and a cassette was sent to the student's home address. It was then up to the student to decide where to use the cassette, before returning it, so the cassette could be used at home, if the student had a machine, or at a local study centre.

In practice, the main student usage was at home. Very few students used the facilities in the study centres, although the provision of rented equipment in the study centres cost more than half the whole project. Consequently, the machines were eventually withdrawn from centres, although students could still borrow cassettes. Thus this scheme failed to solve the problem of access to television for those without their own VCR machines, although it substantially improved access to those who were unable to watch the broadcasts (see Brown, 1983).

Secondly, when the study centre is used as an alternative to home delivery, students usually require to access the media individually and to use the media in conjunction with other components of their course (e.g. the text, assignments, etc.). This requires individual, independent study. Open University study centres by and large, though, are organised around group activities, i.e. around classrooms. The VCR machines were located in classrooms in the study centres, which tended to be at adult education centres or further education colleges. With VCR machines placed in open classrooms primarily used by other students, it is perhaps not surprising that 57 machines were stolen in the first year of the scheme.

Some institutions keep copies of all television programmes at study centres for use by students. For instance, the Open University of the Netherlands provides copies of all its broadcasts on video disc at its 13 local centres. However, even if students can access centres regularly, such a practice becomes viable only if there are few centres, or few programmes, or if programmes have a short 'life'. For instance, the British Open University has 1,500 television broadcasts transmitted in any one year, and over 250 study centres. To provide a copy of each programme in each centre would require a total of 375,000 copies, with 50,000 cassettes or discs being replaced each year.

Video cassettes lend themselves to group activity. However, such use either needs to be deliberately designed into the whole teaching package, or alternatively, tutors will need encouragement and training to use video recordings of broadcasts in their face-to-face sessions. Open University experience suggests that tutors generally prefer to use their limited time covering other aspects of the course than the broadcasts. In any case, such group uses of video are quite different from providing a back-up to home study, which is usually done on an individual basis.

Students need to be isolated from one another when studying individually through media. This requires study carrels, headphones, and multiple copies of equipment and course material. Unless technology facilities in study centres are readily available at times and at places where most students can use them on an individual and private basis without queueing, or for group activities arranged well in advance, it is not a good idea to rely too heavily on study centres for media delivery. It is also very expensive in terms of equipment, and demands a great deal of the time of regional staff to organise and look after such facilities.

The UK Open University's experience suggests that locating equipment in shared learning centres to 'equalise' student access to equipment is not a viable strategy, especially if the bulk of the learning can be done at home.

TEACHING AND LEARNING

Applications

To give some idea of the extent and variety of such kinds of instructional television applications, a brief overview is given of a selection of applications in Europe and North America.

Narrowcasting

Brey (1991) and Hezel Associates (1993) conducted thorough reviews of the use of television (and other telecommunications media) for higher education in the USA. Brey for instance found that 'by 1994, 80 per cent of community colleges and 78 per cent of universities will have distance learning programmes' and that 'video cassettes, public television stations and cable television are the three most frequently used technologies . . . in 1991 and will remain so in 1994.'

The major use of television for higher education in the USA is for the relaying of lectures or classroom teaching from one site to classrooms on other campuses. While most use of television for undergraduate teaching in the USA is confined within state boundaries, there are about 30 regional or national initiatives. The National Technological University (NTU) in 1991/92 offered 11 Master of Science degree programmes to 4,500 enrolments, and 440 short courses to more than 100,000 technical professionals. The teaching originates from 45 collaborative universities. Programmes are up-linked from these sites, and broadcast by satellite to 419 sites in 129 different organisations, including the US Air Force and many of the major US corporations (National Technological University, 1992).

Lionel Baldwin, the President of NTU, reports:

Many courses are broadcast in real-time, so that NTU students can interact instantaneously with the instructor by telephone or fax. Many students however view the programmes asynchronously, using video-tapes of broadcasts, because this mode provides the needed flexibility for working adult learners. For these students, interaction with the instructor is by telephone during office hours, electronic mail via the

NTU computer and INTERNET, and the regular flow of hard copy assignments either by mail or, increasingly, by fax.

(Baldwin, 1993)

Baldwin cites evidence that the grade point average for students on NTU courses is significantly higher than for campus-based students following similar courses in 'regular' universities.

In Canada, the two provinces where television is being used on a regular basis for distance delivery of undergraduate courses are Saskatchewan and British Columbia. In 1991/92, the Saskatchewan Communications Network (SCN) was used by the Universities of Regina and Saskatchewan to deliver a total of 15 first year courses to 1,400 students. A further 1,250 students were similarly served by Saskatchewan Institute of Applied Sciences and Technology. This system uses satellite and fibre-optic cable transmission to provide live, interactive, one-way video, two-way audio to more than 90 classrooms across the province. Students in these programmes performed equally as well as on-campus students (SCN, 1992).

In British Columbia in 1992/93, seven different institutions used broadcast television to deliver a total of 421 hours of telecourses across 89 different courses. These programmes, part of courses for credit distributed via television on the Open Learning Agency's Knowledge Network, are received via satellite and cable networks in homes across the province. Some of these courses are based on acquired tele-series; others involve original programming. Emily Carr College of Art and Design has gradually built up television-based courses so that a full first year programme is now available at a distance anywhere in the province.

EuroPACE, established in 1987, was a consortium of multi-national companies (including IBM, DEC, Hewlett-Packard, British Telecom, Thomson, etc.), using both satellite and computer communications, to deliver a Programme of Advanced Continuing Education in Europe to companies throughout Europe, drawing on key researchers in European universities and companies (very much following the NTU model). This was funded partly by sponsorship and partly by the sale of courses. In 1994, EuroPACE and Eurostep, another organisation that provided services to member education and training organisations wishing to transmit by satellite across Europe, merged. In general, though, narrowcast instructional television has struggled in Europe, possibly because of the dominance of relatively well funded national educational broadcasting organisations.

Videoconferencing

The advent of compressed video, and lower tariffs because of more abundant channels of communication through satellite and cable systems, have led to a rapid growth in video conferencing applications in education and training.

Satellites can be used in several ways for video conferencing. The most common is to use one-way television transmission via satellite to a wide variety of sites, with 'live' audio-telephone communication back from the sites. The major advantage of satellite transmission is that transmission costs are independent of distance, within the (very large) area covered by the satellite.

There has been considerable corporate use of video conferencing in the USA, mainly for in-house training between several sites across the continent, partly because of the savings on travel that can be made. A VSAT (Very Small Aperture Terminal) is a relatively small ground-station for transmitting and receiving narrowband satellite signals. The US Army is using the Hughes InteleConference VSAT satellite system for training reservists across the USA. It provides multi-site, two-way video conferencing operating at between 256 and 384 kbps (depending on the application). It is not yet desk-top, but is room-to-room, and can handle two-way video between any two sites at once, plus simultaneous audio between all sites. Video linking between sites can be transferred in mid-conference ('passing the baton'), as the PC-based control system enables any site to be the uplink. The PC control system comes with a simple user interface, and can be located at any single site.

Thus, satellite transmission is useful when there is a large number of receive sites (e.g., cable stations, schools, learning centres, individual learners at home), and where most of the visual communication is from the centre to the periphery (e.g., a lecture, followed by discussion).

There are, though, several disadvantages of one-way video and two-way telephone conferencing via satellite. There is no visual communication from receive sites; the television signal has to reach a (high-cost) transmission uplink, which can be a problem for live lectures generated at sites away from such facilities; all receive sites require (relatively low-cost) reception equipment; television transmission time may be expensive, or not available when required.

Point-to-point video conferencing using terrestrial links, such as telephone, cable or micro-wave links, is frequently used when institutions have campuses on different sites. The Mississippi 2000 project and Vision Carolina both use digital fibre-optics to provide full, two-way television between schools, and also to link in to college campuses (Northern Telecom, 1991). The main purpose of the networks is to link rural high schools in order to equalise access to specialised teaching. Four high schools, two university campuses, and the state educational television centre were networked on the Mississippi 2000 project. There was a computerised, PC-based network control, which could be operated from any site. Each fitted classroom had remote controlled cameras and remote acoustical control, plus a four-quadrant screen, and a podium control for the teacher. Students used a push-button system to respond to questions. Vision Carolina is developing two networks, one based on Charlottetown, with 11 sites, and one on Wilmington, with five sites.

The Open Learning Agency has a private video conference link between its learning centre in Prince George and its headquarters in the lower mainland, 500 miles away, to facilitate the delivery of training between the lower mainland and Prince George. It is an integrated system network that allows for telephone, fax and data transmission, as well as video conferencing. The agency leases 56 kbs capability on a 24 hour basis, with the capability of switching 'on demand' to 364 kbs capacity as required for video conferencing applications. The aim is to link the centre at Prince George to other educational institutions in the north-west of the province, and eventually integrate this service into a province-wide learning network.

Where ISDN services are widespread, as in Australia, they are being extensively used for video conferencing in education and training. Latchem, Mitchell and Atkinson (1993) have provided a comprehensive review of educational video conferencing in Australia:

> As at March, 1993, 20 of Australia's publicly funded universities had videoconferencing facilities at 41 sites and over 20 sites were operational in the technical and further education (TAFE) sector with many more planned for. Thirteen of the remaining universities had plans to install such facilities and the number of sites could increase to 80–100 over the next few years. The most common form of videoconferencing system involves two-way video and audio, transmitted as compressed digital signals via . . . ISDN at 128kb/s.
>
> (Latchem, Mitchell and Atkinson, 1993)

However, the lack of standardisation around ISDN in North America means more variation in the kinds of two-way educational video conferencing application.

Video cassettes

Video cassettes have been used both at Stanford University in California, and the University of Aston in Britain, for 'tutored video instruction'. This entails the centralised production of usually well-illustrated lectures, with the programme being copied on cassette and distributed to local centres (often in work-sites), where the programme is watched by a small group of local learners, with a tutor to facilitate the discussion. Sometimes the 'central' instructor is available for questions or discussion by telephone with the local group. The important feature here is the ability of the groups to discuss the teaching material and ask questions, either of the tutor or the central instructor.

Durbridge (1982) studied groups of experienced teachers taking an education course at a distance who came together to a local site to view and discuss video cassette 'case-studies' of children learning in a classroom. She found that students who studied the same case-study material in isolation tended to view the programme only once, straight through, and lacked confidence in their interpretation of the material, while those who watched in groups stopped the cassette, viewed the material several times, felt more confident in their interpretations, and were able to identify a wider range of phenomena from the case-studies.

It seems then that if television programmes are made to stimulate analysis and interpretation of case-study material, the opportunity for group discussion may be critical for some students in achieving such learning objectives.

Video discs

Video discs can be used in several ways: either in a stand-alone form, in the same way as a video cassette, but with much more precise and convenient control; or combined with a micro-computer. Without a computer, they can be used to access large banks of images, such as pictures in an art gallery, biology cells, or 'encyclopedias' of animals, either as stills or in motion. They can be used for special purposes, such as playing back in slow motion for analysis of accidents, or for precise viewing control of medical operational procedures.

More commonly, video discs are computer-controlled, so that the student is guided to work through different parts of the television material, with activities or tests of learning built in. These applications are discussed in more detail in the next chapter.

Instructional strategies

There is a great deal of variety in the way that instructional television has been, and is being, used in delivering distance education programmes. Such programmes can vary along any of the following dimensions:

lectures/discussion panels	unique presentational characteristics of television
low-cost	high-cost
live, interactive	pre-recorded
programmes to classes/groups	programmes to individuals
sole medium	mixed-media
'narrowcasting'	'broadcasting'.

In general, instructional television tends to demonstrate characteristics on the left of the table above, and educational broadcasting those characteristics more on the right. In between is a whole variety of different programme styles or approaches, for example 'enhanced lectures', using specially prepared graphics, or drama 'dropped into' a conventional lecture (e.g. a History course at the University of Saskatchewan), or relatively low-cost productions which nevertheless concentrate on the presentational features of television (e.g. laboratory experiments or demonstrations).

The broadcast or 'relayed' lecture, very common in North American universities that teach between campuses, involves the live transmission of a lecture, often delivered in front of a class or group in one location, to a group of students at another campus, or, less frequently, to individuals in their homes or place of work. Students at the remote site in most cases have the opportunity to ask questions or participate in the learning event, usually through an audio telephone link, in which case it may be referred to as 'interactive' television.

There are several reasons why broadcast lectures are the preferred mode of television for university professors. There is very little need to change their normal campus-based approach to instruction. There is plenty of evidence (see Clark, 1983; Moore and Thompson, 1990) that live, televised lectures can be as effective as face-to-face lectures. Exploiting the presentational features of television is usually more expensive – and requires more training and specialist production – than using it for relaying lectures. Professors and administrators therefore need to be convinced that more expensive production techniques lead to better teaching.

There are arguments though for trying wherever possible to break away from the lecture format. The greatest success of televised lectures has been on courses where students already have a good grounding in the subject matter, and/or are motivated to acquire the information (e.g. NTU's postgraduate courses), or where access and convenience is an important factor (e.g. mature working adults with limited time or ability to travel to campuses). There is less experience, and less evidence, of the success of this kind of programming with novice students, i.e. students who are new to a particular subject area, and not familiar with the concepts in the subject area (irrespective of the students' age or experience in studying in other subject areas), or with students with relatively low levels of motivation.

In particular, the lecture format, unless there is a great deal of interaction between individual students and the lecturer, tends to result in what Marton and Säljö (1976) call 'surface processing', i.e. learning focuses on recall and reproduction of what has been taught, rather than on analysis, questioning or re-working of the learning material: 'deep processing', in Marton and Säljö's terms.

In order then to assess the appropriateness of the televised lecture, the question that needs to be answered first is: what are the teaching objectives? Is it merely the transmission of information? Is it deep understanding? Is it the ability to analyse, interpret and synthesise information, to evaluate evidence, or to apply learning to new situations? If the teaching objective is more than the efficient transmission of information, then it is likely to be worth making the effort to exploit the unique presentational characteristics of television.

Portway and Lane (1992) have provided an excellent summary of video conferencing applications in the USA. The tendency to use the traditional lecture or seminar format is even stronger with video conferencing applications than with instructional television, mainly because the compression ratios make it difficult to transmit high-quality moving images. In most of the reported video conferencing applications in the USA, there has been little discussion of the pedagogy of distance education, beyond such comments as 'Classroom teachers need to adapt their methods for TV teaching', and 'They need lots of training to familiarise themselves with the equipment'. Instructional design is not usually an issue that is discussed or reported.

Also, at the time of writing, there have been very few evaluations of teaching through television or video conferencing, apart from straight comparisons with face-to-face lecturing. Users seem satisfied if they can demonstrate that distance teaching by video conferencing is 'as good as' conventional face-to-face teaching. Several reported 'no significant differences', using grade-point averages. None of the studies examined qualitative differences in learning through television or video conferencing.

There is an urgent need for sensitive, imaginative research that looks beyond mere comprehension and recall, that tries to test the quality of learning, and that tries to relate the quality of learning to different methods of using television for different types of target group.

INTERACTIVITY AND USER-FRIENDLINESS

Once recorded on to cassette or disc, television can be used quite differently from viewing a broadcast or participating in a video conference. The tape or disc can be stopped, some parts can be selected for use, and not others, and the same television material can be used as many times as required. Educational institutions have been slow to appreciate the significance of this difference between transmitted and recorded television; viewing behaviour for educational television materials in a pre-recorded form is still dominated by general 'broadcast' television viewing habits, or by the 'lecture' mode of talking and listening.

At Rensselaer Polytechnic Institute, New York State, Stone (1992) produced evidence that flexibility of recorded materials was more important to students than live interaction. An internal evaluation study found that those students on advanced engineering courses who received recordings of live, interactive lectures learned more than those who actually participated in the live, interactive sessions. Follow-up phone calls indicated that the non-interactive students preferred the flexibility that the video cassettes gave them.

Interactivity is also related to student numbers. The opportunity for any individual to participate in questioning or discussion decreases in proportion to the number of students viewing a live interactive programme. One reason for using television is to obtain economies of scale, but this can be at the cost of interactivity. It may be better to provide opportunities for interaction outside the programme itself, through local group discussion or computer conferencing, if the total number receiving a programme is more than 25 or 30.

Another factor influencing interaction is the style of presentation. There is no real need for a live programme if most of the time is taken up by the instructor delivering information. Particularly with video conferencing, instructors need to design the learning experience so that students at the remote site have opportunities or are required to participate on a systematic and regular basis. It may be valuable sometimes to split a video conference into two parts, to allow for local discussion or group work, then return to the video conference to report back to the instructor.

Finally, there is a great need for more systematic research into the relative advantages of 'live interactive' versus pre-recorded programming, in terms of learning effectiveness. There is no firm evidence that two-way live video conferencing is more effective than one-way video plus two-way audio, or even the distribution of video cassettes for individual use.

What we do know is that for most distance learners, it is essential that they can access the television material at the appropriate point in their studies, and that there are learning benefits if they can stop and reflect on what they have just seen before moving on to the next part of the programme, and if they can watch the same scene as many times as necessary to interpret it. Thus while interactivity is essential, the live interactive lecture is not the only, and probably not the best, way to provide this.

COSTS

Video cassettes

In terms of cost, video cassettes impact mainly on distribution, rather than production. Studies at the British Open University have established at what point it becomes cheaper to distribute television material on cassettes through the mail, rather than through broadcasting. The Open University broadcast programmes are usually 25 minutes in length. Thus the most common type of video cassette used by the Open University is an E30 (i.e. 30 minutes in playing time). Furthermore, the university does not give the video cassette to the student, but loans it for the duration of the course; the student must return the cassette after the course ends. In addition to the distribution of non-broadcast video material on cassette, the Open University also operates a student loan scheme for broadcast programmes that they miss or wish to see again, on selected courses. (Less than 10 per cent of the cassettes loaned are lost or damaged per annum.)

Transmission costs were US$435 (£290) per 25-minute programme in 1988. However, to ensure a high proportion of student viewers, two transmissions of each programme at different times were necessary. Thus it cost US$870 (£580) to reach a majority of students for each programme through transmissions. On the basis of its experience in operating a video cassette copying and loan service, the Open University estimated that it becomes more economical to distribute on cassette than to pay for two transmissions when there are 350 students or less on a course (Open University, 1988). In fact, in 1988 more than 40 per cent of all Open University courses had 350 students or less.

Thus the cost structure for the distribution of video cassettes is very similar to that for audio cassettes, as can be seen by Figure 5.1 below.

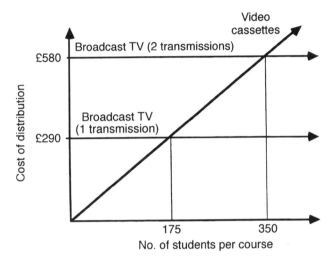

Figure 5.1 Structure of delivery costs: broadcast TV and video cassettes (UK OU)

Narrowcast instructional television

There is not a single cost structure for instructional television, but several, depending on the way television is produced and distributed. It is very difficult to find published data on the costs of instructional television, and practice seems to vary considerably from institution to institution. Since the cost of studios and faculty are seen as 'fixed' and have to be paid, whether or not the facility is used, many institutions do not 're-charge' teaching units for the use of television, since this would discourage use. For these reasons, some hypothetical data will be given, to illustrate the different cost structures for different applications.

Case 1: televised, interactive lectures, repeated every year, distributed by satellite and/or cable

University X is a dual-mode institution. It uses television to reach students in local centres in smaller towns around the province. The university has a studio complex designed for the production of live, interactive television lectures/seminars, and uses a combination of satellite and cable for delivery within the province. In calculating costs a number of assumptions have been made.

If interactivity is to mean anything, the number of students receiving a broadcast has to be limited (probably 50, split between the main campus and the remote sites, is the maximum for any single programme). Beyond such a number, another instructor may need to be hired, and another set of programmes produced (additional 'sessions' in North America).

Thus in this case, each course delivered by lecture/seminar has a total of approximately 50 students registered across 10 different sites. Programmes are one hour in length, and students receive one programme per week per course. Each site has a leased telephone link to the studio.

The experience of most teachers and professors who have used television for instruction is that a televised lecture requires probably at least twice as much preparation time as for a standard face-to-face lecture. Greater care has to be taken not only over graphics, but also over the structure, clarity and length of the lecture. Thus:

Academic time: two days per one-hour programme (including preparation time) = $300.

Studio ($1 million initial cost): maintenance/equipment replacement at 15% per year = $150,000 per year.

Studio crew (director + two technical staff) = $100,000 per year.

Programme budget (materials, e.g. graphics, tape, props) = $500.

Satellite/cable cost per hour: $350.

Telephone costs: $75 per hour (leased lines, across 10 sites, including fixed costs).

One programme per week, over 39 weeks, per session.

Note that 250 students a year could be one course with five instructors, or five courses, each with a single instructor and 50 students. If sessions were longer than one hour, costs would rise more or less proportionately. The fixed costs of production ($250,000 per annum) are averaged across the number of programmes produced each year (e.g. $250,000/117 = $2,137).

It can be seen from Table 5.1 and Figure 5.2 that the unit costs for live, interactive instructional television are surprisingly high. For numbers over 500 per course per year, even the high-cost productions of BBC-OUP start to work out less per student contact hour than live instructional television. In the model used in the previous chapter, the cost per study hour per student for 125 students per course was US$109 (£73) for educational broadcasting, compared with US$67 (£45) for interactive TV. However, by

Table 5.1 Costs of interactive television per student study hour over eight years (hypothetical data)

	No. of students p. a.			
	125	*250*	*625*	*1,000*
	No. of instructors			
	3	*5*	*13*	*20*
	Programmes produced p. a.			
	117	*195*	*507*	*780*
	US$	*US$*	*US$*	*US$*
Development/production				
Production (fixed costs)	2,137	1,282	493	320
Programme budget	500	500	500	500
Academic time	300	300	300	300
Total production costs	2,937	2,082	1,293	1,120
Delivery				
Transmission	350	350	350	350
Telephone interaction	75	75	75	75
Total (per hour)	3,362	2,507	1,718	1,545
Cost per student per hour	67.24	50.14	34.36	30.90
(50 students)	(£44.83)	(£33.43)	(£22.91)	(£20.60)

Note: 3 terms × 13 weeks = 39 weeks

around 500 students per course the unit costs for educational broadcasting start to compare to those of instructional television. This is because each lecture is a separate production, limited to 50 students on average. Each time the lecture is repeated, the costs are repeated.

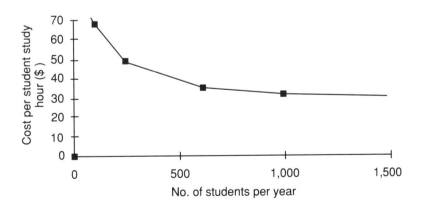

Figure 5.2 Cost per student study hour: interactive TV

Figure 5.2 converts Table 5.1 into a graph. Figure 5.2 once again shows the importance of maximising fixed costs, such as studio overheads. This reduces the average cost per programme substantially, as fixed costs of the studio are averaged out over a greater number of programmes. However, unit costs start to level off after about 250 students per year receiving television lectures, because the 'marginal' costs associated with additional sessions balance out the lower average unit costs for the studio.

In the above example, 20 television-based sessions a year generate 780 programmes; if sessions included two programmes a week, or if the number of television sessions increased above 20 per week, there would be a 'step' increase in studio overheads, due to overtime, or adding new production facilities.

Figure 5.3 illustrates the total costs of live, interactive lectures over an eight-year period. Note that the total operating cost per annum (around $1,200,000 for maximum production at around 780 programmes a year, or $400,000 for 100 programmes a year) is much less than for the educational broadcasting model ($10.5 million/£7 million). The costs for maximum production from one studio will accumulate to almost $10 million, though, over a period of eight years.

This then is the cost of increasing access, and needs to be set against the building and staffing of small, local institutions, and faculty and student travel and lost opportunity costs. Nevertheless, the total annual operating costs are still a significant amount for a university, particularly if the sole purpose is to increase access. Furthermore, if one added incrementally the costs of individual institutions using live instructional television to reach the same numbers as educational broadcasting, the cost comparison would be more favourable to educational broadcasting.

Thus for live interactive programming, the volume of production is

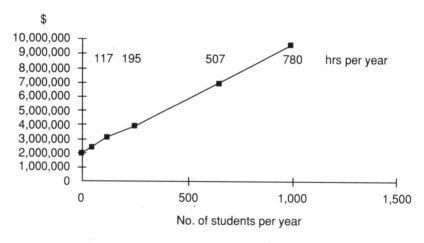

Figure 5.3 Total costs: interactive TV (over eight years)

determined not only by the number of courses using television, and the number of programmes per course, but also by the number of students following a particular course.

Case 2: televised lectures, recorded once and distributed for eight years by satellite and/or cable

University Y has a similar studio complex to University X, for the production of lecture-type programmes. However, these programmes are recorded once, and distributed by satellite and cable each year for eight years, when the course is withdrawn, or revised and re-recorded. Each course delivered by lecture/seminar has approximately 50 off-campus students registered. In calculating costs, the following assumptions have been made:

Academic time: two days per one hour programme (including preparation time) = $300.

Studio ($1 million initial cost): maintenance/equipment replacement at 15% per year = $150,000 per year.

Studio crew (director + two technical staff) = $100,000 per year.

Programme budget (materials, e.g. graphics, tape, props) = $500

Satellite/cable cost per hour: $350; video cassette copying and distribution: $5 per hour.

39 programmes per course (one a week); 10 new television courses a year.

Table 5.2 is based on these assumptions.
In this model, the key factor is that with pre-recorded programmes, the

Table 5.2 Total costs: pre-recorded instructional television (over eight years)

	Courses p. a.			
	1	*10*	*20*	*25*
	Programmes produced p. a.			
	39	*390*	*780*	*975*
	US$	*US$*	*US$*	*US$*
Fixed	250,000	250,000	250,000	500,000
Programme budget	19,500	195,000	390,000	487,500
Academic time	11,700	117,000	234,000	292,500
Transmission costs	13,650	136,500	273,000	341,250
Total (one year)	294,850	698,500	1,147,000	1,621,250
Over 8 years	390,400	1,654,000	3,058,000	4,010,000
Courses (cumulative)	8	80	160	200

Note: 3 terms × 13 weeks = 39 weeks

programmes last for eight years. This enables, for the same annual operating cost, courses to be cumulatively added each year, over a period of eight years, at which point the volume of activity stabilises, as existing courses need replacement after eight years. Thus, if in the first year of operation, 10 courses, each of 39 weeks, were based on pre-recorded television programmes, the total cost for the 390 programmes would be US$698,500. To this must be added the cost of transmitting this course for another seven years ($136,500 x 8 = $955,500). Adding in these, the total cost over eight years would be $1,654,000.

It would stretch most single studio production systems to the limit to produce 780 new programmes a year (20 new courses per year in this model). Somewhere beyond this point, an additional studio and crew would be needed, and the costs of this have been included in the 25 courses per year column.

In this model, the critical factor with regard to total costs is the volume of activity: the more courses, or programmes per course, produced each year, the greater the total costs, as can be seen from Figure 5.4.

Student numbers per course are irrelevant, as far as the television costs are concerned, because there are no variable costs associated with the production and transmission of programmes, unless programmes were to be distributed on cassette. However, there will be additional costs if interaction with students is to be provided via another medium, such as telephone or computer tutoring. The total cost then would be the combination of the two technologies.

Table 5.3 (p. 109) provides data on the cost per student hour related to both volume of production and student numbers per course.

First of all, unit costs are influenced in this model by the volume of production: the more courses/programmes produced, the lower the unit

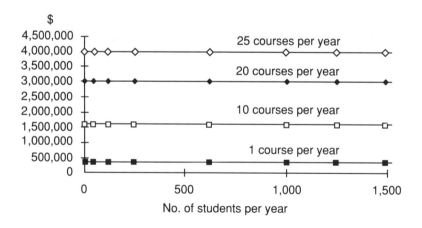

Figure 5.4 Total costs: pre-recorded instructional television (over eight years)

Table 5.3 Costs of pre-recorded instructional television per student study hour (over eight years)

No. of courses (over 8 years)	1,000 students (125 students per year × 8) $	5,000 students (625 students per year × 8) $	10,000 students (1,250 students per year × 8) $
8 (1 per year)			
Production	281,200	281,200	281,200
Transmission (over 8 years)	109,200	109,200	109,200
Total (39 hrs)	390,400	390,400	390,400
Cost per student/hr	10.01	2.00	1.00
80 (10 per year)			
Production	562,000	562,000	562,000
Transmission (over 8 years)	1,092,000	1,092,000	1,092,000
Total (390 hrs)	1,654,000	1,654,000	1,654,000
Cost per student/hr	4.24	0.85	0.42
160 (20 per year)			
Production	874,000	874,000	874,000
Transmission (over 8 years)	2,184,000	2,184,000	2,184,000
Total (780 hrs)	3,058,000	3,058,000	3,058,000
Cost per student/hr	3.92	0.78	0.39
200 (25 per year)			
Production	1,280,000	1,280,000	1,280,000
Transmission (over 8 years)	2,730,000	2,730,000	2,730,000
Total (975 hrs)	4,010,000	4,010,000	4,010,000
Cost per student/hr	4.11 (£2.74)	0.82 (£0.55)	0.41 (£0.27)

Note: 39 programmes per course: 3 × 13 week terms

costs, until another studio and crew has to be added. In this model unit costs stabilise around 650 students per year, irrespective of the volume of production (see Figure 5.5). Costs drop below $1 per hour per student at around 500 students per course and 300 programmes produced, per year.

Table 5.3 also indicates that with pre-recorded instructional television, cable and satellite transmission costs constitute between 68 per cent to 71 per cent of all costs. If cassettes are used to distribute the programmes, instead of cable, the cost of distribution by cassette becomes progressively more expensive than cable once student numbers exceed around 75 students per course (Figure 5.6).

The difference in total television costs over eight years between live interactive and pre-recorded programmes is dramatic (see Figure 5.7).

Unit costs for interactive television stabilise at around $34 per hour, for

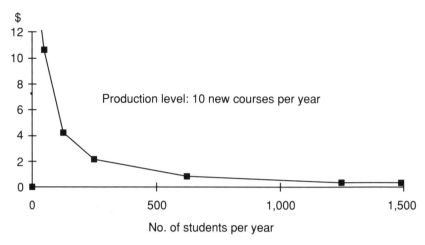

Figure 5.5 Cost per student study hour: pre-recorded instructional television (over eight years)
Note: For Figure 5.5, the average cost per student study hour at 390, 780 or 975 programmes a year production levels is quite close; hence only one line is drawn, at the level of 390 programmes per year.

650 students or more per year per course. Pre-recorded television programme costs never reach this level even for the smallest student numbers and smallest level of production ($25 per student study hour for 50 students per annum, and 39 programmes per year). The reason of course is the amortisation of pre-recorded courses over eight years, giving 400 student users even for a course of 50 students per year.

The disadvantage is the loss of live interaction, and the possibility of the

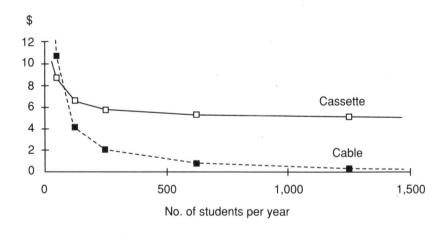

Figure 5.6 Cost per study hour: pre-recorded television (over eight years): cable vs. cassette

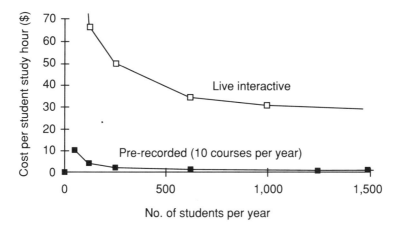

Figure 5.7 Cost per student study hour: interactive vs. pre-recorded instructional television (over eight years)

material becoming dated. However, the difference in costs is so great that other means of providing interaction, such as audio conferencing (at between $3–$5 per student study hour) or computer conferencing ($2–$3 per student study hour), may be more attractive.

It can be seen then that there are major cost advantages of recording programmes and repeating them in later years (irrespective of distribution method). In addition, academic staff time is released for other research, administrative or teaching duties.

Video conferencing

Satellite

Satellite video conferencing, using a satellite broadcast from a central point, with telephone calls from receive sites, has a number of cost elements:

- studio cost per hour (including crew);
- programme budget (presenter, materials, director);
- cost of reception sites (rooms, satellite dish, if not previously available);
- transmission cost per hour;
- local facilitators at each site;
- project management (substantial organisation is needed to put together a satellite video conference across several sites, especially if, as in most cases, it is a one-off event for participants).

There is evidence that private-sector companies will pay for timely, local delivery of training via video conferencing. For instance, the Saskatchewan

Communications Network claims that 'in a recent cost comparison, it was demonstrated that the one-way video, two-way audio format of the Training Network can deliver a programme for less than one-half the cost of a traditional face-to-face meeting for large groups' (SCN, 1992). The cost savings from the Open Learning Agency's delivery of management training by satellite video conferencing has already been discussed in Chapter 2.

Point-to-point

This form of video conferencing links two or more sites through standard or leased lines from telecommunications carriers. Vendors such as CLI, Mitsubishi and PictureTel are offering equipment with a choice of baud rates, depending on the application. The price of equipment depends on the application, baud rates and the extent to which operation is automated. Software and equipment (a miniature video camera) for desk-top video conferencing can be bought for as little as US$5,000. Work-stations for group video conferencing can be purchased beginning at US$20,000 per site. Self-operated automated studios for full digital transmission (2 mega-bits) now range in price up to $200,000 per site, depending on the quality of the signal, the sophistication and size of the video conferencing room, and the amount of building construction needed to make a room sound-proof, especially if conventional classrooms are to be used.

Transmission rates also vary, depending on the telecommunications carrier, federal or state regulatory environments, and bandwidth required. Distance is another cost factor. At the time of writing, there are very few examples of regular tariffs for educational video conferencing, particularly at the higher baud rates. Switched 56 kbs or ISDN-based video conferencing systems can operate at the rate for two standard telephone lines. The Open Learning Agency operates at 356 kbs at a cost of US$244 (C$325) for the first hour and US$187 ($250) for each hour after, between two sites 500 miles apart. This includes a charge for room and technical support. If more than two sites are involved, there will also be video conferencing bridging costs (if there is a suitable bridge available). Going through a central bridge, particularly if distant from the linked sites, will also increase long-distance charges.

In the first phase of Mississippi 2000, there was lively discussion between representatives of teachers, carriers, and Northern Telecom, about transmission costs. Staff from the schools reported that costs averaged $2,300 per school per month, but the carriers were not willing to confirm these costs. On-site costs for equipment and building adaptation (for one room) were between $30,000 and $80,000 per site, depending on whether analogue or compression technology was being used, and the amount of building alterations needed. The main problem with room conversion was sound quality.

Compressed video techniques are reducing dramatically the bandwidth required for high-quality digital video. This is leading to substantial reductions in transmission costs, and more drive towards two-way video applications. Switched 56 kbs services, using two telephone lines, looks like emerging as a continental 'standard' for point-to-point video conferencing in North America.

Video conferencing cost structures are similar in structure to, but different in actual costs from, live interactive television (see Bates, 1994, for a full cost analysis). Costs for serving 125 students or more per year range from US$9 to $18 per hour, or about one-third the cost of live, full bandwidth televised lectures.

The main economic justification for two-way video conferencing comes from increasing teacher/student ratios by sharing instructors between sites, or through a dramatic reduction in travel costs for instructors, and there are special situations in the USA and Canada (e.g., inter-campus teaching with small numbers, rural high schools, small college consortia) where this might apply.

Summary

It can be seen that live, interactive, instructional television is an expensive option. Pre-recorded instructional television, combined with another technology for the purposes of interaction, is a much better option in most cases.

There also appears to be both economic and pedagogic advantages in a consortium approach, where a single programme or course serves students from a number of different institutions. Avoiding duplication of courses should allow funds to be concentrated, thus allowing for a higher quality of production, which in turn would enable the presentational features of television to be more fully exploited, which in turn should result in a wider range of intellectual skills being developed.

Lastly, there is a strong and growing market for original, good quality instructional television that exploits the medium. Market revenues can help off-set original production costs, if the project's financial structure is set up to exploit this opportunity. However, unless the presenter is outstanding in either reputation or televisual skills, there is little 'secondary' market demand for lecture-type programming.

ORGANISATIONAL ISSUES

Curriculum design and team-work

Of all the research evidence, the most common finding is that, whatever style of programme is used, teachers need to adapt their teaching to the medium. There are many studies that indicate that if television is to be used successfully for instruction, it takes more time, and a different technique to lecturing or classroom instruction is required.

However, it is not only teachers who need to adapt. Schramm (1972) claimed that broadcasters bring a different set of professional criteria to educational television: 'Most educational broadcasters tend to talk of a "good" programme in terms of quality; most scholars, in terms of effectiveness.' Lionel Baldwin, the President of the National Technological University in the USA, has pointed out that just as the personal computer freed the control of computers from the white-coated technician, so the new forms of television, such as low-cost video conferencing, allow educational television to be freed from the control of broadcasters.

The trick though is not to throw the baby out with the bathwater. Television professionals bring more than just expertise in managing the technology; they also usually bring skills in exploiting the visual elements of television. If the production people can be made to concentrate on this aspect, rather than the need for 'super-professionalism' in production and technical standards, etc., then television can be fully exploited at reasonable cost: more than just a relayed lecture, but considerably less than a full-blown broadcast documentary.

It will also be evident by now that curriculum design, in terms of identifying the various roles of television, accompanying print materials, tutorial support, and assessment strategy, is critical. Instructional designers can play an invaluable role in helping subject experts define the various teaching and learning needs of a course, and making sure they are assigned to the most appropriate media.

Timing of investment decisions in a particular technology is critical. The technology of compressed video is developing very fast, and costs will continue to drop rapidly for some time for both equipment and transmission. Some of the new compression-based technology applications are too expensive at the moment, but will become cheaper. Others will always have a relatively high cost, when all cost factors are considered rather than just the cost of transmission. Thus, the technology and the potential markets need to be constantly monitored.

NOVELTY

Instructional television, in the form of televised lectures, certainly has little novelty value; such programmes have been available in North America since the mid-1940s. Novelty comes from the use of compressed video or satellites, thereby increasing access or reducing transmission costs, and the ability to bring a return television signal from the 'receive' site.

However, merely replacing one technology with a newer technology does not necessarily bring learning benefits, if the teaching method remains the same. If video conferencing or instructional television is being considered for a course, there should be some justification in terms of the additional visual benefits provided over audio conferencing and/or the distribution of lecture notes, given the additional costs for video transmission.

SPEED

This is one real advantage of 'live' instructional television. Content can be changed quickly, from year to year, or experts brought in quite late to such kinds of teaching. This can be critical for areas where the subject matter rapidly becomes dated. However, this requires programmes to be remade each time a course is offered, and we have seen that there are high costs associated with this.

CONCLUSIONS

Despite the popularity of instructional television, particularly in dual-mode institutions, there are severe limitations in terms of instructional design and learner convenience. The popularity is more with the course provider, who does not have to radically re-think teaching strategies, than with the learners. While students may rate such offerings as satisfactory, they often have no other standard of comparison than the similar methodology of lecture or classroom instruction.

Also, the apparent cost advantages are deceptive. For a single institution with small numbers, the total cost may seem relatively small, but when aggregated across institutions, or when cost per student study hour is calculated, the costs are relatively high, particularly for live, interactive programming.

Even the advantage of interaction between student and teacher is deceptive. Unless the teacher is particularly skilled, and the numbers per class low, the level or quality of interaction is usually poor, confined to a small number of questions from a small minority of participating students.

Nevertheless, there are particular circumstances where instructional television can be appropriate and cost-effective. Both Stanford University and the National Technological University have found 'niche' markets in the USA, for highly skilled engineers requiring up-grading, in areas where learners are in companies facing fierce competition and survival depends on being at the leading edge of technological development. Satellite television gives the NTU economies of scale, and television gives Stanford access to employees at their place of work.

However, for students with little experience of a particular subject area, or for students struggling with the content of a particular subject, or for subject areas where deep or critical thinking is the educational objective, instructional television, particularly where it fails to exploit television's unique presentational characteristics, is not likely to be a cost-effective technology.

6 Print

PRINT: AN OLD TECHNOLOGY UNDER TRANSFORMATION

Ever since the invention of the Gutenburg press, print has been the dominant teaching technology, arguably at least as influential as the spoken word of the teacher. Even today, print dominates as the main technology of teaching in formal education, training and distance education. Why is this? What makes print such a powerful teaching medium, and will it remain so, given the latest developments in electronic communications?

THE TECHNOLOGY

The changes that are occurring as a result of information technology make it necessary to define carefully what we mean by print, since it combines both technological and communications aspects.

Until recent times, print, in the form of words and pictures reproduced from blocks or plates, was the main method by which words and two-dimensional pictures or diagrams could be reproduced on a large scale. Print, however, took over from an already established hand-written medium of communication. Books existed long before the invention of the printing press. Printing did not make a fundamental difference to the representational qualities of books. Indeed, until lithography and engraving became established, the move to printing actually reduced the pictorial quality of books, compared with the beautifully-worked coloured and illustrated manuscripts produced by monks and scribes. The main significance of the mechanisation of printing was to make books available to a much wider public: in other words it made books more accessible.

With the invention of computing, though, both text (i.e. words and other related signs, such as numbers) and pictures can be stored in the form of digitised data, and displayed on screens. Text can also be printed as 'hard copy' on paper. This chapter is concerned primarily with 'hard copy', in the form of printed teaching texts, i.e. text books or correspondence texts, although much of the discussion regarding the representational qualities of 'print' will also apply to text displayed on screens.

Electronic publishing has revolutionised the print industry, leading to greater cost-effectiveness and more flexibility in the print process. All the stages, from author's first draft right through to access by students, can now be handled electronically. At an increasing number of distance teaching institutions, the course author (the subject expert) keys in the draft at an office or home work-station using standard word-processing software. The draft is then distributed either electronically, through a computer network, or by sending a copy on disc to other members of the course team for comment. After the author has made any changes necessary following comments received, an editor/graphic designer/instructional designer (who may be one or more people) will then convert the electronic draft into a final version for printing, including styling (headings, and page lay-out), and diagrams prepared electronically, using more powerful electronic editing and graphic software. The draft is then sent back to the author, who checks the content and lay-out (see Bacsich, 1990, for a detailed discussion of the use of electronic publishing in distance education).

At the Open Learning Agency, the final version is sent electronically to a computer called a file server, where the job is prioritised (queued), then sent electronically for printing on a Xerox Docutech printer, which can run automatically for 24 hours a day, and does the complete printing and binding (although separate colour covers may be added). The system enables 'on-demand' printing. This means that only those copies needed for a particular course term need be printed, thus saving warehouse space.

The Open Learning Agency has used a scanner to convert all its old course material created on metal plates to digital format. In 1995, it is installing computer software, in the form of a multimedia relational data-base, that will enable students to choose the format in which they would like their learning material delivered. Once the learning material is designed, it could be distributed to students in a number of ways: through the mail as printed text, as now; on computer floppy disc or CD-ROM via the mail; called up from home or work through the public telephone service as data; or transmitted by satellite for direct reception at home. The learning materials will eventually include audio and video in digital formats, as well as textual material.

ACCESS

One reason why you are reading this in book form rather than on a computer screen is because at the moment print is more accessible and more standardised than computing. A very strong feature of print is that the same version of a book can be used in any school, college or home. To read this on a screen, you would need an Apple Macintosh computer, or a program that would convert it for use on another type of machine, like an IBM-PC. Even when converted, it may lose all the formatting (paragraphs, headings, and different fonts). Furthermore, learners need no expensive or specialised equipment to use printed material, whereas they need a computer to read text stored as data.

In most compact, densely-populated and reasonably affluent countries, the mail service is fast and efficient. Thus in many Western European countries, print can be directly delivered to every home within two or three days of mailing, using the general postal service. In these countries, delivery is reliable, very few packages going astray. Distance education students may complain about delays in the post, but these are in fact more likely to be due to organisational problems within the distance teaching institution than due to the mail service.

In comparison with Western Europe, though, the postal service in Canada and the United States of America is relatively slow and unreliable, unless the more expensive courier services are used. However, even in Western Europe, there is no doubt that the long-term trend will be away from the use of postal services, which have high costs in terms of labour, especially for residential and more remote areas, as business and industry move more towards electronic means of communication. It will though be many years before every home in the country has the facilities to send and receive text in the form of data, while every home is already accessible by post.

Thus as far as access is concerned, print will have considerable advantages for some time over other technologies, because of standardisation, the ubiquity of the mail service, relatively low delivery costs, and a well developed organisational infrastructure for publishing, distribution and marketing.

TEACHING AND LEARNING

Print and intellectual development

From a teaching point of view, print is by tradition a powerful medium. There is a common assumption that print is the intellectually superior medium – that television, by comparison, 'encourages children to be passive, mindless and unimaginative' (Greenfield, 1984). Certainly, a great deal of education is concerned with factual learning, the understanding of generalised or abstract principles, and with logical argument, and print is a very strong medium for developing and acquiring these skills.

Indeed, some writers such as Postman (1982) have argued that print provided the necessary foundation for intellectual and scientific thought, and that with the coming of television, 'rational' thinking has been severely undermined, as witnessed for instance by the modern political process of electing a president, where image-building, rather than ideas, argument or logic, becomes paramount. Postman claims that it is no accident that with

Ronald Reagan, the USA elected an actor as president. The problem with these kinds of statements is that they have a common-sense plausibility that is nevertheless difficult to prove or disprove scientifically.

Despite these caveats, print does have major advantages for dealing with logical and rational thinking, which require precision, factual accuracy, and clarity of thought. Print lends itself both to consciously critical analysis and to intellectual – as well as emotional – persuasion, by those who have learned the rules of communicating through print. Print is a medium that facilitates what Piaget calls the 'formal operational' stage of intellectual development, which is the manipulation of symbolic or abstract concepts (Piaget, 1970).

Representational qualities

Print can present words, numbers, musical notation, two-dimensional pictures and diagrams. It can also, at a cost, carry full colour illustrations. It cannot directly present movement. Text is linear, although literary conventions, such as parallel developments being represented sequentially or in the form of flashbacks, allow for non-sequential events to be represented.

Illustrations and diagrams in texts provide an intermediate stage between direct experience and abstraction, because they can be used to give more concrete or physical representations of abstract ideas or concepts. Illustrations and diagrams give added flexibility to text, by providing alternative approaches to the representation of knowledge, thus adding variety to a student's learning.

Through text print can precisely represent facts, abstract ideas, rules and principles, and detailed, lengthy or complex arguments. It is good for narrative or story-telling, and in the hands of a skilled writer can lend itself to interpretation and imagination. Because print can handle abstractions well, it can be a very dense medium, in that a single book can contain a great deal of 'coded' information. Print is still the great storehouse of knowledge.

Print then has traditionally been the main means of presenting information in education. Print can also be both very precise or deliberately ambiguous. Alternative explanations or approaches can be handled, but only in a sequential manner. Print therefore does allow students to develop higher level skills of interpretation, synthesis and evaluation, as well as comprehension. It is not surprising then that print is still the dominant medium in higher education.

INTERACTION AND USER-FRIENDLINESS

Interaction

All forms of reading require interaction between the reader and the text. Iser (1978) states that:

> [Reading] sets in motion a whole chain of activities that depend both on the text and on the exercise of certain basic human faculties. Effects and responses are properties neither of the text nor of the reader; the text represents a potential effect that is realised in the reading process.
>
> (Iser, 1978)

Iser points out that the meaning of the text is something that the reader has to assemble, leading to what Iser calls an 'aesthetic response': 'although it is brought about by the text, it brings into play the imaginative and perceptive faculties of the reader'.

Thus a text is not a neutral object; its meaning depends on the interpretation of the reader, whether it is a work of great literature or a car mechanic's manual. Therefore, if the reader is to obtain meaning from a text, there has to be an interaction. What differentiates distance learning texts from other kinds of printed material is a deliberate attempt to structure explicitly a student's response to the material. This may be done in one of several ways:

- detailed objectives expressed in measurable outcomes;
- a system of headings and sub-headings that make explicit the structure of the text;
- self-assessment questions within the text;
- activities – and model responses;
- summaries;
- examination or assessment questions;
- model answers to exam questions.

Research on how students process text (see, for instance, Marland *et al.*, 1990) indicates that while such 'organisers' of student reading can be helpful, they have to be used with care if students are to process information at a 'deep' rather than a 'surface' level.

Print then can range from highly structured, 'controlled' texts, interspersed with very frequent and explicit activities, representing a behaviourist approach to learning; to dense, loosely structured text, with few headings, and little guidance given to the student as to how to interpret the material, other than that indicated by assessment questions, which may be few, and require broad-ranging answers. The choice of approach will depend on the nature of the subject matter, the experience and previous level of education of the learner, and the type of learning that the teacher believes to be important. Print then is an extremely flexible teaching material, and can be designed to suit a wide variety of teaching approaches and purposes.

Nevertheless, a major weakness of print is the difficulty it has in assisting students who have failed to understand parts of the text. While good print design tries to reduce the extent of misunderstanding, there will always be occasions where alternative explanations or a different approach are required for those students who have difficulties. In other instances, students are often unaware of their failure to understand, and this is often where an intervention from a tutor is most necessary.

Another weakness of print is its difficulty in providing feedback for questions that have a variety of acceptable responses, or which require complex or elaborate responses, or for challenging and 'discussing' the appropriateness of students' responses to in-text questions. Furthermore students can easily go to the printed 'feedback', where answers or 'discussion' of the activity are provided, without actively engaging in the exercise. In-text questions or self-assessment exercises may be too frequent or too trivial to stimulate deep processing. Feedback through print is also less appropriate for more practical forms of learning requiring the development of social or psycho-motor skills.

Thus one important role of a tutor is to provide the necessary interventions to assist students in learning from texts, and in particular to help students challenge the material where appropriate, and to challenge or clarify students' own interventions. To provide this kind of feedback and interaction for students studying at a distance, most distance teaching institutions have established an elaborate system of part-time tutors, who use correspondence by mail, the telephone, or regular local face-to-face sessions for interaction with students. Nevertheless, such field support for students is very expensive to provide.

User friendliness

A major advantage of printed material over other technologies is that it is self-sufficient: it does not need another piece of equipment to make it accessible to the learner. It is generally conveniently portable, and hence can travel easily with the learner without additional expense. Because techniques such as indexes, content lists, page numbering, chapters, and headings are well-developed, information can be quickly accessed, even by relatively untutored users. Print can also be quickly scanned by the reader.

Properly printed text has many advantages over both screen-delivered text and text printed on printers linked to desk-top computers. Printed text is portable, easily accessible, easy to skim and search, relatively cheap to deliver, can provide higher quality graphics and design, and above all is easier to read, compared with either materials printed on a home or office printer, or, even more so, screen-based text.

For these reasons, students in general still prefer to read print, rather than text on a computer screen. For instance, a survey of over 2,500 computer-literate Canadian post-secondary students found that printed text books were still the single most popular choice of format, chosen by 49 per cent of those sampled. Computer disc was preferred by 22 per cent, CD-ROM by 14 per cent, and access via networking by 15 per cent (Environics Research Group, 1994).

Technical developments over the next 10 years (e.g. the introduction of colour and large-screen monitors, and better quality low-cost printers; improved indexing software; increased portability of computers) may change students' preferences. The relative advantages and disadvantages of print over electronic text, in terms of learning effectiveness, does need to be researched more thoroughly, to provide stronger empirical grounds for decision-making.

One of the problems with print in most distance education systems is that there is a three-way flow of textual information between students, tutors and the central institution. Students submit their assignment by post to the tutor, who then marks the assignment, often on a form with three copies. The tutor then sends the assignment to the headquarters of the distance teaching system, so that the grade can be recorded, and the marking checked and standardised, then the assignment is returned by headquarters to the student.

One consequence of this is that the students usually must wait at least 10 days between submitting an assignment and receiving back the tutor's comments and/or the assignment grade. This 'turn-round' time on assignments is a major weakness of distance education, as studies by Rekkedal (1978) have shown.

In order to exploit the benefits of text, a great deal of effort has to be put into developing learners' skills in reading and writing. In fact, these are extremely difficult skills to develop. Even in advanced, developed countries, up to 30 per cent of adults have difficulties reading tabloid newspapers – generally measured to require the level of reading achieved by the 'average' 7-year-old! So, despite its familiarity and pervasiveness, text is not so user-friendly, as far as learners are concerned, as it may at first appear. Learning to read – and learning to write – have become educational goals in themselves, and require a great deal of time and effort. Furthermore, intellectual development requires more than just the facility of reading. The ability to manipulate words and ideas is both facilitated by and dependent on print, but also requires a great deal of tuition to achieve. There is therefore heavy investment in the education industry to make print work.

It is significant that most people teaching at a college level or above have obtained great facility in both constructing and using text for their work. Indeed, their ability to publish research papers and to give papers at conferences is a key factor in their professional advancement as college and university teachers. A great part of their working life is based around the skills of reading and writing. It is not surprising then that for many post-secondary teachers, print is a favoured teaching medium: they are familiar with it, they have ability to use and manipulate it for communication purposes, and they have progressed in their careers as a result of their skills in reading and writing. This provides an in-built advantage for print, in terms of its acceptability to academic staff.

For many students, though, print is increasingly becoming only a relatively small contribution to sources of information; for instance, only 38 per cent of a national UK sample of adults listed print (newspapers, magazines, books) as their main source of information about the Arts, compared with 41 per cent who listed television (IBA, 1988). Despite the amount of education and training that goes into making people skilled in using print at school, for many people it remains a difficult medium to learn from.

COSTS

The costs of printing in distance education are quite difficult to calculate, because of the complexity of the design and production process, the difficulty of assigning a proportion of a multiple-media product to print alone, and in particular the difficulty of assigning academic staff costs to one element of many related activities. However, it is possible to give rough ball-park figures.

Development costs

These are the costs of developing print materials from scratch. In a traditional single-mode distance teaching institution, the specially designed print component (the correspondence text) usually takes at least half the total student study time. If the supplementary printed material (the audio–visual notes, assignment questions and student assignment notes, etc.) is also included, print probably accounts for nearly two-thirds of student study time. What is more difficult to calculate is how much time academics spend on print development, compared with their other

Table 6.1 Notional allocation of academic time at a distance teaching university

Activity	Days	%
Weekends and holidays	140	38
Research	40	11
Administrative duties (committees, etc.)	10	3
Sub-total	190	52
Teaching days:		
Course maintenance	16	4
Summer school	14	4
Sub-total	220	60
Developing new courses	145	40
Total	365	100

activities, such as course maintenance and revision, tutoring, and research.

However, Rumble (1986) has suggested a basis for dividing academic time at the British Open University, and building on that, the following estimates are given in Table 6.1.

Historically, over the 20 or so years that the British Open University has been operating, the academic staff have each averaged roughly one unit, or approximately 12–14 hours of student study time, per year, of which 6–10 hours will be spent by students on reading print. Given that academics spend a notional figure of 145 days a year on course development, and assuming that they spend roughly a half to two-thirds of that time on print-related activities, the following estimates can be made:

- 75–100 academic days on print development for every unit produced;
- about 10 academic days for each hour of print study;
- about US$600–$675 for academic time for each hour of print study (based on UK academic salaries in 1988).

As well as the academics, there are editors, photographers, graphic designers, educational technologists, course administrators and secretaries involved in the development of printed material. An editor's work-load is about 20–24 units a year, and course administrators and educational technologists average about two courses a year. It would not be unreasonable to assume that the additional staff cost at least as much as the academic time for each unit of print, which would bring the total development cost up to around US$1,500 per hour on print materials.

The Open University estimates that the total costs of developing a full credit course (32 weeks study totalling approximately 400 hours study) can be anywhere between £500,000 to £1 million (US$750,000 to $1.5 million), or between US$2,000 and $4,000 per study hour, depending on the amount of television, whether there is a home experiment kit or summer school, etc. If print takes about two-thirds of student study time, this comes to around US$1,500 to $2,250 per hour of student study time on print, or between US$375,000 to $600,000 for the print development costs of a full credit course. Taking all the different ways of calculating costs into account, a development cost of US$1,500 per study hour of print material is not likely to be wildly wrong for the British Open University.

Distribution costs

Printing

Distribution costs, unlike development and production costs, are variable, in that they are dependent on the number of students enrolled in a course. At the British Open University, an average cost of printing from final proofs of the main text of 32 units of 36 pages each for a one-year course

Table 6.2 Printing costs (from bromides), 1988, UK OU

No. of copies	Price	Average cost per student	Average cost per unit	Average cost per study hour
	£	£	£	£
(a)	(b)	(c)	(d)	(e)
1,000	14,432	14.32	0.45	0.07
5,000	37,568	7.51	0.23	0.04
10,000	62,688	6.27	0.20	0.04
		[(b)/(a)]	[(c)/32]	[d/6]

Note: No. of units = 32; no. of bindings = 16

totalling about 400 hours study, in 16 bindings, single colour, in 1988 was as in Table 6.2.

There are several points to note from Table 6.2. Although the printing cost for 10,000 copies is over £60,000 (US$90,000), the printing cost per student for all 32 units is only £6.27 ($9.4), and per unit is only 20 pence (30¢). For a smaller run of 1,000 copies, the average printing costs per student are just over double (45 pence, 67¢). If we assume that students spend approximately half their study time reading the main correspondence texts, the printing cost is about 10¢ (7 pence) per study hour for 1,000 students and 6¢ (4 pence) per study hour for 10,000 students. Thus, although not insubstantial, particularly for large courses, presentation costs tend to be minor compared with development costs.

Postage, packaging and storage

In addition to the costs of development and printing, there are warehousing, packaging and mailing costs to be added. At the British Open University, in 1988 enough copies of the main correspondence texts were printed to last for four years, then a re-print from the original plate was done for the remaining four years of a course, although for foundation and larger second level courses, print was ordered for a maximum of two years at a time.

Consequently, warehousing costs can be considerable. For a projected total student population of almost 100,000 on undergraduate, diploma and full associate student courses in 1990, the total warehouse costs for the Open University were around £500,000 ($750,000), about half of which was related directly to the storage of course units and supplementary material (home experiment kits are another major warehouse cost), giving an average warehouse cost per student per annum at around $3.75 (£2.50) to $4.50 (£3) for print materials. The cost advantages then of large print runs and the immediate availability of materials must be off-set against the increased costs of storage.

Packaging costs are also substantial. An average mailing to a British

Table 6.3 Delivery costs per student, per course, 1990, UK OU

	£	US$
Warehousing	3.00	4.50
Packaging	6.00	9.00
Mailing	5.00–8.00	7.50–12.00
Total	14.00–17.00	21.00–25.50

Open University student may include the following separate teaching items:

● four different correspondence texts (= one block of four weeks study);
● a block guide;
● supplementary reader articles;
● notes on the audio-visual materials;
● an assignment question, with notes;
● two different audio cassettes;
● a stop-press sheet, with amendments or corrections and course news;
● a contents list.

For each mailing of the course material (normally eight for a full credit course – 32 weeks – in the first year, then between two to three mailings in subsequent years), all these materials need to be collated, packed and mailed. With 100,000 students across nearly 200 courses, this is a major logistical exercise for the British Open University; despite this, the packing costs averaged about £6 ($9) per student per full credit in 1990.

Lastly, there is the cost of postage. The British Open University has special contracts which average out at between £5 to £8 per student per 32-week course. The delivery costs are summarised in Table 6.3.

Total costs

In arriving at a total cost for print, a distinction has to be made between the core correspondence texts, and a substantial amount of supplementary printed material. At the British Open University, correspondence texts are printed by commercial printers, while the bulk of the supplementary material is printed in-house. To some extent, then, the costs of the supplementary printed material are fixed.

In summarising costs, I have combined both the development and printing costs for supplementary printed materials with the £250,000 ($375,000) estimated for the development cost of the correspondence text, to give an overall development cost of £400,000 ($600,000).

Table 6.4 summarizes these costs. These figures relate only to printed teaching material, and not to time students spend on other activities, such as assignments or studying the audio-visual materials.

Table 6.4 Costs of printed teaching materials: UK Open University

	1,000 copies		5,000 copies		10,000 copies	
	£	%	£	%	£	%
Cost head						
Development	400,000	93	400,000	78	400,000	65
Printing (CTs)	14,432	3	37,568	7	62,668	10
Storage	3,000	1	15,000	3	30,000	5
Packaging	6,000	1	30,000	6	60,000	10
Mailing	6,500	2	32,500	6	65,000	11
Total	429,932	100	515,068	100	617,668	100
(US$	644,898		772,602		926,502)	

It can be seen that while costs increase as the number of students increases, the main cost is in development and production of materials.

With development costs of £1,000 ($1,500) per study hour, for 1,000 students the average development cost is £1 ($1.50) per study hour, and for 10,000 students 10 pence (15¢) per study hour. Thus for 1,000 students the development cost is 15 times the actual printing cost, while for 10,000 students, the development cost is about 2.5 times the cost of printing.

Figure 6.1 shows the total cost over eight years for producing and distributing print material at varying volumes of activity. Table 6.5 converts these into costs per student and per student study hour, assuming that students spend 250 hours a year on the printed texts. Figure 6.2 shows the steep drop in cost per student study hour as student numbers per course increase.

These figures show clearly the economies of scale for print-based

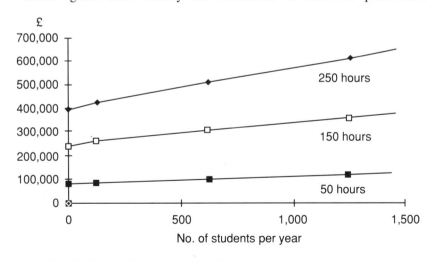

Figure 6.1 Total costs for print, over eight years

Table 6.5 Costs of printed teaching materials per student and per study hour: UK Open University, 1989

	1,000 students (125 students per year × 8) (£)		5,000 students (625 students per year × 8)		10,000 students (1,250 students per year x 8)	
	Per student	Per study hour	Per student	Per study hour	Per student	Per study hour
Cost head						
Development	400.00	1.60	80.00	0.32	40.00	0.16
Printing (CTs)	14.43	0.08	7.51	0.04	6.26	0.03
Storage	3.00	0.01	3.00	0.01	3.00	0.01
Packaging	6.00	0.02	6.00	0.02	6.00	0.02
Mailing	6.50	0.03	6.50	0.03	6.50	0.03
Total	429.93	1.74	103.01	0.42	61.76	0.25
(US$	644.89	2.61	154.51	0.63	92.64	0.37)

distance education courses produced from scratch. Courses with just over 100 students a year are four times more expensive per student than courses with 600 students or so per year. Even so, for courses with 250 students a year or more, total print costs work out at well under £1 per study hour per student, or $2 per hour for about 200 students a year.

These publishing costs are not too dissimilar to those of commercial publishers developing standard text-books for use in schools and colleges. Indeed, the British Open University has been able to underwrite substantially the costs of print production on some courses through co-production deals with commercial publishers, who recover their costs through sales of

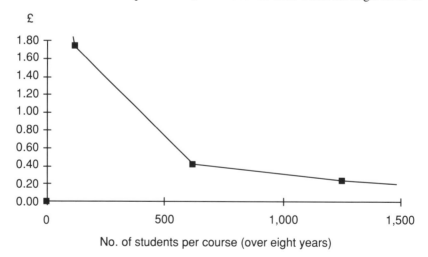

Figure 6.2 Cost per student study hour: print (UK OU)

the materials to the general public. On other courses, substantial revenue has been generated by the Open University marketing its own materials, both to the general public, and to other distance teaching institutions.

The economic impact of electronic publishing

Since 1988, the British Open University has introduced electronic publishing, which should have reduced printing costs to some extent. A cost-benefit analysis of the Open Learning Agency (Bates, 1992) indicated that although the total cost (hardware, software, networking and training) of introducing a fully electronic publishing system (which meant putting a computer on virtually every desk and installing a Xerox Docutech printer) was about US$1.5 million, by 1992 the agency's print costs had been reduced by around US$375,000 a year (this includes staff savings and revenue generated from external contracting – other savings in warehousing are not included in these figures). Thus the capital investment was recovered in four years (five if opportunity interest costs are included). However, while electronic publishing has led to substantial savings in copy editors and printing, there are still substantial development costs on the academic and instructional design side.

The development process and the price of quality

Although print costs per study hour, particularly for large courses, are not high when averaged over a course life of eight years, the British Open University development costs of around $1 million per 32-week course are substantial. Why does high-quality university-level printed distance teaching material cost so much to develop? Need it be so expensive? And is it of high quality?

The UK Open University course design model

The British Open University course production system is based on the course team, which may have up to 30 different people from a range of disciplines and job categories working on it. As well as the Open University's own academic staff, one of whom will chair the team, there will usually be a television and radio producer from the BBC, an educational technologist (concerned with pedagogic design), a print editor (concerned with literary style, typography and graphic design), and a course manager, concerned with budgets, deadlines, and arranging and recording course team meetings.

The course team will discuss the detailed contents and structure of the course, which is usually broken down into blocks of several weeks' study, or single units of one week's study. Members of the course team will be allocated responsibility for the development of particular blocks or units.

Each printed text will usually go through three separate drafts. Each draft will be discussed or commented on by several at least of the course team. Each course will have a paid external assessor from another university, who checks and comments on all the material, and who must give written, formal approval before the course can be offered to students. Additional external block assessors may also be used, especially where the course is inter-disciplinary. Typically, a course will take two to three years to be developed before delivery to students, then the course will be offered for an average of eight years before being withdrawn or remade.

It is this process of discussion by a range of people with different skills and knowledge that ensures that the material is comprehensive, well-structured, accurate, clearly written and coherent. It enables the development of topic-based or inter-disciplinary courses, as well as the more traditional single-subject based course, and enables new curricula to be developed, embracing and integrating a wide range of perspectives, theories or approaches.

This process of peer-group analysis and discussion prior to course delivery is considered essential for courses with perhaps 5,000 students a year; if poorly designed, such a course could have damaging effects on many students long before changes could be implemented, for once a printed course is finalised and delivered, it is extremely difficult and expensive to correct or change. In an integrated course, changes in one part of a text often have knock-on effects in other parts of the text or television programmes.

Some flexibility is built in through additional supplementary print materials, which are printed and replaced each year. These may contain notes on how to study the course, the students' assignments, any corrections, notes on the broadcasts, and collections of articles from journals. Because these are finalised much later than the main texts, they are usually less expensively printed using in-house facilities.

The British Open University course team approach, with its extensive discussion on teaching materials and teaching approaches, on design and lay-out, is labour-intensive, and consequently high cost. These costs are justified on grounds of high quality materials and use by large numbers.

On the other hand, the process is lengthy and bureaucratic. Many academics feel they are driven by the print production system, with academic decisions subordinated to production decisions. The main academic short-coming of this process has been the difficulty in altering texts once handed over for printing. The high cost of replacement means that courses tend to last beyond an acceptable length of time without alteration or improvement. Also, the process distances the teachers who originate the teaching material from their students, both in time and in interaction.

Alternatives to the British Open University course-team approach

It is not surprising that distance education institutions with courses with relatively low student numbers per year (i.e. less than 200) have found less labour-intensive methods to produce course material. For instance, as well as buying in courses produced by a wide range of institutions and adapting them for local use, the Open Learning Agency of British Columbia, Canada, does not have its own full-time academic staff to develop courses, but contracts in subject specialists from other universities and colleges to prepare materials, which are then transformed into distance teaching materials by the full-time instructional designers and editors employed by OLA.

Its development cost for a 13-week term, print-based course is around US$37,500 (C$50,000), which when converted to the equivalent of a 32-week course works out at about US$90,000, or about one-tenth the cost of course production at the British Open University.

In some dual-mode institutions, the on-campus teaching forms the basis for the off-campus teaching, in that lecture notes are converted to duplicated or printed materials distributed to off-campus students. This is very much cheaper, but raises serious questions about the quality of the printed material.

Protecting quality

There are three different aspects to quality in printed distance teaching materials: the quality of layout, graphics and print presentation (print design); the quality of the academic content, in terms of comprehensiveness, balance and accuracy (content); and the quality of the educational design, in terms of clarity of objectives, the way the content is organised and structured, and the quality of student activities and assessment (instructional design).

The danger is that by lowering the costs of development the quality of the print materials may also deteriorate. Distance educators believe that printed teaching materials must be of a high quality because of the particular circumstances of distance education students. These students cannot be assumed to have such easy access to their teachers as campus-based students, nor do they have such strong peer-group support in their learning context. They are therefore much more isolated, and therefore need materials which are clear and easily understood.

Thus while costs of development of print material can always be reduced, the price may well be increased drop-out or attrition, or lower levels of achievement. Although it is difficult to prove that reducing quality in print design leads to greater drop-out, the enrolment, completion rates and examination results of institutions with high standards of design, such as the British Open University and the Open Learning Agency, compare very favourably not only with other distance education institutions but also with conventional institutions.

Thus the cost of producing good quality print materials for distance education is high, and is likely to remain high; however, these costs can be justified when student numbers exceed 200 or more per course per annum, or even fewer if sales and co-production deals can be used to off-set the costs.

The costs of tutoring

In costing print, I have excluded the very substantial costs of correspondence and face-to-face tutoring, which provide the essential interactive component of the teaching. Despite all that can be done through good design to make print an interactive medium for the learner, it is essential to provide in addition a 'real' tutor, for reasons given earlier.

As well as the tutor costs, there are also the very substantial costs of the administrative support systems required to manage the tutorial system. In both the Open Learning Agency and the British Open University, the part-time tutor system constitutes at least 20 per cent of all operating costs. Whatever the technology, there is a need for real tutor interaction, but the cost will vary depending on the technology's ability to incorporate two-way interaction with a real tutor. With print, these additional tutorial costs are a critical factor. It is beyond the scope of this book to develop a costing methodology for face-to-face and correspondence tutoring, although this needs to be done.

Summary

It is important not to get hung up too much on the actual costs of the two institutions used here as examples. The aim of this section has been to identify the various stages of the development and delivery of print materials, to look at the relationship between the costs of different stages of the process, and the relationship between costs and student numbers. As a result of this analysis, the following conclusions can be drawn:

- the major costs come in development, rather than in printing and distribution;
- the major development costs are academic time and instructional design; these costs can be reduced but at the risk of reducing the quality of instruction;
- print is a low-cost technology for courses with more than 200 students per annum, given an eight-year course life;
- electronic publishing reduces costs except in the areas of academic development and instructional design, and improves the flexibility of print production;

- print requires substantial support from part-time tutors, which in itself is a major additional cost factor.

ORGANISATIONAL ISSUES

With regard to the production and distribution of print, book publishing is a highly organised industry, because of its long history. Consequently, the human skills and the procedures necessary for the production and distribution of print materials are well established. There is a very strong organisational infrastructure supporting the distribution of print material, from well-established educational publishing companies, through high street bookshops and public libraries, to comprehensive coverage by postal services. Furthermore, there is a highly formalised system of education and training for people working in publishing and printing. Specialist colleges provide training in the more vocational aspects, such as printing and graphic design, while managers and editors are usually drawn from graduates in literature, classics or history.

One common feature of technology-based systems is the demarcation of skills and professional boundaries. For instance, each of the following jobs concerned with the production of print materials may be found within a distance teaching institution:

- subject expert (author, consultant, academic);
- instructional designer (course developer, educational technologist);
- editor;
- librarian;
- graphics designer (illustrator; lay-out consultant);
- proof-reader (copy editor);
- printer.

Several approaches have been adopted with regard to the organisation of these jobs. At single-mode distance teaching institutions, most of these jobs exist separately, resulting in considerable division of labour, and with it a clear differentiation of salaries between different jobs, and the creation of different departments concerned with each function (e.g. Faculties, Institute of Educational Technology, Publishing). Subject experts and educational technologists have full academic status, including tenure, while editors and graphic designers have less favourable salaries and conditions of service.

In smaller institutions, one person may combine several of these jobs. Sometimes, particularly in dual-mode institutions, the job of converting academics' lectures or prepublished text books into distance teaching material is seen primarily as a 'technical' job and therefore something to be left to the print shop or media resources centre to do. Instructional designers may be seen as nothing more than glorified editors.

However, a major difference between traditional educational publishing and publishing for distance education is the role of the instructional designer. This distinction has arisen because in distance education, learners may need to be totally independent, and cannot necessarily fall back on a teacher for help in understanding or motivation. Thus distance learning texts have to combine both information-giving and direct teaching. The responsibility therefore for learning is shifted away from the face-to-face teacher to the teaching material itself. Converting the texts handed over by subject experts into printed material suitable for distance education requires more than just the traditional skills of a publishing editor; it also requires teaching skills.

It may be argued that academics or subject experts also have teaching skills. However, few university, polytechnic, college or industrial research staff have more than a rudimentary training in teaching methods. In any case, the skills needed to design good quality print material for distance learners are specialised. They include organising and structuring the whole course, setting realistic learning objectives, identifying accurately the level of ability and knowledge of the target group, assessing realistic study loads for students, selecting appropriate media and technologies, and designing appropriate student assessment and course evaluation procedures. These are in addition to skills in advising on writing style, illustrations and layout, and avoiding unclear or confusing prose. These latter skills may or may not overlap with those of traditional editors (who themselves usually have no training in teaching methods).

Because of the need to work as part of a team, and the problems of status within the teams, social and communication skills are equally as important as technical skills for such instructional designers. However, finding people with the appropriate instructional design skills is not easy. With the increasingly rapid expansion of open learning and distance education projects, especially as part of in-house company training, there is a growing need for properly trained people in this area.

Even in institutions where each job is clearly demarcated, there is often a good deal of overlap in the areas of work, and academics with experience of designing distance learning material often acquire many of the skills of the educational technologist and editor. This can and does lead to conflict and organisational manoeuvring between the different departments responsible for these different jobs.

Also, electronic publishing technology is further blurring the demarcation areas. Computer-graphics and word-processing packages replicate some of the skills of a graphic designer or editor. In some ways, the previously differentiated skills are now converging back to the original subject expert who is skilled in using word-processing.

Nevertheless, few academics or subject specialists have been trained in or have the skills of instructional design, editing and graphic design, and even if they can pick up such skills as they go, many would still prefer to limit their activities to producing drafts of texts and to research. If high-quality printed teaching material is to be designed, the whole range of skills is required, and therefore it is important that each institution responsible for the production of printed teaching materials has people with these skills.

Also, in a single mode distance teaching institution, there may be perhaps over 20 different courses in various stages of production and over 200 in actual presentation in any one year. The activities of one department – such as a faculty – inevitably influence the activities of another, such as the print shop. Late handover of draft texts by academics can cause bottlenecks in editing, design and the warehouse. The decision to replace or delay a text, while perhaps justifiable on academic grounds, will have budgetary implications for other departments. Therefore skilled project management is essential to manage efficiently the process of production and distribution.

This can be a major problem in dual-mode institutions. If print materials are to be delivered on time and to high standards, all departments have to work together. Academic staff sometimes find it difficult to subordinate their autonomy to the needs of a production process. However, a well-defined and disciplined operational process is essential for the timely production of high-quality print materials for distance education.

NOVELTY

The main novelty element in printing these days is electronic publishing, and related to this, the storage of large quantities of text material in digital form, on CD-ROM or even video discs. While electronic publishing does provide opportunities for cost saving and flexibility in production, it will be some time before electronic delivery, either through computer networks or CD-ROM, becomes a reality for home-based learners.

SPEED

This is probably the major weakness today of print as a teaching technology. It takes a long time to develop high quality printed material. Once produced, it is difficult to change. Often, supplementary printed material has to be produced and distributed to students to accommodate errors (especially where this may affect assignments) or major changes since the material was originally produced (e.g. new laws, new developments in a particular field, etc.).

Although electronic publishing allows for printing on demand, and also allows changes to be made more easily, changes in one part of a text usually have knock-on effects in others, such as page numbering, reference lists, etc. The cost of making changes to printed materials has been a major obstacle to course evaluation in the large single-mode institutions;

even when evaluation has shown texts to require alteration, there is often no budget for changes in content or structure or for re-printing.

Nevertheless, in many subject areas, the ability to make changes regularly over a period of time, other than for evaluation reasons, is not critical. Indeed, the economies of scale and the high cost of replacing 'courses has led many distance teaching institutions to run print-based courses virtually unchanged for 10 years or more. However, this is becoming increasingly untenable in many academic subject areas.

CONCLUSIONS

Despite the importance of computerised information storage and communication, print will continue to be a major teaching medium, and is likely to remain so well into the twenty-first century. This is because print will remain more accessible and convenient for learners than digitised text, since no special equipment is needed to use print.

Print is an extremely valuable teaching medium, able to carry large amounts of information in a condensed form, and is ideal for courses requiring high levels of abstraction, and where logical thinking or argument is required.

However, learning from print requires high levels of skill from both the learner and the designers of print material. The teaching material itself has to be designed specifically to help people who may not have strong literacy or study skills, and who have to study for the most part independently.

The main limitation of print is the time required for the development of high quality text, and it is difficult to see how this can be reduced substantially without affecting quality. Despite the high development costs of about US$2,250 an hour of study material in the large single mode institutions, the print unit costs for courses of 250 students or more a year are still very low as far as higher education is concerned, below US$1.50 per study hour per student, including delivery. However, because of the weakness of print in terms of student interactivity, print needs to be complemented by a teacher. This in distance education requires the establishment of a costly and comprehensive tutorial system.

There is much more differentiation of labour in the production of distance and open learning materials, although electronic publishing may reverse this trend. In several open universities, the course team has proved to be a crucial mechanism for harnessing and integrating the various skills required, although other mechanisms are also possible. Instructional design skills are essential.

Institutions often have difficulties with the structural organisation of the various groups of staff concerned with the design of materials, because of the overlap of professional roles, the added costs of non-faculty staff concerned with design, and the relative newness of such functions in educational institutions. Lastly, professional project management is essential if courses are to be produced and delivered in an efficient manner.

Thus print is, and will remain, a most important technology for open and distance teaching.

7 One-way audio
Radio and audio cassettes

AUDIO: THE ORIGINAL LOW-COST, FLEXIBLE TEACHING MEDIUM

Audio is perhaps the most undervalued of all the media. Audio technologies are cheap, easy to use, accessible, and generally educationally effective; they are not exotic, though, and as a consequence tend to be ignored or undervalued by educational decision-makers. For this reason, Schramm (1977) called audio-based technologies 'little media'.

A great deal, but by no means all, of the educational uses of audio centre around the human voice. Durbridge (1983) notes that, compared with print, the human voice can have an informal quality that is not so easily transmitted in academic print. The human voice can be modulated, i.e. it contains variations in pitch, tone, pace, volume and emphasis, and these cues are invaluable to the learning process.

There is a wide range of audio technologies now available to educators. These can be divided into one-way and two-way technologies:

One-way	Two-way
Radio	Telephone (point-to-point)
Audio cassettes	Audio conferencing
	Audio-graphics
	Narrow-band satellite transmissions

We shall see that audio is becoming less and less a separate medium, but is both being combined more and more with data, print and video, and is becoming increasingly digitalised, to the point where it will soon be difficult to discuss audio separately from other media as a teaching medium.

RADIO

Radio has been used in education for over 60 years. It has in that time been used in many different ways for education and training.

Access

Radio is accessible to more people than any other single technology. Millions of people around the world who cannot read or do not have access to television have a radio set. In developed countries, almost all households have at least one radio set (UNESCO, 1986). In the United Kingdom, 99 per cent of all Open University students had a radio suitable for receiving the university's transmissions. Even in many developing countries, access to radio is widespread, and increasing year by year.

One problem of access is ensuring that students are able to listen when the programmes are actually broadcast. A great deal of research on the accessibility of radio programmes to its students was carried out at the British Open University (see, for instance, Grundin, 1981). It was found that even when a programme was broadcast at the optimum time, the maximum number of students able to listen at that particular time was never more than two-thirds. There were always students who were unable to listen at any particular time, because they were at work, travelling to or from work, or had other unavoidable commitments that prevented them from listening.

However, a judicious combination of two different times would enable over 90 per cent of students to be able to listen to the programme on transmission. Thus to ensure delivery to nearly all students, two transmissions were required. Recording for subsequent replay can alleviate the problem, but radio is less easy to record remotely than television, because most radio/cassette machines do not have timers as standard equipment (unlike video cassette machines).

Despite these difficulties, radio is generally an extremely accessible technology for teaching, and can reach certain target groups, such as the illiterate and very poor, better than other technologies.

Teaching and learning

Radio has been used in many ways in education (see Bates, 1984, for a full review). Its uses include school broadcasting, informal general education, social action programming, and adult basic education and literacy. There are more than 20 radio literacy schools in Latin America, largely sponsored by the Catholic Church, which use radio, combined with specially prepared print materials, and face-to-face classes, often run by the local priest. These radio literacy schools have been very successful in teaching literacy to the *campesinos*, the poor farmers of Latin America (see Fuenzalida, 1992).

Radio has also been used for direct teaching in Australia, where the Radio Schools are used to link children in isolated farmsteads in the outback together with a teacher located many hundreds of miles away. Two-way radio is used (the farmsteads having short-wave receive and transmit radios), enabling the children to participate directly in the lesson (parents provide the back-up support). Thus the teacher operates very similarly to a classroom teacher, except that the children are at a distance.

A $20 million USAID programme advocates a direct teaching approach through radio that, it claims, 'offers hope for 100 million children in the poorest nations who cannot attend school' (Agency for International Development, 1990). The approach is based on the use of interactive radio instruction (IRI) for teaching core curricular subjects (e.g. maths, Spanish, English, science and health education), and has been applied in 14 developing countries.

Distance teaching universities in Spain, Thailand, Sri Lanka and Indonesia all use a significant amount of radio as part of their course provision, as do, to a lesser extent, distance teaching universities in Britain, Israel and Pakistan. As well as its immediate teaching role, radio is often used by distance teaching universities for its publicity and recruitment value. It should be noted though that radio's publicity value is not high when transmissions are restricted to late at night or early in the morning.

One use of radio is for relaying lectures by professors. In the British Open University, though, at the peak of its use of radio, this format was used for only about 20 per cent of the programmes, even though students often wanted or expected this use of radio (Meed, 1974; Bates *et al.*, 1981). More frequently it was used for:

- discussions of course material or issues covered in the printed materials;
- alternative viewpoints to that contained in the printed material (e.g. guest speakers);
- source material for analysis (e.g. children's speech patterns);
- 'performance', including poets reading their own poetry, dramatisation of literature, musical performance;
- providing aural experiences: music, language learning, analysis of sounds;
- collecting the views or experiences of specialists, experts or witnesses.

However, as audio cassettes became more popular at the British Open University at the beginning of the 1980s, radio's role became more restricted to relating course material to current events and up-dating a course over its eight-year life, providing corrections or course news (such as information on examinations or help with examination technique), and overviews or summaries of units or blocks.

Interactivity and user-friendliness

Perhaps one of the greatest advantages of radio is that it is an easy and familiar technology for most people. No special skills are required to operate a radio set, and even people with low levels of literacy can learn from radio. Nevertheless, there is some evidence that there are listening skills that need to be developed, if students are to get the most from radio as an instructional medium.

One of the main weaknesses with radio is the difficulty of two-way communication between the teacher and the learners. In theory, phone-in radio programmes provide an opportunity for interactivity between students and the teacher, but the level of interactivity and participation rates are often low, when this format is used.

There are several reasons for this. First of all, a relatively large number of students is required to generate sufficient questions; producers have been nervous about going live with no questions coming through, even when students have been called and primed in advance. Secondly, it means making the programme new every year, thus increasing costs. Also, where phone-in programmes were tried at the Open University, feedback showed that they are not usually popular with enrolled students (Bates *et al.*, 1981). The questions generated did not usually relate to the individual problems that other students had; or students were not interested in the views of other students. Thus radio phone-ins appear to be a less acceptable form of participation and interaction to students than, for instance, audio conferencing via telephone.

Also, there are strong cultural differences that influence the student's ability to respond effectively to radio programming. Brown (1980) for instance found that students' use of radio at the Open University was strongly correlated with their previous use of general radio. Before they enrolled with the Open University, Arts students, for instance, tended to listen to radio drama and documentaries, while science and technology students tended to listen primarily to news bulletins and pop music. Once enrolled, Arts students listened much more to the Open University radio programmes on their courses than the Maths, Science and Technology students. Arts students apparently brought general skills in listening to radio which they were able and willing to transfer to the similarly-formatted Open University programmes. Science and technology students were not accustomed to listening to extended talk programmes, and were less willing to accept enrichment programmes. It is also likely that radio is a more acceptable teaching medium for cultures with a strong aural tradition.

A major weakness of radio is its ephemerality. Many distance education students find it difficult to be available at a fixed time on a regular basis. The advantage of being able to listen to recordings of programmes, at times that suit the learner, in comparison with listening to a radio transmission, is substantial. In a survey of student listening on 88 different courses (Bates *et al.*, 1981), programmes that were listened to on transmission received an average student helpfulness rating of 3.42 (on a five-point scale, where 5 = very helpful). When the same programmes were listened to as a recording, the average helpfulness rating was 3.79. (Given the size of the sample, and the narrowness of the rating scale, this difference was highly significant statistically.)

Nevertheless, one should not underestimate radio's power to stimulate the imagination or provoke strong student support. Those students at the British Open University who did listen to the radio programmes on a regular basis tended to rate them highly. The Open University research clearly indicated large individual differences between students in their reactions to radio, with Arts students in particular showing strong positive reactions.

Costs

Because of the reduction in the use of radio in the 1980s at the Open University, it is necessary to go back to 1981/82 to get full cost data. In 1981/82, BBC-Open University Productions (BBC/OUP) spent £746,000 (US$1,119,000) on the production and transmission of audio material, equivalent in production to 280 × 20-minute radio programmes. The Open University broadcast 24 hours 20 minutes of radio per week over a 33-week period. Virtually each programme broadcast received two transmissions. The production figure of 280 programme equivalents refers to actual demand from the university; the BBC estimated that it had the capacity to produce 350 programme equivalents.

Thus the cost of BBC/OUP radio programme production in 1982 is estimated to average about US$2,860 (£1,907) per 20-minute programme or US$8,581 (£5,721) per hour (Bates *et al.*, 1981). The figure of £1,907 per programme was obtained by dividing the total production costs (£534,000, including overheads) by the number of programmes produced (280). The direct (or variable) cost though was only about £315 (US$472) per programme, or £945 (US$1,417) per hour. This covered costs such as travel, fees to contributors, and copyright clearance incurred in the making of a radio programme, and did not include the cost of the producer or studios, which were treated as overheads. Overheads are those costs (studio staff, administration, rent, heating, etc.) that have to be borne irrespective of the number of programmes produced, i.e. they are fixed costs.

Excluded from these costs are those for the time of the Open University academics involved in the development and production of the programme. This is extremely difficult to calculate, but a rough estimate would be an average of two to three days per programme, if one includes programme planning and discussion, script preparation, collecting material, and recording time (the preparation of accompanying student notes should be considered as print costs). A rough figure of £200 (US$300) at 1982 prices would be a reasonable estimate for academic time per programme.

Transmission costs were around £75 ($112) per transmission (or £150 ($225) per programme per year, as each programme was repeated). Thus transmission costs were £225 ($337) per hour for single transmissions, and

Table 7.1 Costs of radio: UK OU, 1982

	Actual 280 programmes p.a		Maximum 350 programmes p.a.	
	per programme £	per hour £	per programme £	per hour £
Development/production				
Academic time	200	600	200	600
Production (overheads)	1,592	4,776	1,211	3,633
Direct production	315	945	315	945
Total production costs	2,107	6,321	1,726	5,178
(US$	3,160	9,481	2,589	7,767)
Delivery				
Transmissions (two): 1 yr	150	450	150	450
Transmissions (two): 8 yrs	1,200	3,600	1,200	3,600

£450 ($675) per hour for repeat transmissions. Note that for transmission, these were direct, marginal costs, since they covered just the extra costs of extending the times of an already established national transmission network.

Table 7.1 summarizes these costs.

Two calculations have been made in Table 7.1, one for the actual production load in 1982 (280 programme equivalents), and one for the maximum load (350 programmes). It could be claimed that if the full production load had been reached, the average costs would have been reduced by about 20 per cent. What prevented the maximum production level being reached was the lack of academic time and demand.

Thus the average production cost of a 20-minute programme in 1982 was US$3,160 (£2,107), or $9,481 (£6,321) an hour. Production for a single programme can be fixed, i.e. once produced and recorded, it can be used as many times as required, unless the programme is broadcast live. If the programme is broadcast live, it has to be re-created each year, in which case the cost is recurrent each year. Generally, Open University radio programmes are expected to last the life of a course, i.e. eight years on average.

Although there are some exceptions, the Open University rarely broadcasts live programmes. Nevertheless, one of the main advantages of radio is its speed of production and its capacity for up-dating. For this reason, radio programmes on some courses tend to be withdrawn and re-made over the eight-year period.

Total costs and cost per student hour

Table 7.2 sets out the total costs of radio programming over an eight-year period (i.e. one production cost, assuming no remakes, and eight × 2

Table 7.2 Total costs of radio: UK Open University (over eight years)

Production level (in one year)	150 programmes 50 hours £	280 programmes 93 hours £	360 programmes 120 hours £
Cost head			
Fixed	446,800	446,800	446,800
Programme budget	47,250	88,200	113,400
Academic time	30,000	56,000	72,000
Transmission	180,000	336,000	432,000
Total	704,050	927,000	1,064,200
(US$	1,056,075	1,390,500	1,596,300)

transmission costs, as each programme is repeated). Costs are calculated for production levels of 150, 280 (actual) and 360 programmes (maximum capacity).

Figure 7.1 shows the total costs for radio at these varying levels of production. It can be seen that radio costs are constant, irrespective of the number of students.

Table 7.3 converts BBC-Open University production and transmission costs into costs per student and per student study hour. Once again, this calculation is not straightforward, since students may spend more than just the length of the programme studying the programme material, especially if the students record it and play it back several times, or hear the repeat as well as the first transmission, or if the programme makes reference to printed notes or other printed material.

Account also needs to be taken of the utilisation (listening) rate. The average listening rate for OU radio is consistently under 50 per cent, i.e. for

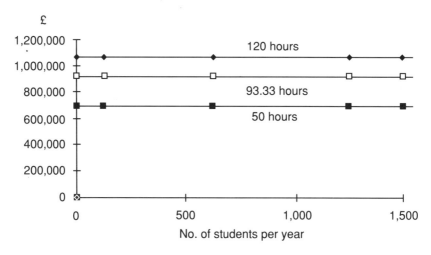

Figure 7.1 Total costs for radio over eight years

Table 7.3 Costs of radio per student and per study hour: UK OU, 1982

	1,000 students (125 students per year × 8)		5,000 students (625 students per year × 8) Cost (£)		10,000 students (1,250 students per year × 8)	
	Per student	Per study hour	Per student	Per study hour	Per student	Per study hour
Cost head						
Production*	67.42	6.32	13.48	1.26	6.74	0.63
Transmission*	38.40	3.60	7.68	0.72	3.84	0.36
Total (radio)*	105.82	9.92	21.16	1.98	10.58	0.99
(US$	158.73	14.88	31.74	2.97	15.87	1.48)

Notes: 32 × 20-minute radio programmes, transmitted twice each year
* The cost per 'listening' student will be double these figures, to take into account the 50% of students who do not listen

any single programme, less than 50 per cent of the students on that course would listen to it in any fashion. In 1981 the listening rate was 47 per cent. Furthermore, it was found (Bates *et al.*, 1981) that of those who did listen, only about 20 per cent listened to more than a single transmission of the same programme.

It is simplest then just to consider the study time as equal to the length of the transmission. In calculating the costs in Table 7.3, I have assumed an allocation of one 20-minute programme per week, over a 32-week course, with each programme broadcast twice each year, which is usually what is allocated to OU foundation courses. This gives a total production cost of £67,424 ($101,136) for 32 programmes, and a total transmission cost per year of £4,800 ($7,200). This averages about £13,000 ($20,000) a year per programme over an eight-year life for a series of 32 radio programmes, or about £400 ($600) a programme each year.

The costs vary from about US$158 (£105) a student, at $15 (£10) per study hour, for courses with 125 students, down to $15 (£10) per student, at $1.50 (£1) per study hour, for a course with 1,250 students a year, assuming an eight-year life. These figures show clearly the economies of scale for radio. Radio costs per student for courses with just over 100 students a year are ten times higher than for courses with 1,250 students or so per year. If utilisation is taken into account (less than 50 per cent of students listening to programmes), then the cost per listening student is doubled. Figure 7.2 presents the cost per student study hour in graphical form.

Courses needed to have over 1,250 students a year before unit costs dropped below $1.50 (£1) per student study hour; on the foundation courses, though, each with more than 6,000 students a year, radio costs came down to 30¢ (20 pence) per hour.

BBC radio production costs are not the cheapest that can be found. However, the sharp separation of costs between the Open University and

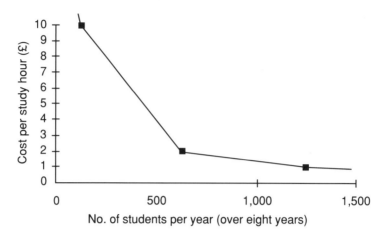

Figure 7.2 Cost per student study hour: radio (UK OU)

the BBC does allow the full costs of radio, including administrative over-heads, to be fully identified in this example. What is important here is not the actual costs, which will vary from institution to institution, but the relationship between the different costs, which are likely to be more consistent across institutions.

Organisational and political issues

In many European countries, it is the public broadcasting organisations who provide the educational radio programmes. Some public broadcasting organisations go to considerable efforts to involve the educational system in the planning and utilisation of the educational radio programmes. For instance, the BBC has advisory councils for both schools and continuing education radio, and also regional education officers who liaise with schools and colleges. In a number of developing countries, educational radio is directly funded by relevant government ministries.

There are instances in some countries, particularly in Latin America, where educational institutions have negotiated access via a commercial channel, but this is rare. The Latin American Radio Literacy Schools and some universities in the USA have negotiated licences for their own radio stations. In several other countries (e.g. Thailand) the ministry of education has its own radio channel. In general, though, educational institutions or organisations, including ministries of education, have had great difficulty in directly accessing radio transmission facilities, and this has been a major inhibitor to greater use of radio in education.

Even when educational institutions do obtain access via public or commercial broadcast services, the educational programmes are often relegated to a ghetto of poor transmission times. For instance, in 1988 the majority of the British Open University's radio programmes were being broadcast after 11.30 pm or before 7.00 am.

It should however be noted that the most convenient times for Open University students (between 6.00 pm and 9.00 pm) is one of the least used periods by general radio listeners (in the UK, less than 2 per cent of the general population listen to radio between 8.00 pm and 11.00 pm). In general, educational radio (as distinct from public service programming) has more or less disappeared in North America; in Europe, increased competition from commercial channels has resulted in some public broadcasting organisations dropping educational radio altogether, while in others it has become increasingly marginalised.

Novelty

Radio is unlikely to attract much external funding or interest, except for unusual applications, such as narrowband satellite transmission and reception.

Speed

This is a major advantage of radio. Programmes can be produced and transmitted to large numbers very quickly, often within 24 hours. Thus radio can be used to link contemporary events, such as strikes, international incidents, and political events, to the course materials, as they happen. Radio can be invaluable when corrections or last-minute changes of plan are necessary.

The immediacy of radio can help in even more dramatic circumstances. For instance, in 1971, just after the Open University opened, there was a major postal strike. Radio was used to inform students to obtain their course materials from local centres, and to submit their assignments in the same way; in October 1988, at a time when many Open University students were due to take examinations, Britain was hit by a major hurricane. Many roads were blocked and rail services disrupted; some students had their homes damaged or were even injured in the storm. Radio was used to inform students about alternative examination arrangements.

Summary

Radio is extremely accessible, and can be used to reach even poor people in the least developed countries. It is also likely to be of interest where low cost is considered essential, although there is evidence to suggest that print can still be substantially cheaper per student study hour. Radio has also been used for a very wide range of educational applications, and radio is a quick and easy medium for students and teachers to use.

However, newer technologies such as television (for visual presentation), audio conferencing (for two-way interaction) and audio cassettes (for student control) are stronger instructionally. Thus in deciding to use radio, a very careful assessment needs to be made of its benefits and weaknesses for the particular target group it is to serve.

AUDIO CASSETTES

When I am pressed to say what I think is the most cost-effective teaching medium, I tend to answer: 'Audio cassettes plus print'. I believe that audio cassettes are the most underrated technology of all in open and distance learning.

Audio cassettes have basically replaced the open-reel tape recorder and the gramophone record for use by both learners and teachers, with the possible exception of records (or compact discs) for some activities requiring the playing of music. The audio cassette has an advantage over both records and the emerging technology of CD-ROM in that it can both record and replay at low cost.

Access

Audio cassette machines are now as common-place in most countries as radio receivers. The last survey of British Open University students' access to audio cassette machines in 1985 showed that 95 per cent had audio cassette machines at home suitable for study purposes (Grundin, 1985). Most of the few students without an audio cassette machine said they would purchase one if they felt it was necessary for their studies.

Even in developing countries, audio cassette machines are common. For instance, in Afghanistan in 1977, I was surprised to find audio cassette players more common among the Kutchi nomads than radio receivers. The reason for this was that the radio airwaves were controlled primarily by government, and used for official information and 'cultural' programming, while the Kutchis used the audio cassettes for playing popular music.

Teaching and learning

There are several quite different uses of audio cassettes. The first is to record radio programmes. Because broadcasts often come at times that are inconvenient, or do not fit the times when students want to study, the programmes are recorded and played back at the time that suits the learner ('time-shift' recording). Students at the British Open University tended increasingly to record radio programmes for replay at a later time to coincide with the rest of their study pattern, and we have seen that they rated the radio programmes as being much more useful when listened to as recordings, rather than live, on-air. However, when using cassettes to record radio transmissions, the programme format and style is of course that of a continuous, uninterrupted radio programme.

A second use of audio cassettes is not very different instructionally from that of a recorded radio programme, and that is where audio cassettes have been used to record lectures or lessons, often delivered in a face-to-face classroom context, but also made available as a cassette, with supporting lecture notes, which include diagrams, formulae, etc, to off-campus students who for reasons of distance were unable to attend personally. The major difference with radio programmes is that the production is less professional, and therefore depends very heavily on the quality of pre-sentation of the individual professor or teacher; also, such cassettes tend to be twice the length at least of an average educational radio programme (50–60 minutes, compared to 20–30 minutes). This use is quite common in dual-mode institutions, which have both on-campus and off-campus students following the same course.

The third use, and the one which is the most cost-effective, is where the cassettes are deliberately designed to exploit some of the control features available to users of cassettes, such as stopping, re-wind, and repeat. This can lead to a format that is very different from a radio programme. Thus the cassette can be broken up into a number of discrete, non-continuous segments. Activities can be built in, which require the student to stop the cassette and return to it later. Most important of all, the cassette can be tightly integrated with other learning material. Some of these roles are summarised below:

- talking students through parts of the printed material: text (e.g. analysis of arguments); formulae and equations (explaining and discussing); illustrations, graphs, diagrams and maps; technical drawings; statistical tables;
- talking about real objects that need to be observed (e.g. rock samples, reproductions of paintings, metal fatigue in examples sent as part of a home kit);
- talking students through practical procedures (home experiments, computer operation, etc.) so their hands and eyes are free for the practical activity rather than needed for written instructions;
- analysing human interaction (e.g. decision-making; personal experiences; conduct of meetings): here the role of print and audio is reversed, in that the text is used to help analyse the audio material;
- providing feedback on student activities: cassettes allow answers to be more easily tucked away, thus encouraging students to make more effort to answer the questions themselves rather than search for the answers.

Interactivity and user-friendliness

The importance of audio cassettes as a teaching medium is far greater than just the additional convenience of 'time-shift' recording. Audio cassettes

Table 7.4 Control characteristics of broadcasts compared with cassettes

Broadcast characteristics	Learner implications	Cassette characteristics	Learner implications
Fixed schedules	Time and place dependent/sets pace	Available when required	Convenience/use when appropriate for study
Mass audience	Poor quality times/ popular appeal/ recruitment	Targeted audience	Learner specific
Ephemeral	Non-retrievable non-interruptible	Permanent	Repetition/analysis
Continuous	Thinking 'on the run'/made for the 'average' student	Stop-start facility	Reflection/activities/ individual pacing/ mastery
Holistic	Synthesis/overview/ summary	Segmented	Integration with other media/re-structuring

increase the *control* that both students and teachers have over the medium. Table 7.4 compares the control characteristics of broadcasts (audio and video) with those for cassettes, and the implications for learners.

One of the characteristics of broadcasts is that because they are open to everyone, there is a tendency to make them understandable to the general public, in an entertaining style. This is especially important if one of the main rationales for using broadcasts is to encourage listeners to take courses at the institution.

Cassettes on the other hand can be much more narrowly targeted, designed to meet just the needs of enrolled students, or to encompass a specific teaching approach. One of the constant findings from the research on radio and television at the British Open University was that registered students wanted very different styles of programmes from general listeners (or viewers) interested in watching or listening to educational programmes. Enrolled students wanted the programmes to deal with specific areas of difficulty, or to provide help or an approach that was not available through other media used in a course. They did not like, or in the end use, programmes that adopted more entertaining styles, if they could not see an educational purpose beyond mere interest or general relevance; in the most part, registered students wanted didactic programmes (Bates *et al.*, 1981).

We have also seen that the ability to retrieve content, to go back over it, and to listen to it several times, is important for students. Even the same material as in a broadcast was more highly rated when available in a recorded form. The replay facility is extremely important where the teaching intention is to go beyond mere comprehension, and to develop higher level learning skills of analysis, evaluation, etc.

Perhaps the most interesting finding of the research comparing radio and audio cassettes, though, is that the ability to design cassettes differently can enable learners to interpret and analyse material more easily than through broadcasts. Broadcasts tend to be made in a continuous, 'seamless' format; the general broadcaster's intention is to keep the listener listening. Cassettes, though, can be designed, through the use of stopping instructions and segments, followed by activities, to encourage not only stopping, but mastery learning through repetition, interaction with the learning materials, and reflection; examples of situations or correct answers can be hidden on the tape until the designer considers the learner ready for the feedback.

The combination of all these features means that well-designed audio cassettes, when combined with print and other materials, can result in high levels of interactivity between the learner and the learning material. The learner is not limited to a narrow range of pre-determined responses, but can be encouraged to think individually and interpretatively, although feedback on the learner's responses is still limited to what is already in the materials.

The advantages are not all on the side of cassettes. The continuous format of radio programmes can be useful for advanced students who can 'think on the run', and since such programmes tend to be complete in themselves, or holistic, they are excellent for presenting a summary or an overview of a topic, where the broader picture is more important than the detail. On the other hand, the ability to stop a cassette and do an activity, and to design a cassette in discrete segments, allows students to move easily between the cassette and other learning materials, thus tightly integrating the cassette in the study process.

Another reason for the popularity of the audio cassette at the British Open University was the greater control academics felt they had over the design of the material. The production of a radio programme was more of a separate event from the design of the textual material, involving a producer who controlled the process. Audio cassette design, though, could be developed in parallel with the development of the textual material. Professors sometimes used a cassette recorder at home to 'rough out' the interplay between cassette and textual material. Even in this situation, it is important to produce a polished script and have the cassette properly recorded in a studio, but the producer here is more of a technician than in the case of a radio programme.

Costs

Production

The BBC/OUP claim that the production costs of audio cassettes are exactly the same per hour as for radio. While this may be reasonable when cassettes are made to the same high production standards as radio programmes, with outside recordings, and broadcast-standard BBC staff producers, recording engineers, editors, etc., educationally effective audio cassettes can be, and have been, produced much less expensively. This does not mean that cassettes require less skill in production, but cassettes aimed at an individual student for study purposes need not contain the same kind of content or format as would a radio programme, with its implicit need to appeal to the general listener as well as to the committed student.

The production cost differences between radio and audio cassettes are nicely illustrated by the British Open University experience. As well as access to the BBC production facilities, the university also operated a small audio studio, with its own technical staff. Audio production costs in 1981 through this studio averaged approximately US$1,350 (£900) an hour, plus the cost of academic time. This was about one quarter that of BBC/OUP radio production.

Even so, the two services are difficult to compare. The OU/AV services were able to produce only about 60–100 'radio programme equivalents' per year, and their production costs did not usually include fees to external speakers, use of copyright material, or overheads for buildings, heating or administration (which could amount to another 40 per cent of production costs), all of which are included in BBC/OUP costs. The technical staff in the OU/AV service were also on much lower salary scales than BBC producers and technicians. Also, in 1979 and 1980, student ratings of BBC-produced cassettes were higher than those produced by OU/AV services (3.89 compared with 3.66). Basically the two production facilities were providing different services. What it does illustrate though is that audio cassette production costs are at most the same as for radio, and can be a good deal less.

Distribution

The cost of copying, labelling, packing and mailing a 60-minute (C60) audio cassette, *and* the cost of the cassette itself, was calculated by the Open University to be 50 pence (75¢), including handling and clerical costs (cassettes are normally included with the mailing of the correspondence texts, which keeps down the mailing costs). Despite inflation, this figure of 50 pence remained stable between 1980 and 1988, as copying equipment and packing techniques improved. At the British Open University, students keep the cassettes, as it costs more to recover them.

The big difference between radio and audio cassette distribution costs is that audio cassettes have variable costs, while the variable cost for radio transmission is nil. In other words, an extra cost of 50 pence is incurred for each student who receives an audio cassette, while for radio, the transmission cost is the same, whether one or a million students listen.

The key issue is the point at which radio becomes cheaper than audio cassettes for distribution. This is simply calculated by working out the number of students who could receive audio cassettes for the same cost as a

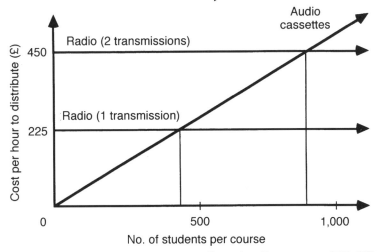

Figure 7.3 Structure of delivery costs: radio and audio cassettes (UK OU)

radio transmission. If we take for the sake of argument a C60 cassette, this would be equivalent to three 20-minute radio programmes. The cost of transmitting three programmes (once each) in 1980–81 was £75 × 3 = £225. At 50 pence each, 450 cassettes could be distributed for the same price as three single radio transmissions. Thus for courses with less than 450 students, audio cassette distribution would be cheaper than a single transmission, and would be cheaper than repeat transmissions for courses with less than 900 students. This can be more clearly seen from Figure 7.3.

Table 7.5 Comparative costs of audio production: BBC-OUP vs. OU-AV: UK OU, 1982

	BBC/OUP 280 programmes p.a.		*OU/AV* 60 programmes p.a.	
	Per prog. £	*Per hour* £	*Per prog.* £	*Per hour* £
Development/production				
Academic time	200	600	200	600
Production (overheads)	1,592	4,776	380	1,140
Direct production	315	945	33	100
Total production costs	2,107	6,321	613	1,840
(US$	3,160	9,481	919	2,760)

Delivery *No. of students* *per year*	*Radio Transmission* *costs per hour*		*Audio cassette Distribution* *costs per hour* *(C60 cassette)*
	Single £	*Repeat* £	£
450	225	450	225
900	225	450	450
2,000	225	450	1,000

Table 7.6 Total costs for audio cassettes: UK OU (over eight years)

| | Level of production per year | | |
| | 60 hours | 150 hours | 250 hours |
	£	£	£
(a) Total cost: production only			
Fixed	30,780	92,340	123,120
Programme budget	6,000	15,000	25,000
Academic costs	36,000	90,000	150,000
Total	72,780	197,340	298,120
(US$	109,170	296,101	447,180)

Distribution costs: 50 pence (75¢) per student per hour of material

(b) Total costs: production (once) *and distribution (over 8 years)* No. of students per year			
0	0	0	0
1	73,020	197,940	299,120
125	102,780	272,340	423,120
625	222,780	572,340	923,120
1250	372,800	947,340	1,548,120

Total costs and cost per student hour

Table 7.5 provides comparative costs for BBC/OUP audio (radio or audio cassettes) and OU/AV cassette production, and differences in delivery costs for radio and audio cassettes. OU/AV production costs have been increased in Tables 7.5 and 7.6 by 40 per cent, to allow for overheads.

Total costs and costs per study hour

The Open University used a small audio studio, with a technician, for its own audio production. The maximum capacity was around 60 hours of programming a year. Thus to increase to 150 hours would have required a three-fold increase in fixed costs, and four-fold for 250 programmes a year. Costs of distribution of audio cassettes are variable. Table 7.6 indicates the total costs for audio cassettes. Table 7.6 (b) is presented in graphical form in Figure 7.4.

It can be seen that unlike radio, audio cassette costs escalate rapidly as student numbers increase. While audio cassette costs are much lower for lower volumes of production and/or smaller student numbers, by 150 hours and 1,250 students a year, there is only a small difference between audio cassette and radio costs.

Table 7.7 gives costs per student and per study hour for cassettes produced both by BBC/OUP and OU/AV, and compares these costs with

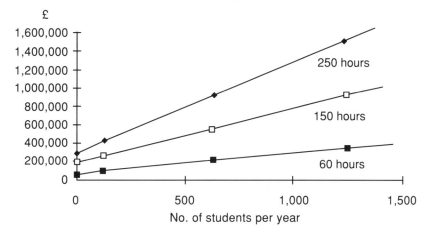

Figure 7.4 Total costs for audio cassettes, over eight years

radio and print, for an allocation of 11 C60 audio cassettes (an average figure for an OU course of 32 weeks, and roughly equal to 32 radio programmes in length).

It should be noted for both radio and audio cassettes that these are not usually used to replace print. Particularly where print and audio cassettes are integrated, the costs should therefore be combined. This gives a cost for the British Open University in the range of £4 ($6) per study hour for low-cost audio + print and £11.66 ($17.50) per study hour for radio + print, for 125 students per year, dropping to around £1 ($1.50) per study hour for all forms of audio + print for courses with around 1,000 students a year.

Since audio cassettes in general replaced radio programmes at the Open University, their introduction did not lead to any increase in the total costs of the system; indeed, there were some slight savings from the reduction in transmission times.

Organisational issues

Audio cassettes can easily be designed and distributed without the need for high-tech facilities. If a simple recording studio is not available on campus, many cities have audio recording studios which can be hired for little cost. Similarly, while the British Open University has its own high-speed cassette duplication facilities, it is not usually difficult to find commercial companies able to copy from master tapes at similar costs to those cited in this chapter. While it obviously helps to have technical support in the form of an on-campus A/V service, most teachers should be able to organise the production of their own material without a great deal of cost or effort.

It is the design of the accompanying printed material that is likely to be more demanding, since considerable care is needed to ensure that the

Table 7.7 Costs of audio cassettes per student and per study hour: UK OU, 1982

| | 1,000 students (125 students per year × 8) | | 5,000 students (625 students per year × 8) | | 10,000 students (1,250 students per year × 8) | |
| | | | Cost (£) | | | |
	Per student	Per study hour	Per student	Per study hour	Per student	Per study hour
Cost head						
Production (OU)	20.24	1.84	4.05	0.37	2.02	0.18
Transmission	5.50	0.50	5.50	0.50	5.50	0.50
Total (OU/AV)	25.74	2.34	9.55	0.87	7.52	0.68
(US$	38.61	3.51	14.32	1.30	11.28	1.02)
Radio (£)	105.82	9.92	21.16	1.98	10.58	0.99

Note: Figures are for an allocation of 11 C60 audio cassettes

students can easily find the appropriate places in the text or tape, and can move from one segment to another, and from cassette to print and back again, in a smooth and obvious way.

Figure 7.5 shows typical stages in the design, production and delivery of audio cassettes at the British Open University.

Novelty

Despite the fact that few institutions make heavy use of audio cassettes, they have little novelty value, and certainly not enough to excite funding agencies.

Speed

While cassettes are not difficult to design, if they are to be integrated with textual or other materials, their production is determined to some extent by the speed of print design and development, which can be slow. However, they are relatively easy to change and up-date, although this will incur additional reproduction costs.

Summary

Audio cassettes, especially when designed to be integrated with text, are a low-cost, highly effective one-way teaching technology. They are low-tech, and hence easy for both teachers and students to use.

One or two distance teaching institutions use audio cassettes extensively in an integrated manner, exploiting the control characteristics of audio cassettes. In a period of less than five years, radio transmission at the

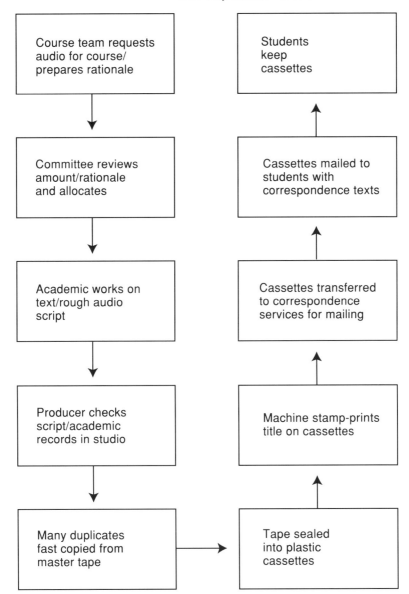

Figure 7.5 Production and distribution of audio cassettes (UK OU)

British Open University dropped from 28 hours a week to just over six hours a week, while the amount of audio production actually increased, but almost entirely for cassette distribution.

The British Open University each year distributes more than 750,000 hours of audio cassette material to students. Perhaps the most telling comment though on the value of cassettes used in this integrated way comes from a comment made by a student during an evaluation by Durbridge (1981): 'It's like having your tutor in the room with you.' However, audio cassette design that achieves that 'tutor over your shoulder' feeling is still comparatively rare in most institutions.

8 Two-way audio
Telephone teaching and audio-graphics

TWO-WAY AUDIO: THE START OF 'THIRD GENERATION' DISTANCE EDUCATION

Telephone-based audio technologies have become increasingly widespread and important in distance education. The telephone has teaching characteristics that strongly differentiate it from the 'mass' media of broadcasting and print.

THE TECHNOLOGY

Audio

Voice telephone on a person-to-person basis is one important form of contact between student and tutor in distance teaching. Many open learning systems make use of this technology. Nothing more than a standard telephone for both the student and tutor is needed, and a reasonably efficient public telephone network.

Another use of the telephone in teaching is for audio conferencing. Audio conferencing requires the use of a special telephone switchboard called a bridge, which allows several lines to be connected simultaneously, so someone at one site can hear and be heard by all the others. In some countries, private bridges can be installed on an institution's internal switchboard; alternatively, the public telephone system may offer an operator-controlled audio conferencing facility.

Where several people meet together at one site to participate in an audio conference, a telephone loudspeaker and individual microphones improve the quality of the sound. If the calls are to students in their home or office, they are unlikely to have such equipment, although some answer-phones have an in-built microphone, loud-speaker and sound recorder, which allow for not only hand-free operation but also recording of the conversation for later analysis.

Audio-graphics

One obvious disadvantage of teaching by telephone is the lack of a visual element, and in particular the lack of diagrams or illustration to accompany the voice. Some teachers who use the telephone extensively for teaching go to the trouble of preparing supporting print material or notes well before the telephone lecture or conference, then mail or fax the notes to the receiving sites.

However, developments in technology now allow for the parallel transmission of images with voice via standard telephone lines. Using common microcomputers with a special plug-in board and software loaded from a diskette, colour graphics – handwriting, text, diagrams, and simple animation – can be generated easily by a teacher or student. A variety or combination of devices can be used to create images:

- a standard computer keyboard, using cursors;
- a 'mouse', i.e. a device that can be used to manipulate or move images on a screen;
- an electronic pen and tablet, that uses a grid reference system to draw on the screen;
- a light pen that appears to draw on a TV screen;
- a video camera that records moving pictures, from which the computer 'snatches' still images, and digitises them.

These images can be converted into digital codes (data) that are stored as 'frames' then edited on the computer as required, or transmitted via the telephone line to remote sites. The package of data and sound is then decoded back into its original form using similar equipment at the receiving sites.

In addition, students at remote sites can in turn create their own visuals, and transmit them back to the tutor in real time. Because the visual signals are transmitted as a digital 'audio' code, the visuals can be recorded on one track of a standard audio cassette, with the sound on the other track. Thus with careful editing a closely integrated audio–visual package can be prepared, and either played back using an audio cassette player in a classroom context, or prepared in advance for transmission by telephone.

Slow-scan television also digitises video signals from a camera, and sends them through standard telephone lines. It can take about 20 seconds to transmit a still frame of someone's face this way using the standard telephone system.

New developments

One major limitation of standard public telephone systems has been the relatively high cost of telephone teaching; another has been the difficulty of sending data or images by telephone because of the limited capacity of the analogue copper wired telephone network and electro-mechanical exchanges. The more complex the image (e.g. movement, colour), the slower the transmission. However, the introduction of satellite technology, all-digital exchanges, and fibre-optic cabling are already having a major impact on telephone services.

In particular, the introduction of ISDN (integrated services digital networks) will allow much greater quantities of information, including images and data, to be carried at much lower cost. ISDN is basically a digital telephone system, i.e. sound (and images and data) are sent in the form of digital codes. This allows much more information to be packed into the same physical carrying capacity of the old analogue copper wired telephone system. For instance, conventional voice telephones operate at transmission speeds of 1.2 to 2.4 kbs (kilobits per second). ISDN can operate at transmission speeds of between 56 and 128 kbs (depending on the wiring and networks) over the same copper wires, enabling much more information, such as images, data and voice, to be carried for a similar cost.

However, even ISDN cannot be used for delivering full video transmission into homes over existing copper wires (full-motion colour television requires 90,000 kbs). ISDN therefore is ideal for 'middle-range' data, such as audio-graphics and integrated voice, or for the distribution of large quantities of computer data, such as data-bases. ISDN also works well over a 'mixed' or hybrid transmission system. Thus ISDN signals can be sent through copper wire, fibre-optic cabling, micro-wave, radio or satellite transmissions.

In order that the data can be moved between different places and across different types of transmission and equipment, the data must be packed in standardised ways. As well as agreed standards, ISDN also requires a certain type of telephone exchange and sub-exchanges, so it may take many years for a whole national telephone system to be switched over to ISDN. ISDN is likely to be available first in central business districts of large cities, followed by connections to the down-town areas of other major cities, next by connections to suburban areas, and lastly to more remote areas.

The implications for education of ISDN, plus related developments in satellite technology and fibre-optics, are two-fold: the costs of communication will drop rapidly, as these services come into place; and the range of information that can be carried economically will widen dramatically. Thus it will be possible to send voice, data, and moving pictures relatively cheaply across increasingly greater distances.

There is no doubt that these new services will offer major opportunities for teaching. However, while these new services will eliminate some of the technical limitations that have hampered greater use of telephone teaching, and while these services will provide opportunities for new types of teaching, experience from telephone teaching indicate that there are some lessons already learned that will apply just as forcefully to these new technological developments.

ACCESS

During the 1980s, home access to the telephone system increased dramatically in most Western developed countries. In the UK, the number of homes with a telephone increased from 54 per cent in 1974 to 86 per cent in 1991. In North America, over 90 per cent of homes have at least one telephone line. While there are some significant variations both regionally and in terms of age and income groups, in general, in most developed countries, the telephone does provide home-based access to a high proportion of potential students.

Currently, most audio-graphics systems require two telephone lines per work-station, one for the sound and one for the data/graphics. Also, audio-graphics need specialised computing facilities. For these and other reasons, access to audio-graphics is likely to be in classrooms or learning centres for some time, at least until targeted students have their own micro-computers with integrated audio-graphics facilities at home. ISDN, though, will allow sound, data and images to be delivered simultaneously via a single telephone line, and will thus substantially reduce the line costs of audio-graphics.

TEACHING FUNCTIONS

Figure 8.1 sets out in diagrammatic form some of the most common modes of telephone teaching and audio conferencing. Mode 1 represents a tutor communicating on a one-to-one basis with a single student. Many distance teaching institutions have used mode 1 for individual tutoring and counselling, with print and other media providing the direct teaching. While this mode is rarely used as the main source of teaching, it can provide critically important tutorial support or counselling to students studying at a distance.

To encourage greater student–tutor contact, some distance teaching institutions require their tutors to initiate the first call to students, as there is substantial evidence that students are often reluctant to call tutors. Other institutions set 'office hours', when students can call their tutors, and know they are available for tutorial advice. Some institutions offer call-free services, where the call is automatically charged to the institution, even if initiated by the student.

Mode 2 represents a teacher or tutor in contact with a group of students at a remote site. This is sometimes used when teachers are in one institution (and may incidentally have 'live' students before them in a classroom), and the remote group is at another campus, or in another institution. In this mode, it is generally used for direct instruction. No bridge is required in this situation, as only one remote site is connected.

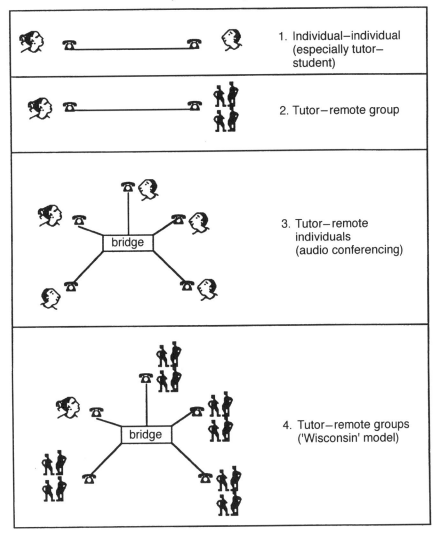

Figure 8.1 Four modes of telephone teaching

Mode 3 links a tutor with a number of individual students at individual sites – usually students at home. Through the use of a bridge, every person can speak to and hear every other person. If two people speak at the same time, usually the loudest prevails, so there are skills required to manage such an audio conference.

The number of sites that can be linked at any one time depends on the size of the bridge. A more serious constraint is the number of students who can be effectively taught or tutored in this way at any single time.

Generally, about seven sites/individuals is optimum, if a high level of interaction between teacher and student is to be maintained.

A number of institutions have used mode 3 extensively instead of (optional) face-to-face tutorials, especially where students are scattered over a wide area. The telephone tutorials provide students with an opportunity to analyse and discuss the teaching materials provided through other media (print, television, and audio cassettes).

Mode 4 in the figure links a tutor in one site to several groups of students at different sites. (This is the same as mode 2, except a bridge is required.) Many universities and colleges in North America and Australia have used mode 4 for direct instruction, with lectures delivered to remote sites, and students calling in with questions to be answered by the lecturer.

In this situation, audio conferencing is the main form of direct instruction, although students will often be required to read set text books or find library references. The University of Wisconsin in the USA has an extensive network of centres across the state linked to its audio conference bridge. It has used a variety of devices to create images, including slow-scan television, in support of its audio conferencing network. There have also been trials of audio-graphics in the Universitas Terbuka, Indonesia, the University of the South Pacific, and the British Open University.

In the latter case, audio-graphics were used extensively over a three-year period between 1981–83 to deliver tutorials into 15 study centres in one region of England (East Midlands). Over 600 students on more than 30 different courses participated. A local tutor could be connected to up to seven different study centres. Students came into the study centres and set up the equipment themselves. The audio-graphics tutorials were used instead of face-to-face classes, to support the mixed-media courses (print, broadcast television and audio cassettes or radio). While the experiment was successful in educational terms (McConnell and Sharples, 1983), it was terminated for cost and technical reasons (Bates, 1983).

The Open Learning Agency ISDN Distance Learning Trial was sponsored by several organisations seeking to analyse the feasibility of using ISDN communications technology and multi-media work-stations for educational delivery in British Columbia. The project was a partnership between the Open Learning Agency, the Vancouver School Board (VSB), the BC Telephone Company (BC Tel), and MPR Teltech (a research subsidiary of BC Tel), and was funded by the Federal Department of Communications and the provincial Ministry of Advanced Education, Training and Technology. It was one of the first educational applications of ISDN technology in North America.

The project employed ISDN technology and multi-media work-stations developed by MPR to connect four VSB Adult Learning Centres in a distance learning network. During the spring of 1992, the VSB offered two high-school upgrade courses – *Western Civilisation 12* and *Introduction to Math 11* – as part of the ISDN Distance Learning Trial. By 'pooling' students in an electronic classroom, the VSB was able to increase the number of courses available at each learning centre, and students were able to attend classes at the centre of their choice (Black and Harasim, 1993).

One other mode of operation is really a variation on modes 1 and 3. Students may be encouraged to set up self-help groups. For instance, usually after a face-to-face meeting, students may exchange telephone numbers. This may be just between two students, who call each other to discuss the course; or it may be a whole group that arranges its own conferences, but uses the institution's facilities.

Robinson (1984, p. 129) found in a study she conducted that telephone tutorials with either individuals or small groups (mode 3) were effective for the following tasks:

- to clarify student difficulties with course materials;
- to promote student discussion of specific issues and topics;
- to exchange interpretations of or debate a case or thesis;
- to discuss problems of recent written assignments, or strategies for tackling forthcoming ones;
- to discuss, analyse or work through previously-circulated materials (maths problems, graphs, diagrams, illustrations, raw data, etc.);
- to analyse a written text or musical score;
- to present short case-studies;
- to role-play an exercise;
- to practise and evaluate sight singing on a musical course;
- to negotiate the design of a project.

and she found the following were *not* considered effective:

- lecturing;
- constructing a complex diagram from scratch;
- impromptu tutorials or unprepared topics;
- tasks involving a large number of texts or sources;
- groups with constantly changing membership;
- some science, technology and maths topics where dynamic visuals were required;
- conveying lengthy and detailed instructions.

Lastly, the telephone can be heavily used for administration, allowing for information to be disseminated to regional staff, for meetings, to avoid staff travelling to headquarters, and even for training staff.

Table 8.1 summarises the different purposes and modes of organisation of the telephone in education.

Table 8.1 Purposes and modes of organisation for telephone use in distance education

	Purpose and frequency		
Organisational mode	*Direct teaching*	*Tutoring/counselling*	*Administration*
1 One-to-one	Rarely	Frequently	Frequently between individual staff
2 Tutor with one remote group	Occasionally, especially on split campuses	Rarely	Rarely
3 Audio conferencing	Rarely	Frequently, particularly when students are too scattered to meet face-to-face	Frequently for meetings to bring in remote staff
4 Tutor with several remote groups	Frequently at Wisconsin	Rarely	Occasionally, between groups of staff at different campuses

INTERACTIVITY AND USER-FRIENDLINESS

Garrison (1989) claims that:

> Teleconferencing represents a paradigm shift in facilitating and support-ing learning at a distance. . . . Of all the means used to support distance education, teleconferencing most closely simulates the transaction between teacher and students in a contiguous or conventional form of education. The exchange is conversational in nature, it may be sponta-neous, and it is immediate. In these respects teleconferencing differs from all other technologies used to bridge the distance in distance education.

(Garrison, 1989, p. 66)

He identifies three 'defining characteristics' of teleconferencing:

- a group method of learning;
- regularity and immediacy of two-way communication;
- suited to small and widely dispersed target groups.

For these reasons, Garrison claims that 'few if any traditional classroom techniques are not adaptable to teleconferencing'.

There is a key difference between the kind of audio conferencing advocated by Garrison (modes 2 and 4) and the kind offered by the autonomous distance teaching institutions, via modes 1 and 3. In Garrison's model, audio conferencing is an extension of the classroom lecture to remote sites, and is thus the main form of instruction. For the autonomous distance teaching universities, it has mainly been used instead of the optional, local face-to-face classes which supplement the print-based teaching (mode 3), or to supplement correspondence teaching (mode 1).

Garrison is making two distinct claims for teleconferencing. The first is that teleconferencing is unique in distance education in providing inter-action between teacher and student (and between students) of a quality not achieved by other technologies (such as correspondence or computer conferencing). The second is that it can emulate traditional classroom teaching. Both these claims need careful examination.

The first has been challenged by Holmberg (1990). He claims that teleconferencing is not so much a paradigm shift as a natural evolution of distance education. He also makes the point that 'Distance education can be – and often is – exclusively based on *non*-contiguous communication and wholly individual study.'

This is an important argument, and it is not co-incidental that Garrison is North American and Holmberg European. Garrison argues that because teleconferencing allows classroom-style instruction to be extended beyond the classroom and across distances, it is therefore superior to print-based forms of distance education, even when mediated by correspondence tutoring. This is because, like most higher education teachers, he believes that:

> dialogue and negotiation are essential. . . . Interaction to facilitate and support the educational process must be seen as the central feature of any educational transaction *including* distance education . . . the relative advantage of audio-teleconferencing is a consequence of the quality of interaction and support it affords.
>
> (Garrison, 1989, pp. 66–68)

Garrison's arguments reflect a view of distance education that is much more common in North America and Australia, where distance education is conducted in the main by dual-mode institutions, than in Europe or Asia, where distance education is designed and delivered by autonomous dis-tance teaching institutions. Put simply, the North American or dual-mode assumption is that the traditional form of group, face-to-face instruction is the preferred and most effective form of higher education, at least, and that the closer distance education can directly imitate this, the more effective distance education will be.

The Europeans, on the other hand, have designed and developed forms of distance education that place emphasis on the need for flexible learning opportunities that enable independence on the part of learners, and have tried to develop forms of teaching that are deliberately quite different from the traditional 'face-to-face' approach of classroom teaching. Courses from autonomous distance teaching institutions are based on breaking down the instructional and learning requirements and allocating different tasks to different elements, such as print, telephone and correspondence tutoring.

There are good reasons why the two approaches to distance education are so different. There has been a much greater tradition in North American colleges and universities of providing off-campus teaching as an extension of the traditional college. There is also a tradition of students working their way through college, thus extending the time needed to qualify, with the result that North American colleges have been more flexible in providing opportunities for more mature students.

By contrast, before the establishment of the Open University, universities and colleges in the United Kingdom, for instance, had a poor record of providing opportunities for off-campus learners. The state grant system also led to most students being full-time, and hence young. Consequently, separate institutions solely devoted to distance education had to be created for a target group quite different from those of the conventional universities and colleges: mature adults no longer engaged in full-time education, most of whom had families and were working.

The main concern of these single mode distance teaching institutions was to provide learning opportunities that fitted the lifestyle of mature adults: the greater the flexibility, the better. Requiring students to attend even local centres at a set time on a regular basis severely restricted that flexibility. There was therefore no need for the newly created distance teaching institutions to be bound by extending classroom teaching to distance learners; indeed, this was seen as likely to be more of a handicap than an advantage.

The argument that true knowledge can come only through questioning and dialogue is as old as Plato and the Socratic Dialogues. I too believe that it is extremely important for learners, especially but not exclusively at a higher education level, to be able to freely question, discuss and challenge, not only with teachers, but with other learners as well. However, is, as Garrison claims, the quality of interaction better through modes 2 and 4 audio conferencing than through that provided by the print-based institutions or through computer conferencing?

The autonomous distance teaching institutions try to provide that inter-action through a variety of ways: design of print material that encourages interaction and questioning by the individual learner in isolation; use of postal services, and increasingly the telephone, for individual tutor–student communication; and a variety of group, face-to-face arrangements, such as evening classes, weekend day-schools, or week-long residential summer schools.

Certainly, there can be more opportunities for spontaneous interaction in a classroom setting than through correspondence tutoring; however, both depend entirely on the way the teacher controls the situation and structures the teaching. Badly prepared lessons are no better and often a great deal worse when delivered through teleconferencing.

Immediacy and spontaneity, even in a well-controlled and designed audio conference, are not always possible to achieve. There are 'rules of discourse' which need to be applied, such as taking turns, and not inter-rupting. Tutors need to, and tend to, take more care in managing an audio conference than a classroom interaction, to compensate for the lack of visual cues; while this leads in fact to more effective teaching in most cases, audio conferences tend to be more inhibited and less spontaneous than classroom settings.

Robinson's list of advantages and disadvantages of audio conferencing also indicates that audio conferencing is best used *in conjunction* with other media. Garrison's claim that: 'While most teleconferencing makes use of print materials they do not have to be highly structured and attractively packaged', tends to over-emphasise the role of audio conferencing. Students still can benefit from individual study, as well as group study; they will therefore benefit from well designed print material, even when weekly audio conferencing is also available. Garrison's claim is not so much about the quality of the teaching experience, but about the limiting context under which dual mode institutions 'whose main function is not distance education' have to operate.

Similarly, Garrison's claim that teleconferencing can emulate the tradi-tional classroom setting may also bring a wry smile to the face of experi-enced teleconference teachers and, even more so, students. The statement is true, but not without much greater effort in most cases. This is because teleconferencing is not so user-friendly as a face-to-face class, even when delivered at a local centre.

For students at home, a one-hour audio conference can be an immensely tiring experience, especially if the telephone is a traditional handset. Taking notes while holding the phone can be done, but is not convenient. The quality of the sound is dependent on the quality of the worst line in the conference. Audio conferencing in mode 3 (individuals at home linked together with a tutor) is often most valuable for people in more remote communities, whose lines are often the oldest or least well maintained in the telephone system.

Teachers need consciously to use techniques to ensure participation of all connected students, otherwise a student could die in the middle of a conference and no-one would know. Handbooks on teleconferencing tech-niques can run to over a hundred pages (see, for instance, Open University, 1982 or Burge, 1987). The lack of visual clues is a major handicap, and even where audio-graphics are provided, they are relatively awkward to create and use in an interactive session. Lastly, and this is a major barrier for many students, participants have to be available at a set time and usually a set place on a regular basis.

Despite this, students often rank audio conferencing highly, where the alternative of a face-to-face session does not exist, or is even more inconvenient. Thus Garrison is right in asserting that in the Canadian context of courses with small numbers of students, relatively efficient telephone networks, and relatively affluent students or institutions able to bear the costs of telephone lines and on-line tutors, audio conferencing can play a more central role in distance teaching. Even here, though, it is important to use it in conjunction with other media, and does not invalidate the use of other forms of communication, such as written comments on written assignments, or computer conferencing.

In other contexts, and in particular where large numbers of students are to be taught at a distance, or where the telephone system is not efficient, or where tutors are not skilled at designing and conducting conferences that encourage and support student interaction, then other forms of communication such as correspondence or mail are likely to be essential, and indeed more appropriate.

COSTS

Factors influencing costs

Costs of teaching by telephone will be influenced by several factors:

- the mode and purpose of the teaching;
- the distance between participants;
- the pricing structure (tariffs) of the telephone company;
- the availability of special services, such as leased lines, ISDN and fibre-optic networks;
- the extent of regulation governing competition and monopoly of services;
- the policy of the teaching institution regarding payment of line-charges by students and tutors.

Pricing policies

There is great variation in practice between institutions, and even more so within an institution, between what is charged to a student, and what is not. Distance teaching institutions in particular have difficulties in drawing the boundary between what the student pays and what the institution pays. Nowhere is this more apparent than in policies regarding telephone call charges.

Some institutions offer call-free services, where the call is automatically charged to the institution, even if initiated by the student, to encourage greater student–tutor contact. In other institutions, costs of telephone calls are borne directly by the students.

Where telephone tutoring is used in support of other media such as print, telephone teaching tends to be seen as a replacement for 'optional' face-to-face lectures, where these are uneconomic. The logic in such institutions of making students pay the line charges is that the institution does not pay for student travel to face-to-face sessions; why then should it pay for telephone costs?

Robinson (1990) reports that at the British Open University:

> Audio conferencing is almost always cheaper than the cost of a face-to-face tutorial *when the travel costs of all participants are taken into account.* The more usual calculation done compares only the tutor's travel costs (paid for by the university) with the cost of a conference call. On this basis the cost of the conference call may not always be less.
> (Robinson, 1990)

It could be argued that telephone teaching is not used as much as it might be in distance education because students are charged for using the service; on the other hand, it is very difficult for institutions to control costs if students are allowed to charge back all their calls.

One general approach is for all 'development' costs to be paid by the institution and all delivery costs to be recovered from the students, either in the form of a flat fee or through a set of direct costs for each service provided. This means that students are responsible for the variable costs, and in this way an institution can accommodate everyone who wishes to enrol for a course (provided they can afford the fees), since fees cover marginal costs. (Under such a policy, students would logically pay for not only their calls, but also for calls *from* the tutor.)

However, if students pay the direct cost of their telephone calls, the more remote a student, or the further a student is away from the tutor, the more it will cost the student to use the telephone for study purposes. Thus although students may have equal *access* to telephones, they do not necessarily have equal *costs* to bear in using them. One argument for allowing students to charge their calls to the institution is that this avoids cost disadvantages due to distance. One approach is to allow students a set number of charged calls (irrespective of distance); over that limit, the student pays.

Private networks

Another factor influencing costs is whether institutions have to go entirely through the public telephone system, and are charged per line and the amount of use, or whether they have access to a private network. If telephone teaching goes through the public network, line costs are *variable*, being dependent on the number of students, the distance of the call, and the amount of use.

However, in some countries, private lines can be leased (rented) by an educational institution from the public telephone organisation or a telephone 're-seller'. The lease is a flat annual fee. Once the lease is paid, there are no further charges for calls between sites covered by the lease. Thus a college in one part of an educational system can offer courses not only to its own on-site students, but also to students at its own satellite campuses or at other colleges elsewhere in the state or province, with no direct cost to the college for the telephone lines, once the lease has been paid.

This is particularly useful for small colleges or schools, where there are insufficient students or specialist staff at one site to teach a particular subject, but by 'pooling' students across several schools, a viable number can be reached for a class. Leased lines also provide a means of equalising telephone costs for more remote colleges or schools.

The Open Learning Agency leases lines that connect with most government offices, colleges and universities within the province of British Columbia, from a government agency, BC Systems Corporation (which in turn leases lines from the main carriers). OLA not only uses the audio conferencing system for its own courses, but manages it on behalf of the other post-secondary institutions in the province.

OLA provides a conference bridge service for the colleges and universities. It pays an annual fixed charge of C$150,000 (US$112,500), plus C$780 (US$585) per line, for this service (this includes all uses, not just audio conferencing). This is a *fixed* cost, since the figure is independent of the amount of use.

In addition, there are charges for calls that go outside the system. Calls from outside this particular leased system are charged at the rate to the nearest system 'point'. Thus if someone calls into their local college, they will pay at the rate to their local college, even though the college switchboard may then be networking them into an audio conference across the whole province.

In many countries, regulations prevent the linking of a leased network to external public lines, because in this way those not part of the leased network are by-passing the long-distance calls of the public telephone company.

Bridge costs

Audio conferences can be set up by the local telephone company. There is usually an administrative charge for doing this, in addition to the line charges. For institutions though that use audio conferencing extensively, it is usually cheaper to buy and operate their own bridge, provided the institution has an adequate number of telephone lines.

Technology in this area has improved rapidly during the 1980s, bringing down the cost of bridges. In 1990, a 40-port (line) bridge cost US$75,000. It is relatively easy to calculate whether or not to buy a bridge, if traffic can be estimated. Dividing the cost of the bridge plus the cost of providing one's own bridge operator, by the administrative charge of the telephone company, enables one to calculate the number of conferences that need to be made to make purchase more cost-effective than using the audio conferencing service of the telephone company.

Some private companies offer conferencing services by leasing lines from the telephone company, and using their own bridge. If they can generate enough traffic, their services can work out more cheaply than the public telephone company's.

Audio-graphics

The cost of audio-graphics equipment has dropped rapidly in the last few years, from US$20,000 a work-station down to around US$5,000 today ($2,500 for the standard computer, and $2,500 for the software and peripherals – modem, graphics tablet or electronic light pen).

The OPTEL audio-graphics system can operate on one telephone line for both graphics and voice, but needs a modem, and only works with IBM-compatible machines. Other systems such as VIS-A-VIS at the time of writing require two telephone lines, one for voice and one for data, if the pictures are to synchronise with the voice; however, VIS-A-VIS can be used on local area networks without a modem, and can be used with both Macintosh and IBM-compatible machines. Using two lines of course doubles the cost of delivery. ISDN enables sound and data to be transmitted synchronously on a single telephone line.

Cost examples

Nowhere is there greater variation between institutions in cost policies than in telephone teaching. Given this wide variation in practice between institutions, any example chosen of the actual costs of telephone teaching is likely to have limited relevance. However, by using examples, we can explore the *structure* of telephone teaching costs. I will base my examples on costs and practices at the Open Learning Agency.

Example 1: Direct teaching by audio conferencing using leased lines

Where telephone teaching is the primary medium used, the teacher may be paid a set fee, which includes curriculum development, choice of set books, advice on supplementary reading, setting and marking of assignments and examinations, and tutoring/counselling of his or her students.

At the Open Learning Agency, a fee for a 13-term course (roughly 150 hours of study) would be approximately C$3,000. Such a course would include a three-hour telephone tutorial, consisting of a lecture (sometimes given by a guest specialist, who might be paid in addition to the teacher) followed by an interactive discussion between students and teachers. Students would also be able to call the teacher during set office hours for individual consultation.

The line charges can also be calculated in a variety of ways. The direct

Table 8.2 Direct fixed cost of OLA audio conferencing service, 1990–1991

Fixed costs per annum	C$	US$
Operator costs	40,000	30,000
Bridge costs (amortised over 8 years)	12,500	9,375
Leased lines: C$780 × 40 =	31,200	23,400
Other costs	8,000	6,000
Total	91,700	68,775

fixed cost of the Open Learning Agency's audio conferencing unit was C$91,700 in 1990–91 (see Table 8.2).

The Open Learning Agency in 1990–91 provided 1,185 hours of audio conferencing. This works out at a direct fixed cost of C$77 (US$57.75) per hour.

The average 'class' size for an Open Learning Agency course delivered by audio conferencing is about 12. Handling more than 12 individuals at 12 different sites becomes difficult, and interactivity for all students starts to drop off rapidly. (Larger numbers can more easily be handled for one-off events, linking groups of students at multiple sites.)

The instructor's cost of C$3,000 for 13 weeks at 12 hours a week, divided by 12 students = C$1.60 (US$1.20) per student per hour. (This includes all the work of the teacher, not just time spent on audio conferencing.) There are probably additional costs, such as guest lecturer fees, mailing and library costs for supplementary reading, etc.

Using a leased line service, the instructional costs per student will increase with the number of students in steps of 12, but not the direct telephone costs, until all 40 ports are being used. There is an additional cost for calls going outside the leased network and beyond local calls to the nearest leased 'node', e.g. to students' homes in more remote areas. In 1990–91, these averaged about C$2 (US$1.50) per student per hour, plus another C$2 per hour per tutor, across all participants.

Calculating costs for audio conferencing is particularly complex. Up to three sessions, each with 12 students and a tutor, can be handled simultaneously on a 40 port bridge. With each session lasting three hours, up to nine sessions could technically be handled per day, or 45 per five-day week. However, many sessions will be held in evenings or weekends, when students are at home.

In these calculations, I have assumed a maximum of 45 sessions per week (probably too high); once the number of sessions exceeds 45, an additional operator, bridge and leased lines will be needed. Table 8.3 provides data on the three points where these costs would increase. Combining these figures leads to Table 8.3.

A number of points need to be noted from Table 8.3. First of all, 120 students per annum may refer either to one course of 120 students, with 10

Table 8.3 Costs of audio conferencing per student study hour over eight years (based on OLA costs, 1990–1991)

	120 students per annum (10 tutors) C\$	625 students per annum (52 tutors) C\$	1,250 students per annum (104 tutors) C\$
Semi-variable costs			
Operator costs	320,000	640,000	960,000
Bridge costs	100,000	200,000	300,000
Leased lines	249,600	499,200	748,800
Other costs	64,000	128,000	256,000
Sub-total	733,600	1,467,200	2,264,800
(US\$	550,200	1,100,400	1,698,600)
Tutor contracts	90,000	468,000	936,000
Student phone costs	224,640	1,170,000	2,340,000
Tutor phone costs	18,720	97,344	194,688
Total (8 years)	1,066,960	3,202,544	5,735,488
Total (1 year)	226,970	400,318	716,936
Cost per student/hour	C\$9.50 (US\$7.12) (£4.75)	C\$5.47 (US\$4.10) (£2.74)	C\$4.90 (US\$3.67) (£2.45)

Note: 3 terms × 13 weeks = 39 weeks

tutors, or 10 different courses, each with 12 students and one tutor, or various combinations in between. In each case, though, the cost per student/hour works out the same.

Another point to note is that these figures refer just to the cost of the audio conferences themselves, and not to the actual time spent on the course as a whole. The audio conference itself is only one quarter of the weekly workload for students.

Figure 8.2 shows that costs do not decline as smoothly as Table 8.3 suggests. Figure 8.2 indicates the points at which extra operator, bridge and line costs impact.

Table 8.4 indicates why audio conferencing appears an attractive option when student numbers are low.

Teaching departments often are not expected to pay towards the fixed cost of an already existing service. Thus it is possible to offer a course with relatively low initial costs, compared with, for instance, a print-based course. However, when the fixed costs are included, and the costs applied to larger numbers of students, repeated each year over eight years, Figure 8.3 indicates that audio conferencing is not so attractive, from a cost perspective.

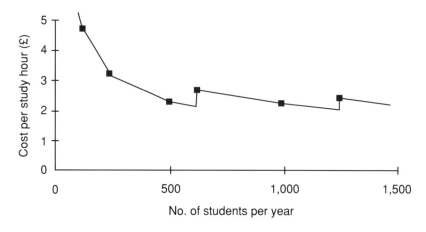

Figure 8.2 Cost per student study hour: audio conferencing (OLA)

Example 2: tutorials using audio conferencing via direct lines

For telephone tutorials used in support of other media, such as print, tutors tend to be paid on an hourly rate, which was approximately C$22 per hour in the OLA in 1991. For a class of 12 students, this works out at C$1.83 per student per hour. In addition, a fee related to numbers of students may be paid, to cover the costs of assignment marking. In most cases, tutors get some form of re-imbursement for their outgoing telephone calls to students, sometimes with a set limit.

Without leased lines, long distance charges in British Columbia, Canada, average 22¢ per minute at mid-week evening rates, or C$13.20 per hour per line. In addition, there is a 'bridge' cost of C$9 per line per hour, to cover the cost of the bridge operator.

A one-hour telephone tutorial for 12 students, each in their own home or individually at remote sites, paying direct line costs, would work out at as shown in Table 8.5.

Audio costs drop if, for instance, several students are at a local centre, or if there are face-to-face students in the presence of the tutor, although then

Table 8.4 Audio conferencing costs for one 13-week term for 12 students

Item	C$	US$
Tutor contracts	3,000	2,250
Student phone costs	936	702
Tutor phone costs	78	58
Total	4,014	3,010
Cost per student	334.50	250.87
Cost per study hour (12 hrs per week)	2.14	1.60

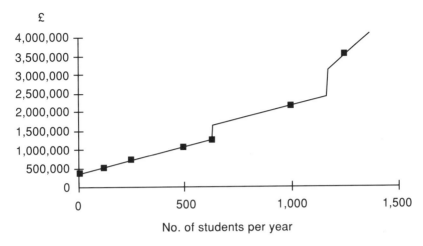

Figure 8.3 Total costs for audio conferencing over eight years (OLA)

there are costs of loudspeaking telephones, microphones and possibly rooms, to be factored in, as well as student travel costs. The cost per student can also be reduced by increasing student numbers per tutorial, but at the risk of reduced interaction. Adding a one-hour audio conference per week for a print-based course with approximately 125 students a year will roughly double the cost of the course.

Costs for audio-graphics will always be higher than for straight audio conferencing. If two lines are required, the line costs double, and the costs of the special equipment for generating and receiving graphics also add substantially to the costs.

Costs: summary

The structure of costs for teaching by telephone are very different from those of one-way media, such as print, broadcasting and cassettes.

Where telephone teaching is the primary teaching method, the fee paid to the teacher could be considered part of the 'development' or 'production'

Table 8.5 Cost per student for one-hour telephone tutorial (based on 12 students at individual sites)

Breakdown of costs	C$	US$
Share of tutor's fee per student	1.83	1.37
Line charges ($13.20 for each of the 12 lines)	13.20	9.90
For bridge overheads – operator, equipment, etc.	9.00	6.75
Shared cost of tutor's line fee/bridge operator cost	1.85	1.39
Total per student per hour	25.88	19.41

costs of a course. Where tutors are using the telephone for tutoring or counselling, in support of other media, such as print, tutors' fees could be considered as delivery costs. However, irrespective of the mode of telephone teaching, both production and delivery costs are directly related to the numbers of students on a course, unlike one-way media. Thus the structure of telephone teaching costs is similar to that of the costs of classroom teaching, although the level of costs is different.

The important point is that telephone costs are variable, i.e. they rise roughly proportionate to the number of students using the service, unlike the one-way technologies of print and broadcasting. Audio conferencing becomes increasingly more expensive per study hour than print, radio or audio cassettes as course numbers exceed 150 students a year, but for courses with less than 100 students, audio conferencing is likely to be cheaper than developing a print-based course from scratch.

However, these economies may be true only at an institutional level; at a system level, several institutions in the same educational jurisdiction may be offering identical or similar courses by audio conferencing. A common print-based course may work out considerably cheaper than several independent audio conference delivered courses.

When ISDN and fibre-optic technology are well-established, telephone costs are likely to come down, but because tutor contracts make up a significant proportion of audio conferencing costs, reductions in line charges will not have a dramatic effect on the overall cost.

ORGANISATIONAL ISSUES

It is no coincidence that the greatest use of audio conferencing for direct teaching is found in dual-mode institutions. First of all, such a use of the telephone is a direct extension of the classroom, and can be used as a direct substitute for face-to-face teaching. Although some adjustment has to be made to the technology, the basic teaching approach is the same. Audio conferences can, indeed have to, be scheduled in the same way as face-to-face classes, and therefore academic staff can fit these in to their normal work patterns.

Where a relatively large number of courses are taught in this way, an educational institution may appoint one or two technical staff to manage the bookings and to provide technical support, especially if voice conferencing is supplemented by graphical facilities, such as slow-scan or audio-graphic equipment.

One major disadvantage though of courses offered by audio conference in dual-mode institutions is that this is often merely added on to an academic's teaching work-load, without extra pay, or even consideration for promotion; indeed, it may eat into the academic's research time. Also, many such courses have to be given outside regular teaching hours, in evenings or week-ends, because of the requirements of working students.

On the other hand, large national autonomous distance teaching institutions are organised around the production and delivery of learning materials, with long lead times between initial design and delivery. Audio conferencing is separated from the design of teaching materials, and tends to be used as a support medium, with its organisation and operation delegated to regional staff and part-time tutors. Courses in general average well over 100 students a year, and direct teaching by audio conferencing would therefore be expensive. In such institutions, audio conferencing in support of other learning materials tends to be limited to substituting for optional face-to-face tutorials, where students are too scattered to meet together.

NOVELTY

After a stable period of almost 100 years of relatively small steps in the capability of the telephone system for teaching purposes, we are seeing an explosion of activity in the areas of voice, data and image transmission. Audio conferencing, audio-graphics, ISDN services, fibre-optics, facsimile, viewdata, and other telephone services have led, and will lead, to a great deal of experimentation in education.

Funds will flow from government and the private sector for educational trials, partly to encourage technological development and hence commercial competitiveness, and partly to stimulate services to a point where the take-up of the service makes it economical, or at least justifies earlier infrastructure investments.

It is therefore even more essential that educators ask themselves – and potential sponsors – questions regarding access, costs, teaching purposes, user-friendliness, and organisational implications before embarking on projects which may have technological glitz, but may not be either valid educationally, or economic as a sustainable system. At the same time, there is a genuine potential to develop more interactive, more exciting learning opportunities through greater use of the telephone.

SPEED

Finally, one very important advantage of teaching by telephone is that courses can be set up quickly, and are easily adapted and modified as new knowledge is generated.

CONCLUSION

Telephone teaching provides far greater facility for two-way communication than the 'one-to-many' form of print and broadcasting, resulting in a much more equal distribution of communication between student and teacher (and also between students).

While the telephone is readily accessible to home-based students in North America and Western Europe, this is not the case in many other parts of the world, where lack of access, unreliability and poor sound quality make telephone teaching impractical. Nevertheless, many countries are rapidly up-grading their telephone systems, and telephone teaching will become more and more viable as systems improve.

9 Computer-based learning and multimedia

COMPUTERS – THE ULTIMATE EDUCATIONAL TECHNOLOGY?

> In asking what computers can do, we are drawn into asking what people can do with them, and in the end into addressing the fundamental question of what it means to be human.
>
> (Winograd and Flores, 1986, p. 7)

From out of the considerable exaggeration and overselling of the benefits of computers in education, three significant developments can be observed: the move to multimedia, enabling a wider range of educational applications of computers; the use of computer networks for communication purposes; and a change in philosophy, from computers as teaching machines, to computers as tools to empower learners and teachers.

THE TECHNOLOGY

Mainframe or minicomputers are used by many of the largest distance teaching institutions. These computers are needed to keep and manipulate large quantities of data, such as student records, staff records, tutor payments, financial data, stock control, etc. Mainframe computers require highly skilled staff to operate and maintain them. These more powerful machines are usually accessed from multiple locations, such as offices.

However, as computers become more powerful and more compact, mainframe computers are becoming replaced by smaller, but still powerful machines, called *client servers*, which are dedicated to a particular application (such as student records), but which can also be linked to each other to share and combine information.

Microcomputers allow users to process information locally. Microcomputers can be used for word processing (preparing letters, papers, documents, accounts), maintaining data-bases (lists of addresses, or lists of courses, etc.), desk-top publishing, including page design and printing, preparing or running computer-assisted learning materials, and for communications through electronic mail and other services. Microcomputers can also be connected to mainframe computers or client servers, allowing data to be input to and collected from the mainframe or client server via the local microcomputer. As microcomputers become more powerful, they can also be used as client servers themselves.

The actual information stored or generated is called *data*. Software and data may be stored on floppy discs, which can be physically removed from the computer and stored externally, or on a hard disc, which may be embedded within the machine or may be an external piece of equipment, or on CD-ROM.

CD-ROMs operate similarly to a video disc but store data digitally. Although a compact disc can store over 300 times more data than a computer floppy disc, it has a limited capacity for storing full-motion video compared with a video disc, although large numbers of 'single frame' colour graphics can be stored on a compact disc, and compression techniques now enable more than 30 minutes of digitised moving video to be stored. At the time of writing, students and teachers cannot record but only play back from both kinds of discs, although compact disc mastering (recording) equipment can now be purchased for around US$5,000. As with video discs, there is relatively little material suitable for education already available on compact disc, although this is improving.

Interactive video is a term that has been used to describe the combination of a computer and (analogue) video disc or video cassette player. With the use of a special board in a computer, the analogue video (and audio) signal from a disc can be integrated with computer-generated data, providing full multimedia integration within a single work-station. Full motion video from discs (or cassettes) can be combined on the same screen with text and graphics generated by the computer, either taking the whole screen with 'overlays' or 'windows' for text; or with the video itself in a 'window' on the computer screen, with text or computer-generated graphics in the remaining area. While both video cassette and video disc machines can be linked to a computer, computer control is more precise and access is quicker on a video disc or CD-ROM.

Software called *authorware* can be created that allows someone with little knowledge of computer programming to design computer-based learning materials, by using pre-designed *templates*, which guide the developer of the instructional material who, using the authorware templates, enters data, such as subject information, diagrams, questions, answers, and alternative pathways through the material.

When information can be shared between several terminals through a system of inter-connected cables, this is called a *network*. If the network is within one campus or institution, it is called a local area network, or *LAN*. Networks can be very useful for exchanging information between computers and for accessing mainframes and other servers. LANs can also carry electronic communications such as electronic mail (*e-mail*).

Within a single distance education institution, it is important to ensure that mainframes, client servers and microcomputers can all inter-connect with one another without too much difficulty, as there will always be a need to move information from one system to another. For instance, work prepared by an academic on a microcomputer may need to be transferred to a client server for the next stage of electronic publishing. This need not be a physical link, in the form of connected cables, but it does mean that data generated from one computer and stored on discs can be read by another machine, without losing document formatting or control codes, etc. This is facilitated by standardising on a particular operating system and word processing software.

Although computers got their name originally from their power to process long or complex numerical calculations, they now serve a wide range of functions. Furthermore, as computer processing power increases, it becomes possible to do tasks on microcomputers today that computers 100 times their size could not do even 10 years ago. The key trends are:

- increased storage capacity, through improved microprocessor chip technology, external hard drives, and compact discs – the greater capacity of the latter enabling digitised audio, video and graphics to be stored;
- multimedia: integration of video, audio and text within the architecture of the computer itself;
- development of software which provides easy-to-use tools for computer applications, including multimedia integration, enabling those without professional training in computing to create learning materials;
- while prices for a computer work-station suitable for education are unlikely to drop much below US$1,000 or £1,500, processing power and functionality are rapidly increasing for the same price;
- increased networking capacity through the use of *servers*, i.e. networked computers that share common information, and act like digital telephone exchanges or switches;
- progression to common operating standards, allowing material developed on one kind of computer to be used 'transparently' on another kind;
- a move to more flexible 'interfaces' between the human user and the computer, through voice commands and voice recognition, pointing and hand gestures to control programming, and artificial intelligence to enable computers better to interpret human commands and requirements.

It will be many years before this rapid development in computer technology starts to slacken off. Thus computers will become more and more powerful, while their functionality and ease of use will continue to improve.

DIFFERENT APPLICATIONS OF COMPUTER-BASED LEARNING IN OPEN LEARNING AND DISTANCE EDUCATION

Computers have a wide variety of applications in distance education and open learning:

- administration;
- student assessment;
- communications;
- desk-top and electronic publishing;
- computer-based learning;
- electronic distribution of materials.

It is essential to manage all these services in an integrated way. Increasingly, the technology enables widely differing administrative and educational functions to be better integrated. Thus registration, tutor allocation, delivery of materials, on-line teaching and student assessment can all be handled through the same computer service. However, since the focus of this book is on educational rather than administrative issues, I will discuss primarily the use of computers for teaching and learning.

ACCESS

Factors influencing access

There are several major factors to be considered before the decision to teach through computers in open learning and distance education is made.

Demographics

Currently, personal computers are found in less than one third of homes in most developed countries. The most recent census in Canada found that approximately 25 per cent of all households in British Columbia had a home computer in 1991 (Statistics Canada, 1992). Even fewer would have had modems. There was a heavy bias towards high income families in home computer ownership, the average household annual income of home computer owners in British Columbia in 1991 being C$63,000 (US$47,250).

However, this is an area where access is changing rapidly, and distance education students tend to have a slightly higher level of access to home-based technology than the general population, as Table 9.1 indicates.

Black *et al.* (1994) found that of a random sample of 482 Open Learning Agency students in 1984, only 23 per cent said that they did not have convenient access to a computer for study purposes and 60 per cent said

Table 9.1 Convenient access to computers for study purposes by distance education students

Date	% at home	% anywhere	Country	Reference
1986	18	33	UK	Kirkwood, 1987
1987	36	56	Holland	van Meurs/Bouhuijs, 1989
1989	79	95	Norway	Rekkedal, 1990
1991	46	82	Canada	Conway, 1991
1994	60	77	Canada	Black *et al.*, 1994

they had a personal computer at home. (This study was conducted *before* OLA started offering courses requiring a computer.)

It can be seen then that in countries like Canada, computer access is now becoming widespread amongst distance learners (OLA courses attract students from a much wider range of backgrounds than students in conventional Canadian universities – see Black, 1992).

Standardisation

Another factor affecting access has been the variety of incompatible computers owned by students. Studies at the UK Open University and Athabasca University found that no single common computer system dominated in terms of home ownership. Conway (1991) found that Athabasca University students had between them computers from 27 different manufacturers.

To keep down the cost of development of computer-based learning, it is highly desirable to standardise on one complete system specification. Establishing a common computing standard for all courses has several advantages. Students for instance know that once they have purchased equipment, they will not need to change their personal computers when moving to another course.

Fortunately, though, the technology has advanced to the stage where standardisation is becoming less of an issue. For instance, the computer conferencing system recently installed by the Open Learning Agency (FirstClass Server) can be used with Windows and Macintosh operating systems without problems. Furthermore, in 1994, 54 per cent of Open Learning Agency students had convenient access to an IBM PC or clone, and only 19 per cent to other makes. If programmes requiring either IBM/clones or Macintosh machines had been offered to students in Spring 1994, 69 per cent of currently registered students could have participated, without the need to purchase a machine.

One limiting factor of establishing an institution-wide home computing policy is that in order to ensure maximum access, there is a tendency to set standards to the lowest possible denominator. This means that some of the more advanced uses of computer-based learning, using multimedia, will not be available in the near future for home-based learners, because at the moment such applications require powerful personal computers and peripherals such as hard discs or CD-ROMs that increase the cost of the workstation. Again, this is a situation that will change quite rapidly by the year 2000 (see Chapter 12).

A major issue, at least in some countries, seems to be gender bias; Kirkwood (1987) suggests that men are much more likely than women to have access and to use home computers, and this has been confirmed by more recent North American studies.

Institutional policies

A number of approaches have been adopted by distance teaching institutions to facilitate access to computers for students. The UK Open University made arrangements with a national computer wholesaler for students to be able to buy equipment direct from the wholesaler at a reasonable discount, including home delivery. Through the same wholesaler, the university also established a rental scheme, which enabled students to rent a computer, monitor and printer for £150 (US$225) for one year. This was particularly useful for students who only wanted to take one course requiring a computer, or who wanted to try out a computer course without committing themselves to any further courses.

When in 1988 the UK Open University developed its first course to use computer-mediated communications, about 35 per cent of students already had a suitable machine, or made their own arrangements for access; a further 38 per cent of students rented a machine; the remaining 27 per cent purchased a machine in order to take the course (Rumble, 1989). The British government provided a one-off grant to the Open University to help with some of the start-up costs of computer-based courses, enabling the university to cut the fee for the course from £150 to £100.

Because of the concern over access, the UK Open University insists on a strong justification from its course teams before students are required to use a computer for studying. One strong justification is when the course topic is information technology. Courses aimed at certain professional groups (such as managers, accountants, computer scientists, professional engineers) could also assume a high rate of access to computers. Some courses in subjects not directly concerned with computing may require students to have access to a computer, because the course includes a strong component related to the use of information technology (e.g. the use of census data-bases in a course on human geography).

Lastly, a few institutions (e.g. New Jersey Institute of Technology, Jutland Open University in Denmark) supply computers to students (Wells, 1992). Supplying or renting machines to students may sound like an expensive option, but we shall see that this may actually cost less than other more conventional approaches to distance education.

Access via study centres

Making it easy for students to purchase or rent machines is certainly likely to be better than requiring home-based students to go to a study centre to access computer facilities. Wells (1992) indicates clearly in her survey of empirical studies of CMC that study centre attendance is not a preferred option for most home-based distance learners.

Lorentsen (1989) found low usage of computers by Danish students who had to use a local study centre compared with those who had access at home, and she also found that home-based students performed better, in that they learned more quickly and were more participative.

The UK Open University located computer terminals in its study centres as early as 1970, for students following a number of maths and science courses. A report to its external Visiting Committee (1988) stated that:

> Tutorial CAL, where this relied upon study centre based machines, proved not to be very successful, largely because students had to expend time and money to travel to study centres. Experiments showed that some of these problems could be overcome if students had access to PCs at home.
>
> The Open University (1988, p. 24)

If study centres are to be used, they need a role different from providing back-up to home-based students who do not have access at home to computers.

The Open Learning Agency has attempted to overcome these problems by setting up a limited number of 'dedicated' learning centres with advanced technology (video conferencing, computer-based training, multimedia, including video discs and CD-ROM linked to computers) not available in homes or most workplaces. The centres have full-time staff, who supervise equipment, schedule facilities and provide support for learners. Learners can 'drop-in' between shifts or jobs, and can have individual learning programmes developed with the help of local centre tutors/counsellors.

These centres are operated in collaboration with local colleges, businesses and government, and are not aimed primarily at independent distance learners studying liberal arts programmes for a degree or college programmes for a diploma, but at people in the workforce requiring upgrading and basic skills. The learning centres have been established only when particular target groups and funding support have been identified.

Workplace training

Some companies provide special on-site 'drop-in' training centres, where workers can access computer-based training equipment. Other companies (for instance, Lloyds Bank in the UK) have installed equipment such as computer controlled video disc players specifically for training at local work-sites; others, such as the Abbey National Building Society, have provided computer-based training via the employee's desk-top computer (Employment Department, 1991).

In British Columbia, employers lease work-stations and associated course materials, such as video discs and computer software, for training in the workplace, from Open Learning Agency learning centres.

The Open Learning Agency is targeting some of its computer courses to certain categories of work-placed training, where learners are expected to have access to computers for work purposes.

Defining the target group

It is clear that for some time to come, substantial numbers of potential distance learners will not have access at home to a personal computer, and even fewer will also have modems. There are also income and gender biases in home access in directions contrary to those who see distance education as a means to open access to disadvantaged groups.

At the same time, there are particular target groups for whom access is not a major issue. While requiring *all* students to have access to a personal computer will exclude many potential distance learners, it is also not wise to put a blanket ban on any course that would require the use of computers. There are groups for whom access to a computer is not a major problem. There are arrangements that can be made to overcome student access problems, and access to computer technology in the home and the workplace will improve over time.

It is important then for an institution to have a coherent long-term strategy for computer-based delivery, and a student computing policy that is well communicated both to staff and to potential learners, and which is reviewed periodically. It is also important to monitor closely home access for computers, and the changing markets for open and distance learning.

TEACHING AND LEARNING: PRE-PROGRAMMED COMPUTER-BASED LEARNING

There are two quite different forms of teaching via a computer: pre-programmed computer-based learning, or CBL; and computer-mediated communications, or CMC. Multimedia, at the time of writing, is mainly a more sophisticated version of pre-programmed computer-based learning.

Because there are major instructional differences between CBL and CMC, this chapter deals only with pre-programmed computer-based learning, and the next chapter with computer-mediated communication.

There are a number of terms used for pre-programmed computer-based learning (e.g. CBL, CAL, CAI, CBT, CML, CMI), but while there are subtle differences in approach between each of these terms, what each has in common is that the learner works through pre-designed material, inter-acting by answering questions embedded within the materials and choosing options or 'routes' through the learning material. The computer program is also capable of using student responses to questions to control routes through the material, and/or to provide feedback on learner responses to questions. Computer-based learning programmes can also be designed to assess students, and keep records of progress. These records can be accessed by a tutor or instructor (computer-managed learning).

Recent technological developments now enable video, audio, and animated graphics to be integrated within a single desk-top computer. Relatively low-cost desk-top computers (starting around US$2,500 for a full work-station) can now take analogue video and audio from video or audio cassettes, video cameras or microphones, and digitise and compress them as computer data. Software within the machine allows these various sources of data to be integrated into multimedia presentations. Multimedia developments have thus increased the presentational features of pre-programmed computer-based learning.

Adding a video disc or CD-ROM to a computer widens the range of possible applications. There are several ways computer-controlled video discs/CD-ROMs can be used:

- a complete 'package' of video disc/CD-ROM and pre-programmed computer software can be bought in; this needs care, though, to ensure that the computer software and disc are compatible with existing 'playback' equipment;
- a pre-recorded disc (say on animals) can be bought in, and a computer program to integrate with it can be produced (or adapted) in house. Thus the computer program may add additional textual information and diagrams, set tests and require student responses. With recent developments, it is becoming more and more viable for instructors to develop their own integrated multimedia productions using 'libraries' of video, sound, data and text;
- a set of materials can be produced from scratch, developing the video, audio and the computer program at the same time, ensuring their complete integration; this however is extremely complex and expensive.

Video discs and CD-ROM, linked to computers, have tremendous educational potential. However, they require a great deal of sophistication, and can be very expensive to produce. They are likely to be valuable within conventional institutions, summer schools or even study centres, and also at the workplace, where the same training programme is required in many outlets; however, they are unlikely to be suitable for home-based instruction, at least in the near future.

The key feature of pre-programmed computer-based learning is that the learner interacts solely with the computer; there is no direct contact, through the computer, with a tutor, instructor or other students, although a tutor or teacher may be available by phone or at a local study centre.

Pre-programmed computer-based learning can also of course be combined with other forms of instruction, such as books, video tapes, etc. One such example is the Canadian Pathfinder integrated learning system. As well as including an element of direct instruction through computer-assisted instruction, Pathfinder also manages the learners' progress, by testing, tracking work, diagnosing further work, and providing reports on learners' progress.

There has not been a great deal of use of pre-programmed computer-based learning in single-mode distance teaching institutions. In most cases where it has been used, for example in the Open University of the Netherlands, the British Open University, FernUniversität in Germany, and the Open Learning Agency in Canada, students have usually had to go to local centres or residential summer schools to access computers or terminals. However, all students (about 4,000 a year) on the British Open University's Technology Foundation course (T102) are required to have an IBM-PC compatible computer, and the course contains a suite of computer-assisted learning materials to provide additional tutorial help for those students who have difficulty with the numeracy strand of the course (Butcher *et al.*, 1989).

The use of pre-programmed computer-based learning is more common in workplace training, although still not widespread. Van der Brande (1993) states that in Europe, 'the main concentration of computer-based training is in the area of banking, finance and insurance, followed by general manufacturing and the public service sector' (p. 99).

It is also being increasingly used in the retail sector. For instance, in 1987 B&Q plc placed computer-controlled video disc equipment in most of its 236 homecare and garden centre stores in Britain, to train its 12,000 employees (Rubin, 1989). Use for training of professionals is also growing. In Ireland, the National Distance Education Centre, in collaboration with the Institute of Chartered Accountants, has developed a 100 hour programme of self-directed instruction on accounting, which includes 40 hours of practical work on IBM-compatible computers, either on their own work-stations or at 14 study centres across Ireland. Over 2,000 people participated in this course (Van der Brande, 1993).

One common use for pre-programmed computer-based learning in open learning contexts in North America is for adult basic education (ABE) courses aimed at adults who have not completed high school graduation. For instance, the Open Learning Agency has used a system developed by the Jostens Corporation in its learning centres. Learners who need to improve their reading and writing skills can 'drop in' at the local centres, and use the system when it suits them. Pathfinder has been used in similar ways by Native Indians in First Nations Learning Centres in British Columbia (Friesen, 1991).

Benefits of pre-programmed computer-based learning

There are several instructional benefits claimed for pre-programmed computer-based learning:

- *Presentation of information*: it can present and store information requiring low levels of symbolic representation (e.g. words, numbers and simple line drawings) on less powerful and cheaper personal computers, and can present and store information requiring high levels of symbolic representation (e.g. digitised and compressed moving video, audio, and high quality colour animations and still graphics) on more powerful and hence more expensive personal computers or work-stations;
- *Tutorial dialogue*: it can present information and, using embedded questions and learner responses to these questions, can simulate dialogue with the learner;
- *Simulation and modelling*: it is excellent for manipulating quantifiable and rule-governed variables, as in simulations, where students can input data, or supply information, and observe the effects. Usually, but not always, this needs more powerful machines. The Open University of the Netherlands has developed several simulation programmes for its courses (de Vries and Huisman, 1989);
- *Testing*: it is useful for testing learners' knowledge, where the responses can be fitted into pre-determined coded categories;
- *Individualised study*: it allows learners to work at their own pace and to obtain feedback on their progress;
- *Diagnosis*: it can use learners' responses to identify areas where further study is necessary – indeed, it can prevent learners from moving to new learning material until they have mastered previous learning material;
- *Mastery learning*: combining testing, feedback, repetition, and diagnosis, learners can progress to the point where they can achieve correct answers 100 per cent of the time, when assessed;
- *Learner choice*: it can allow learners to select materials, levels of difficulty, or pathways through subject matter;
- *Customisation of learning materials*: more advanced hardware and software now allow learners and local teachers to incorporate new material, such as textual input, audio, video or graphics. This allows teachers to 'customise' pre-prepared materials, and learners to develop

their own multimedia projects, which can be assessed by local teachers or tutors;

- *Adaptation to learning styles*: the application of artificial intelligence techniques and expert systems allows the computer to use a number of different teaching approaches, adapted to learners' responses and learning styles;
- *Motivation*: Friesen (1991) reports the sense of prestige and accomplishment of adult basic education learners using computers to learn, especially where the program uses innovative or amusing techniques for gaining and holding interest.

Limitations of pre-programmed computer-based learning

Despite these potential benefits, there are several good reasons why pre-programmed computer-based learning has not been used to any great extent in distance education:

- *Access to the right equipment*: a major drawback is that good quality pre-programmed computer-based learning generally requires more powerful computers than those currently available for use at home or even work, e.g. CD-ROM players or compression software. Some of the more powerful – and hence more effective – programs require greater memory and power than the cheaper range of computers in homes can handle;
- *Poor teaching strategies*: pre-programmed computer-based learning has been widely criticised for using poor teaching strategies. Van der Brande (1993) claims that 'only 3 per cent of educational software has been written in the context of an articulated pedagogic rationale' (p. 23). There is often a heavy emphasis on drill and practice, and passive 'page-turning'. Learners are usually restricted to a limited range of responses (multiple-choice questions, requiring one key-stroke, or individual key-words). The emphasis has been mainly on comprehension and memorisation of facts and principles. It has not proved an easy medium for developing the higher level learning skills of analysis, synthesis, evaluation, or problem-solving, where there are no fixed rules or procedures;
- *Lack of flexibility*: pre-programmed computer-based learning, where content, questions and answers are pre-structured, has a great deal of difficulty in handling subject matter where learners can provide legitimate but unexpected responses. Learners often get frustrated because they have given a perfectly 'reasonable' response, but it is not 'recognised' as such by the computer. It is not a medium that lends itself to subject matter where there is ambiguity or no 'correct' answers or procedures;
- *Costs*: developing original, high-quality computer-based learning

material is expensive and requires highly skilled designers, if more than drill and practice techniques, or simple memorisation of facts or principles, are required.

● *Professional isolation*: 'ICAI (intelligent computer assisted instruction) has in the main been done by artificial intelligence scientists with little, if any, involvement with educational technology specialists, classroom instructors or very many real learners'; 'there has been no field testing or evaluation of ICAI programmes in realistic classrooms' (Van der Brande, 1993, p. 23);

● *Broken promises*: artificial intelligence and expert systems, while offering great promise, have by and large failed to make much impact on pre-programmed computer-based learning. It has proved remarkably difficult to model real teacher behaviour in a convincing way on a computer.

There is a major problem inherent in pre-programmed computer-based learning, irrespective of its level of sophistication, or future developments in artificial intelligence or expert systems. The underlying assumption of pre-programmed computer-based learning, and artificial intelligence and expert systems, is that human behaviour (including learning) can be represented and controlled through the application of rules and processes derived from and conforming to a scientific, rationalist approach to how humans behave. In particular, pre-programmed computer-based learning is heavily influenced by behaviourism and cognitive science, which reject any element of conscious will as a dominant element of human behaviour.

Winograd and Flores (1986) argue however that 'we need to replace the rationalist orientation if we want to understand thought, language and action, or to design effective computer tools' (p. 26). Pre-programmed computer-based learning, by restricting interaction between humans, and limiting the learners' ability to responding within pre-determined boundaries, constrains the capacity of the individual to personalise the learning, or to create constructions of knowledge that are unanticipated in the design of the teaching material, but still legitimate.

There are, though, changes occurring in computer-based learning which enable a very different approach to teaching and learning. Multimedia enhancements, such as animation, audio and video, while improving the presentational qualities of pre-programmed computer-based learning, do not necessarily change the instructional approach. Virtual reality may eventually lead to new instructional approaches, if costs can be brought down to more realistic levels.

What is much more significant about multimedia are the user-friendly software tools that allow teachers and learners to add, adapt, remove and edit material. This adds a different dimension to computer-based learning. Instead then of the computer program being all-inclusive, controlling both the content and the instructional methodology, reducing or eliminating the role of the human teacher, and forcing the learner into a narrow range of response modes, it is possible to develop instructional strategies that enable joint input from teachers and learners, allowing learners not only to transform learning materials into forms that have personal relevance and meaning, but also to construct new knowledge, new ways of understanding.

For instance, the teacher or learner can select materials from a range of multimedia sources that are relevant to the curriculum. Using objectives and guidelines set by the teacher, learners can re-construct material to demonstrate their understanding and skills within a subject area. We shall see that when combined with computer-mediated communication, computer-based learning can provide a very powerful instructional paradigm for distance learners.

This does not mean that there is no future role for pre-programmed computer-based learning. There are many learning tasks that need to be memorised, or procedures that need to be followed exactly and without error. For such activities, pre-programmed computer-based learning may be the most cost-effective approach, and multimedia enhancement may improve that effectiveness. However, there are many other learning activities for which such a behaviourist, pre-determined approach is not suitable.

INTERACTIVITY AND USER-FRIENDLINESS

Interactivity

One of the main arguments for the use of computers is that they require learners to interact with the learning material. Computers can encourage learners to respond to learning material and get feedback on their performance; the computer can also use that information to guide learners to the next appropriate step in their learning. Computers thus provide learners with much greater overt interaction than other media. This argument can certainly be justified in terms of the *quantity* of interaction; questions remain though about the *quality* of the interaction provided by pre-programmed computer-based learning.

Also, designing good quality computer-marked assignments or feedback questions, with 'credible' but still incorrect 'distractor' answers, requires considerable skill. Students often try to beat the system, by guessing or looking for the obvious answer, rather than giving a correct answer based on understanding or deductive thinking. Nevertheless, in certain areas, such as mathematics, where it is possible to specify definitively correct answers, computer-marked assignments can be useful.

There is a great deal of work going into the development of interactive video and multimedia, because these provide ways to increase the interactivity of learning through visual materials. However, the ultimate value of multimedia will depend on its ability to provide the rich range of interaction and feedback required to allow the learner to respond flexibly and creatively. If students are forced to respond through a pre-programmed software application, the pedagogic benefits of analysis and interpretation available through the audio and video elements of multimedia may be lost, because of the restricted means by which the learner can interact.

Computer games

The most successful use of interactivity, in terms of capturing an audience to a level almost of addiction, has been in the use of computer games. Indeed, 'edutainment', games aimed at the educational market, are forecast as the next 'wave' of educational technology. Loftus and Loftus (1983) early on recognised that computer games are successful because they use well-understood laws of human behaviour to provide stimulus and rewards for game-playing. Loftus and Loftus identified partial reinforcement, and Malone (1980) goal-setting, challenge (i.e. uncertainty of outcome, regulated to the level of the learner) and use of fantasy as some of the key mechanisms that make computer games compulsive.

The issue is not whether computer games are effective as entertainment – they clearly are, and not just with young people – but whether they can be used for effective learning. Loftus and Loftus argued that games can have educational benefits. They can help develop a number of thinking strategies, such as problem-solving, the use of imagery to reinforce memory, and strategy and planning. There is growing interest in MUDs (multi-user domains), where participants on computer networks can interact with games.

What is less clear is how well game skills are generalisable outside a games context. Nevertheless, open learning courses can be designed around games which provide increasingly complex and realistic models of social or economic behaviour (such as *SimCity*) or which provide learning embedded in a 'challenge' requiring the development of an understanding of geography, science or mathematics to problem-solve.

There is also the negative side of games, such as: addiction to the 'rewards' offered by games, gender-related issues, the lack of reality of the rewards, the simulated violence that is often a part of computer games, crude design and tasteless graphics, and negative social effects, such as isolation and an overemphasis on competition and winning. Once again, it comes down to a question of design and educational goals. Computer games can be designed in ways that assist the learning process, and can be useful as one strategy for encouraging learning.

Summary

Computers lend themselves better to more behaviouristic approaches to teaching, where 'unchallengeable' facts or procedures are to be learned. It is not surprising then that computer-assisted learning is more common in training and vocational education than in higher education. This may change as artificial intelligence techniques are applied to computer-assisted learning, but these programs are likely to be expensive to develop and will require powerful machines, making them less appropriate for distance education students.

Much more promising is the new generation of computers and computer software that allow teachers and learners to create or modify their own learning materials, through the use of multimedia editing tools.

COSTS

Once again, this is a difficult technology to cost, for a number of reasons. The power of this technology (in terms of data processing, storage and transmission) is increasing rapidly, thus enabling better quality symbolic presentation such as compressed video and audio. Even more importantly, the software tools that enable the design and development of multimedia are improving, thus dramatically reducing the labour costs associated with the design and development of computer-based learning. Thus cost data from even a few years ago can be very misleading.

A second difficulty in costing is that as the technology improves, so do the range of possible applications. The earlier model of pre-programmed computer-based learning, based primarily on textual communication, multiple-choice questions, and limited student interaction is quite different from a model based on the learner remotely accessing a wide range of multimedia resources, under the guidance of a 'real' but remote mentor, possibly working collaboratively with other students, and constructing and re-constructing multimedia projects or assignments. Not surprisingly, the cost implications are very different for these two models.

It is then not just that costs of hardware, software, and development are changing, but there is no stable instructional model yet from which to define cost structures; indeed, a wide range of new instructional models will develop from networked multimedia applications.

Lastly, mainly for these reasons, there are very few detailed research papers giving accurate costs for production and distribution of multimedia materials.

There is evidence though that at least in industrial and military training contexts, pre-programmed computer-based learning can be more cost-effective than classroom instruction. Van der Brande (1993, p. 112) reported that British Telecom used a CD-ROM system to train its operators to use computerised telephone exchanges. The cost of this system was 6 million ecus, compared with an estimated 60 million ecus for using traditional methods (this analysis includes working time lost by trainees).

Beijderwellen (1990) found that for more than 50 students a year, an interactive video disc program on geology developed from scratch was more cost-effective for the institution than a summer school site visit. (Using the disc also reduced direct costs for the students.)

Schlecter (1988) reported that the costs for a ten-terminal system could range from US$20 to $100 per student contact hour for individualised learning. However, in a later, well-designed comparative study (Schlecter, 1990), he found that groups of four learners per terminal learned faster than individual learners, without any significant differences in learning achievement, and needed fewer support services ('proctors' or tutors). He concluded that 'small group CBT could reduce costs associated with this instructional medium by a factor of five' (p. 333).

Stahmer and Green (1993) have produced some guidelines for analysing the costs of training. They distinguish between three types of CBT production:

- very high-end production/technology value: multimedia, in-house production;
- medium-end development: contracting with a courseware development firm;
- low-end development: buying 'off-the-shelf' materials.

Assuming a CBT 'course' of 27 hours for 150 students using one work-station over three years, and a total of one hour tutor support time per student over the course, Stahmer and Green produced the figures shown in Table 9.2.

Table 9.2 Costs for different levels of CBT development

Levels of development	High-end C$	Medium C$	Low C$
Fixed (production)	571,600	170,000	70,000
Cost per hour	21,170	6,297	2,593
Cost per work-station (1:150 students)	5,000	5,000	5,000
Tutor support per student	80.50	80.50	80.50

Table 9.3 Cost per student study hour for CBT

| No. of students | Type of development | | | | | |
| | High | | Medium | | Low | |
	C$	US$	C$	US$	C$	US$
0	0	0	0	0	0	0
150	145	109	46	34	22	16
250	89	67	30	22	15	11
500	47	35	17	14	10	7
625	38	28	15	11	9	7
1,000	25	19	11	8	7	5

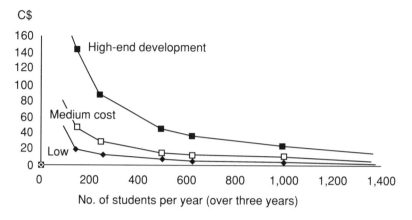

Figure 9.1 CBT training: cost per student study hour

These figures enable the cost per student per hour, over three years, to be calculated, for varying numbers of students, and different levels of production (Table 9.3).

These data are consistent with Schlecter's range of costs, for 'high-end' production. Even at the low end, costs per study hour are still relatively high, compared with some of the other technologies. It must be remembered though that these costs are amortised over three years, compared with eight years for the other technologies.

Figure 9.1 indicates the need for large numbers of learners to use CBT material, particularly for high-end development, if unit costs are to be kept down.

In general, good quality CBL is very expensive to produce. Buying in courseware packages already developed is possible, but as well as the similar problems associated with buying in print or video packages, such as finding appropriate material to fit the needs of the course, there may also be additional problems of computer compatibility, because of the variety of computer systems that students may have. However, new instructional approaches built around multimedia promise lower costs and greater flexibility than the pre-programmed learning approach.

ORGANISATIONAL ISSUES

In some ways, the organisational requirements for the more 'traditional' pre-programmed computer-based learning are similar to those for print, television or other one-way media. There is need for a team approach, which would include a subject expert, and a specialist in the design of computer-based learning. The main argument is whether these specialists should be located in the computer department, or within an academic department, or in an instructional design or materials department. These boundary issues however can become even more pronounced with multimedia developments, since they tend to bring in an even wider range of specialists (television, audio, graphics, instructional designers, as well as computer specialists).

The question then increasingly becomes: who is in charge? It may seem obvious that the academic subject expert would be the team leader, but what is required as well as academic expertise is project management and media selection and design skills. If a true team approach is followed, it probably does not matter in which department individual specialists are located, nor who is team leader. What is more important is a well-defined and agreed project management process, an organisational structure that enables the setting up (and disbandment) of teams of people from various departments to work on particular projects, an understanding of team-work, a willingness to collaborate, and well-organised media support services.

There is a compelling argument for the establishment of a central 'resource' for multimedia development, under a manager and technician, who keep abreast of the technological developments, make sure that appropriate hardware and software are available and installed for easy access, maintain and up-date equipment and hardware, maintain and develop access to resources such as clip art and special effects, provide access to special equipment and skills not available in-house, clear copyright and store newly created material for later use in other contexts, and who help train staff in multimedia design and development.

These organisational arrangements are easy though in comparison to the challenge of re-organising and re-structuring the learning and teaching environment, so that the full potential of computer-based learning materials is developed in a cost-effective manner. Staff in dual-mode institutions will need release from or major re-organisation of their teaching time to be able to create learning materials, the delivery of teaching needs to be re-organised, with less emphasis on lectures, and more emphasis on individualised and small group learning, with teaching staff available on a more informal and accessible basis for academic discourse and dialogue with students. In other words, the whole basis of teaching in conventional universities and colleges needs to be re-organised, and not just for the off-campus students, if the high development cost of computer-based learning is to be justified.

NOVELTY

There is very little novelty associated with the 'traditional' text-based computer-based learning; indeed, its past poor reputation is likely to militate against its use.

However, multimedia, 'edutainment' and virtual reality have very strong 'novelty' characteristics, especially in terms of more powerful symbolic representation and interaction. Nevertheless, we have seen that these are not cheap and easy media to work with, and fancy graphics and low-levels of interaction can be counter-productive in an educational environment. Instructional design remains critical for educational success.

SPEED

Well-designed, pre-programmed computer-based materials take a long time to design, and they are not easy to change, especially if they are based on 'branching' programmes, because a change in one part of the material can have ripple effects right through the programme.

Curriculum approaches based around student access to multimedia resources, with an instructor providing a 'tutorial' or guiding role, can be established more quickly. However, making such programmes work often requires a good deal of support and guidance to learners, who will usually need some time to adjust to this method of learning.

CONCLUSIONS

Pre-programmed computer-based learning can have some advantages in an open and distance learning environment:

- In areas where repetition, mastery and practice are important, computer-based learning can be the most interesting and effective means of meeting these goals;
- Multimedia developments are improving the attractiveness of pre-programmed computer-based learning;
- Developments in software are making it easier and cheaper to create high quality learning materials;
- The increasing ease of importing video, graphics, audio, and text into a multimedia format enable learners and 'local' teachers to construct, adapt or re-structure learning materials, thus widening the range and flexibility of teaching approaches;
- High-cost computer-based learning materials can be cost-effective, particularly when used in a corporate environment, where the costs of more traditional classroom-based instruction are high, and when loss of work-time, travel and accommodation of workers are taken into account.

However, there are still some major disadvantages of using computer-based learning materials in open and distance learning:

- Many students do not have the equipment to access computer-based materials, and especially for multimedia, will not have access for some time at home;
- Although the cost of development is coming down, it is still high; there is still a shortage of good quality, off-the-shelf courseware;

- A great deal of computer-based material (even – or especially – multimedia) is very poorly designed from an educational standpoint;
- Designing good quality educational courseware needs a high level of instructional design skills and a team approach; people with these skills are rare, and the organisational changes needed are beyond the will or capacity of many institutions.

There is no doubt that multimedia pre-programmed material will play an increasingly important role in the future of education. However, progress will be slow, and will depend on the emergence of new curriculum approaches that exploit the ability of teachers and learners to construct their own materials, or re-construct materials accessed from multimedia resource data-bases.

10 Computer-mediated communication

COMPUTERS AS A COMMUNICATIONS TOOL: REVOLUTIONISING EDUCATION?

> At issue is how to create a complex knowledge domain, especially how to build upon and retain the complexity of an environment like computer conferencing so that users learn to be critical thinkers by considering issues and ideas from many perspectives.
>
> (Harasim, 1990, p. 59)

There are two important educational features that distinguish computer-mediated communication from pre-programmed computer-based learning. The first is that the learner can be in contact with teachers and other learners. The second is that remote data-bases can be accessed through electronic networks, and information can be extracted from a data-base and down-loaded into the learner's or teacher's own computer, and stored for later use. Thus any learner or teacher with access to a computer connected to a telephone can communicate with any other similarly connected learner, teacher, or remote data-base, currently mainly in the form of textual messages. The interaction is not so much *with* the computer, as *through* it, to other people or sources of information.

A number of educators are trying to develop new approaches to teaching and learning, to develop new 'paradigms' of education, based on computer-mediated communication. It is still open to debate whether this technology will result in truly new paradigms, or merely allow valued old paradigms to be used more effectively for learners at a distance. Nevertheless, there is a great deal of innovation in the use of computer-mediated communication in education, and it is also one of the fastest growing technologies, in terms of the numbers of teachers and learners who are using it.

THE TECHNOLOGY

Networking

The key element of computer-mediated communication is the integration of the desk-top computer with the public telephone network.

Such services require a local microcomputer or terminal, a communications software package for each local microcomputer, a separate box or integrated chip called a *modem* which converts computer data into a suitable form for transmission via the telephone system, and a connection between the modem and a standard telephone line. Modems can operate at different speeds, depending on the volume of data to be transmitted.

In most cases, a user will have an 'address' (i.e. a telephone number) which will connect the user to a host computer which provides, via software packages, a range of services, such as electronic mail or computer conferencing facilities. Thus an educational institution can establish an 'internal' network of users, using a local area network, and learners and teachers remote from any campus can also be connected to the institution's network, via the public telephone system, thus creating an institutional wide area network. An institution's host computer can also provide 'gateways' or access to other, external networks, such as the Internet. Alternatively, an individual can access other networks and their services directly.

These networks, originally established for military and later research purposes, are now extensive and world-wide. By October 1993, the number of people who were computer networked (i.e. 'on-line') and thus able to send or receive messages to and from anyone else on-line, was estimated to be approximately 35 million (Godwin, 1994).

Services

Computer-mediated communication constitutes a number of different services.

Electronic mail

This is functionally a combination of postal mail and the telephone, allowing for one-to-one communication over telephone lines, but using textual rather than voice communication (although increasingly, digital voice and video is becoming available via computer networks). Learners or teachers 'log-on' from their personal computer to a remote computer, which has software which stores electronic messages in 'mailboxes' according to the electronic address. Users then can access their messages on-line, or download them into their own computer, and reply to messages or send messages to other users by transmitting to the central computer, which then assigns the messages to the appropriate mailbox.

Work-stations and local area networks can be connected via the public telephone system to other networks or sites. For instance, regional offices may be connected to the headquarters for local registration of students, or for entering grades for assignments or even for examinations done locally. Since data can be sent through telephone lines or even by satellite, it is possible to use E-mail for international connections, at very low cost (much cheaper and faster than sending a letter, and cheaper than fax).

Bulletin boards

A number of on-line bulletin boards and journals have been created for open learning and distance education, such as DEOS-L, organised by the American Centre for Distance Education at Penn State University, and available on the Internet. Thus any message or article posted is automatically received by all those who have joined a particular service. These bulletin boards or journals can be 'read-only', or can allow anyone receiving messages to add their own messages.

Computer conferencing

This provides a more sophisticated electronic environment than electronic mail. Mason (1994, p. 50) has summarised the key features of computer conferencing:

- electronic mail to one or more individuals on the system;
- conferences in which a set of participants can read and write a group of messages;
- sub-conferences within conferences so that different topics of discussion can be distinguished;
- user information such as details about participants, lists of conferences, dates of last log-ons, search facilities for particular messages;
- levels of privilege, for initiating conferencing, moderating conferences, removing messages, reading only or reading and writing messages in particular conferences.

As Mason points out, 'one of the key elements of a conferencing system is the structure provided for grouping messages'. This enables the conference 'moderator' or teacher to organise conferences to fit the nature of the subject matter, splitting off topics for further discussion where necessary, and allowing learners to focus on the specific topics of interest to them.

Data-bases

An increasing number of data-bases can now be directly accessed via electronic networks. A data-base is basically any form of content stored in digital format. Thus several encyclopaedias have been made available in digital format and can be accessed through the Internet.

One of the most important data-bases in distance education is the International Centre for Distance Learning (ICDL) library service. ICDL is funded by a number of organisations, including the United Nations University and the Commonwealth of Learning. It is physically located at the British Open University, and has the largest world-wide collection of publications on open learning and distance education. All its entries are catalogued electronically, and the catalogue can be accessed on-line. (The catalogue is also available on CD-ROM.) Full text material supplied in digital format to ICDL is also available on-line, provided the author has given permission.

Off-line editing

Software is now available for some E-mail and conferencing systems that allow users to interact with their messages without being connected the whole time through the telephone system (off-line editing). The user goes on-line, and the software collects all messages and downloads them into the local work-station, then logs (switches) off from the telephone network. The user then responds to the messages at the local work-station, and when finished, the software automatically logs on again, and dumps the responses into the host computer, then logs off. This has two advantages: it reduces dramatically the time on-line, and therefore long distance charges; and it frees up the domestic telephone for other uses.

The technology is still fast developing in this field. One of the main advantages of current technology is that it is relatively cheap and simple to use. There is a move away from 'command-driven' to menu-driven and icon-driven screens, making systems more user-friendly. While most systems are still primarily textual, graphics, voice and video prototypes are already in existence, and will become commonplace soon.

ACCESS

There is a major similarity with computer-based learning in the issues regarding access. There are however some issues that are particular to CMC.

Learners need access to a telephone line. Even in countries with advanced telephone networks, such as Canada, there are people without appropriate telephone access. 'Noisy' lines can cause interference or loss, not all areas have digital switches or exchanges, and modems cannot be used on party lines.

Also, the telephone cannot be used for voice communication when being used for computer communication. Schools in particular may have only one telephone line, which needs to be dedicated for voice use, and there may not be an internal local area network that will hook up the computer in the classroom to the school telephone system. Thus if there is just one telephone line into the home or school, computer communication can tie up the telephone for long periods (particularly since many people become addicted to being on-line). Off-line editing can alleviate but not completely remove this problem, and an increasing number of homes in North America have at least two phone lines, one for voice and one for data, including fax as well as computer networking.

Lastly, one needs a modem as well as a computer and telephone line for CMC. Some portable computers come with an in-built modem, but usually it is an additional expense for learners. Conway (1991) found that roughly one third of the Athabasca University students surveyed had modems. Black *et al.* (1994) also found that 34 per cent of OLA students had access to a modem. Nevertheless, 53 per cent of the OLA students surveyed said they would take a course requiring a modem, and only 25 per cent said they would not (the rest were undecided).

TEACHING FUNCTIONS

There has been a growing use of CMC in open and distance learning since the late 1980s. Wells (1992) has provided an excellent summary of CMC applications in distance education. She identified 93 institutions or networks that had or were offering CMC courses in 20 different countries. While electronic mail may be used occasionally for communications between tutors and students, and for the submission and marking of assignments, computer conferencing is by far the most common form of computer-mediated teaching in distance education.

As with most other technologies, CMC can be used in a variety of ways, from being an optional extra on a course where the main body of instruction is carried by other media, such as print or face-to-face teaching, right through to where CMC is the primary teaching medium. Its use may be either optional or mandatory for the student.

One of the largest single applications has been on the British Open University's second level undergraduate course: DT200: *An Introduction to Information Technology: Social and Technological Issues.* In the first year of the course, 1,364 students registered. The course was developed using an otherwise standard Open University approach, covering a 32-week continuous period, with students expected to spend about 420 hours studying.

The course was made up of specially designed printed course units, a large 'Reader', in the form of a book made up of specially selected articles from journals or books, 16 × 25-minute television programmes, and several audio cassettes. On top of all this was added a computer conferencing component, which linked students and tutors together. As part of the course and student assessment process, students had to log-on, and work on a project via computer conferencing. It can be seen then that CMC was only part of the course, but the course was designed so that students would be at a disadvantage in terms of assessment if they avoided this part of it (see Mason and Kaye, 1989, for more details of this course).

A large number of conferences of different kinds were established for DT200. Each of the 65 part-time tutors was able to establish a conference for their own group of approximately 20–25 students. Several other conferences were also set up, including 'national' conferences on each block, allowing central course team members to participate directly. However, in the context of this course, it was found that many of the individual tutor conferences did not really get going in the first year, so in the second year, conferences were organised on a regional basis.

DT200 is unusual, in terms of the number of students using computer conferencing on a single course. In general, CMC has tended to be used for relatively small numbers of students per course. Wells (1992) found that group size clustered around 25 students per tutor, with some significant variations.

Instructional benefits of computer conferencing

A number of educational benefits for computer conferencing can be identified.

Developing academic discourse

Computer conferencing can be used to develop student skills in analysis, constructing and defending an argument, assembling evidence in support of an argument, and critiquing the work of other learners, as well as the work of other scholars.

Collaborative and project work

Harasim (1989) has stressed the value of computer conferencing for collaborative learning:

> The on-line environment is particularly appropriate for collaborative learning approaches which emphasise group interaction . . . . computer conferencing facilitates the sharing of knowledge and understanding among members of a group who are not working together at the same time or place . . . . the common file of a conference provides participants with a 'shared object' which focuses and organises the group discussions and interactions . . . . The text-based, archived transcript of the interaction facilitates opportunities for reflective interaction . . . . computer conferencing offers opportunities for learning collaborations that have hitherto been impossible.
>
> (Harasim, 1989, p. 52)

Computer conferencing can also facilitate group project work. Several students can work together on a project, which can be assessed. Through the conference archive the 'marker' can assess the contribution of each individual student to the overall project; alternatively, students working together can be assessed collectively.

Knowledge building

Harasim (1990) argues that the collaborative potential of computer conferencing enables students to engage actively in their own knowledge building or knowledge creation, in three ways: through idea generation, idea linking, and idea structuring. Teles (1993) identifies a number of techniques to develop knowledge building through conferencing, under the generic term 'cognitive apprenticeship', i.e. learning 'mediated by access to masters and peers on computer networks' (p. 271). He uses as an example the joint development of a poem between a professional writer and a student in Vancouver. The techniques he lists are:

- *Building knowledge domains*: a mentor not only introduces a learner to the main concepts and facts in a subject area, but also helps develop the necessary cognitive skills;
- *Scaffolding*: this refers to the support, advice, encouragement, and feedback given by the mentor as the learner works towards 'mastery';
- *Reflection*: because of the asynchronous nature of computer conferencing, learners can research and reflect on practice before responding;
- *Exploration*: learners are put in the role of 'experts', to critique or advise on others' work (including the mentor's);
- *Sequencing instruction*: the mentor controls the sequence of instruction (presentation of information, learning of concepts, presentation by learners in their own words of what they have learned, feedback from others);
- *Peer collaboration for expert practice*: co-operatively sharing knowledge with others.

Maximising the knowledge and experience of all participants

This is particularly important for adult learners, who often have specialist knowlege and expertise that is not always available from even the subject specialist. For instance, when I was moderating a 'national' conference on information technology in education and training on DT200, discussion began between three students on the latest technical developments in video disc technology. Each of the students was a professional engineer, working in this field. I was able to encourage them to set up their own separate sub-topic, which other students could read or participate in if they wished.

Increasing equity of participation

Because gender, race, physical appearance, status, or experience are not readily apparent, and because access to conferences can be made available to students and teachers alike, everyone participating is judged solely on the value of their contributions (although this is heavily dependent on the approach adopted by the tutor or moderator).

Cross-cultural participation

Riel (1993) has shown how the ability to link participants in learning circles from different parts of the world through computer conferencing (in this case using the AT&T Learning Network) raises cross-cultural awareness, and brings into the learning process different perspectives from different cultures, a process facilitated by the avoidance of immediate stereotyping through the lack of any obvious visual cultural 'markers', such as gender, race, etc.

Development of reflective writing skills

Mason (1993) identifies three essential elements that when combined make computer-mediated communication a unique communication tool: 'interactive, written exchanges amongst many, widely dispersed people' (p. 23). These features enable CMC to be used to develop writing skills, and especially to help learners reflect creatively on their own writing, as well as on the writing of others. Mason and her collaborators (Mason, 1993) have explored in some detail how computer conferencing has supported and facilitated human communication in written form.

Overcoming social isolation

Mason (1989) has argued that while conferencing cannot substitute for the social life and networks which traditional university campuses offer, it can provide a unique kind of contact and atmosphere. My own experience on DT200 was that conferencing had a revolutionary impact on some students and teachers alike, radically changing the learning context from one of a centrally controlled, hierarchical approach to learning, to one where at least some students not only fully participated, but to some extent took over the communication network to meet their own learning and social needs.

Emotional involvement

Associated with the removal of social isolation, computer conferencing can result in strong emotional involvement for learners in the process of learning and communicating with others which is unusual not only in distance education, but often in conventional education. Johnson-Lenz and Johnson-Lenz (1993) report a number of spontaneous testimonials from computer conferencing participants which indicate that conferencing provided them with a deeply satisfying and emotional environment. For example:

> You have all contributed greatly to both heart and mind and at all times touched me, brought me to deep levels of compassion, made me laugh, lifted me up out of my Why-Oh-Why and most of all listened to what I have to say and responded.

> I feel such a strong sense of sharing with all of you. We approach through this darkened screen and find kindred souls to share with. Thank you all.
>
> (Johnson-Lenz and Johnson-Lenz, 1993, pp. 214–15)

It can be seen then that as well as enabling discussion and informal communication between learners and teachers, computer conferencing can also encourage a more open-ended and social form of learning than pre-programmed computer-based learning, thus being appropriate for subject areas where interpretation and controversy are important. It also provides a means by which students can negotiate their own areas of study.

It is particularly useful for areas where most learners have relevant knowledge and experience to contribute to the learning process, such as in professional development or more advanced level courses. As Johnson-Lenz and Johnson-Lenz point out (p.198), computer conferencing can also support subjective knowledge, such as intuition, as well as objective knowledge, thus allowing for a much more holistic approach to learning and knowledge (including self-knowledge).

Ready access to help and support

Students can use a conference to get help on specific topics, either from their tutor or often from other students. Sometimes other students can provide better understanding or assistance than the tutor. Tutors can also call on help from other tutors, thus maximising the range of knowledge in the tutorial team.

Feedback to and direct student contact with the central academic team

For me, DT200 was the first time in nearly 20 years at the Open University when I felt I was in direct contact on a regular basis with students. I was able to understand better how students were responding to the pre-prepared print and audio-visual material.

Instructional limitations of computer-mediated communication

However, it is not all good news. There are a number of major limitations of CMC in education.

Information overload

This can take many forms. Once on E-mail or distribution lists, one can be overwhelmed by the number of messages arriving daily. I once went on holiday for two weeks, and came back to 800 messages in one computer conference, mainly due to a chain reaction, where the conference I had been moderating was accidently 'transported' by a participant into other conferences, and all the comments from all the other conferences ended up in my E-mail. Even with a strict and focused approach to E-mail, I am averaging about 30 'critical' messages a day, which results in a backlog of over 400 messages after a two-week holiday period.

Peer group pressure often assists instructors in ensuring that trivial messages or 'diads' (conversations between two individuals) do not clog up discussion in the academic conferences. The use of 'spaces' such as student cafés or open forums for those who want to chat is also useful. Nevertheless, most participants new to conferencing (and some who are very experienced) need some guidance to prevent overload.

Similarly, there is now so much information on the Internet, so many interesting bulletin boards and conferences even within a fairly narrow subject topic, that it is impossible to find them all, let alone actively participate. Some commentators have noticed that many of the 'surfers' on the Internet appear to be displaying symptoms of a major psychiatric disorder, ADD, or attention deficit disorder. The arrival of any new piece of information diverts the person away from the task at hand, so that few tasks actually get completed (Schwarz, 1994). There is even a support group now on the Internet for ADD sufferers, which is like asking the inmates to run the asylum.

Emotional absorption

While I am on the topic of psychiatric disorders associated with CMC, there is the issue of emotional absorption, the addictive nature of on-line communication. David Press writes movingly about this phenomenon while studying for an on-line MA from Lancaster University (UK):

> Every moment I had at home, I was sitting at my screen reading what I had downloaded, preparing text, and logging on to upload and read more. . . . Night after night I forgot that my son was still waiting for me to kiss him goodnight. Night after night I said to Gill I would join her in the lounge in a few minutes and then found that a few hours had passed and she was on her way to bed. . . . The peculiar aspect was that

it was like having a party going on in the dining room, but Gill was not invited. Even though . . . the party was invisible to her . . . the fact of its occurrence and her exclusion were plain.

(Press, 1993, pp. 232–33)

David Press managed to get the situation under control before it led to more unfortunate consequences; there are many who have not.

The irony is that most educators would be delighted to see the level of commitment to learning that is often manifested by many who use CMC. Thus emotional absorption needs to be seen as an excess of a good thing, rather than a bad thing in itself.

Limited symbolic representation

To date, CMC has been primarily a textual medium, with all the advantages and disadvantages associated with that medium, with the one exception that it allows for inter-personal interaction. There is a need to have reasonable key-board skills, and a level of literacy that ensures unambiguous communication.

Although some of the newer software is increasingly making use of icons, colour, sound and animation in the opening screens, there are difficulties for most end-users in creating graphics as part of messages in most systems, although file transfer, i.e. inserting an existing computer file (which may contain graphics) into an E-mail or conferencing message, is becoming more prevalent. Nevertheless, the procedures to do this are still clumsy in most programs.

CMC is still waiting for the equivalent of the Macintosh in terms of intuitive, user-friendly operation. This needed development is likely to come before the year 2000 through the use of object oriented programming, with communications software transparently integrated with other forms of programming, such as word-processing, graphics packages, spreadsheets, and multimedia.

Course design issues

Frequently, computer-mediated communication tends to be added to existing distance education courses. For instance, with the DT200 course at the British Open University, computer conferencing was merely added to all the other technologies being used, which created a heavy work-load both for the students and the course team. It was necessary to do this to pilot computer conferencing at the UKOU, as no course team was willing to run the risk at that time of depending more heavily on an untried medium, but as one of the initial course team that designed DT200, I would argue that this is not the best way to use computer conferencing.

Thus, where possible, the role and reasons for using computer conferencing, and in particular its relationship to other media, need to be clearly defined before the course is developed. Computer-mediated communication is rarely a sufficient medium on its own, but there needs to be some trade-off in terms of other media, such as face-to-face tutoring, set readers, or television, depending on the needs of the course. Conferencing is time-consuming for students, who also need to learn how to use the medium, and without careful course design, and firm guidelines to students on its use, it can easily lead to course overload.

To date, there have been very few, if any, distance education courses for credit built around the use of remote data-bases (mainly for the reason that there have not been many data-bases in a particular subject area available on-line for distance teaching purposes). However, this is an area of great promise. Two staff at the Open Learning Agency, Graham Rodwell and Don Black, are investigating the use of Statistics Canada's extensive demographic and social data-bases, based on census data and other surveys, for the teaching of geography and social sciences. These data-bases are available both on-line and as CD-ROMs. Access to remote data-bases would permit students to construct their own project work on-line, with mentoring from both a tutor and fellow students, working collaboratively.

INTERACTIVITY AND USER-FRIENDLINESS

Interactivity is seen as one of the major strengths of CMC. However, while we shall see that it does provide a powerful framework for inter-personal communication at a distance, it also has its drawbacks.

Benefits

Active and interactive participation

Participants can ask questions, develop and participate in arguments and dialogue, respond to conflicting viewpoints, add new information, and receive new information from other learners as well as from teachers or tutors. This can lead to intense academic discourse at a distance. CMC is probably the most powerful of all the technologies currently available to distance educators for this purpose, especially given its asynchronous and archival qualities, which are lacking in audio conferencing.

Freedom from constraints of time and location

Because the central computer stores the messages, which are accessed when convenient for users, communication is asynchronous. Participants can join the conferences over a period of time, reading a 'build-up' of comments from others, and adding their own comments when they are ready. Thus participants do not have to be at a set place or time to participate.

Learner control

Students are able to contribute as much or as little as they want, when they want. If they prefer to 'lurk', i.e. read but not comment, they may do so. Sometimes students will set up their own conference on a topic in which they are interested, but which is not directly relevant to the topic under discussion. Small groups can coalesce spontaneously around a topic of mutual interest.

Limitations

Possible low levels of participation

Wells (1992, p. 15) listed a number of courses with participant numbers, and also the number of messages logged. Table 10.1 is developed from this list.

It can be seen that participation varies considerably, and undoubtedly will have been influenced by the design of the course. In the case of DT200 at the British Open University, in the first year of the course only 26 per cent of students were contributors (defined as leaving at least one message), with an average of 21 messages each for those who did leave a message, and only 53 per cent read or scanned some portion of the messages. Thus nearly half the students did not participate at all. However, CMC constituted less than 20 per cent of the course, in terms of scheduled student time and assesment marks. In Harasim's courses, on the other hand, CMC was a much more central part of the course design; indeed, it would have been difficult if not impossible for students to have completed their courses successfully without active participation in the conferences.

'Lurking' can also be defended, on the grounds that in face-to-face

Table 10.1 Participation rates in computer conferencing courses

Institution	No. of students	No. of messages	Average no. per student	Reference
NKS, Norway	100	1,500	15	Søby, 1990
Dutch OU	53	1,037	20	van Meurs and Bouhuijs, 1989
OISE, Canada	38	3,132	82	Harasim, 1989
	29	3,177	110	
University of Victoria	24	183	8	Muzio, 1989
UK OU	1,364	7,500	5	Mason, 1989

teaching environments, many students do not actively participate, yet often learn. Nevertheless, if a major rationale for CMC is to encourage and develop the skills of academic discourse, active participation from all students is important.

Low levels of thinking

Whereas the previous limitation reflects the quantity of interaction, this one is concerned with the quality. Without good design and moderating skills, it is very easy for computer conferencing to descend into chit chat or low levels of response from students. Merely providing for interaction between learners, or between instructor and students, will not guarantee intellectual development.

One advantage of computer conferencing over audio conferencing is that it is less easy for the instructor to act as an 'information-giver', and thus dominate the interaction. However, in computer conferencing, provision of information can too often be replaced with a vacuum, with no sense of direction in the discussion.

Castro (1988), in analysing the transcript of a computer conference, found that even when a tutor did take a 'strong' role (10 interventions out of 35 messages), most of the contributors ignored the task set by the tutor, and only two participants managed to make their contributions somewhat relevant. The student comments were generally based on personal experience, and the link between that experience and the topic was not developed by the participants.

It is important that the instructor or moderator keeps the discussion focused on critical issues, and helps learners to respond at the appropriate intellectual level. To improve the level of interaction, some of the issues that students are expected to focus on need to be spelled out, and explicit directions as to relevant readings, and criteria for assessing contributions (whether for grading or not), need to be given. This requires the development of a high degree of skill on the part of the moderator, in particular in striking a balance between encouraging a wide range of contributions from students while keeping the discussion focused and at an appropriate intellectual level.

The need for training

Although CMC systems are getting easier to use, first-time students and tutors will probably need to learn both new computer and new study skills in order to use CMC effectively.

It is still necessary for some educational institutions to develop their own manuals for some CMC software currently available, because the manuals either do not exist, or are so badly written that they cannot be used with first-time students. Even if the software is relatively simple to install and use, and is accompanied by a good, clear manual, many students (and tutors) will still need additional help in getting on-line for the first time. If students are also expected to use external networks, such as the Internet, they will need some help to find their way round. It is quite common then for at least the first week of a course (or an extra pre-course session) to be devoted to user training. Some institutions even insist that this is done on a face-to-face basis.

It is just as much a challenge to prepare instructors, tutors and students in the design and learning requirements of CMC. Instructors need to develop skills in identifying the role and purpose of discussion, criteria for assessing the quality of discussion, skills in helping students to participate constructively (and in particular to frame appropriate questions), and the ability to construct an integrated curriculum that combines CMC with other media. While most of these skills are not substantially different from those needed to run a successful face-to-face seminar or audio conference, they are critical for the success of a good computer conference.

Similarly, many students are not ready or prepared for participative learning. Many feel shy or threatened if they are asked to contribute, in case they reveal their own inadequacies; others are used to, and expect, the instructor to provide the information they need. Thus instructors, tutors or moderators require some skill and sensitivity if they are to encourage a wide range of student participation.

COSTS

The major 'external' network used by most educational institutions is the Internet. The costing structure of the Internet is very different from that of the public voice telephone service. Costs are dependent on bandwidth connection, and distance to the nearest 'initial' Internet 'node', rather than total distance travelled by a message or even (at the time of writing) volume. Thus once an institution is connected to the Internet, it pays a 'flat rate' for the connection; the rate is determined by the bandwidth requested. Once connected, there are no additional charges. This means messages can be sent anywhere in the world, at no additional direct cost to the institution.

Although a number of educational institutions have been using computer networking for instructional purposes for some time, the technology is developing so rapidly that there is no standard cost structure yet emerging. Nevertheless, there is still a number of common cost elements that need to be taken into consideration.

Two examples will enable the differences and common features in costing CMC to be explored, and also give some indication of how the technology and costs have changed over a six-year period. The British Open University first introduced computer conferencing in 1988. Following the lead of a number of school districts in British Columbia, the Open Learning Agency in 1994 installed a computer communications system based on software called FirstClass, as part of its own electronic computer network, called OpeNet.

Rumble (1989) conducted a thorough cost analysis of the use of computer conferencing on the British Open University's course *DT200: An Introduction to Information Technology*. This section draws very heavily on his analysis.

Institution-related costs

Research and planning

There are considerable staff costs concerned with researching possible CMC systems, briefing of staff on the advantages and disadvantages of CMC, meetings to get agreement on implementation and to settle policy issues. It is not possible to give a firm figure but the costs are substantial.

Hardware, software and central network costs

The computer conferencing software installed on a mainframe (VAX) computer at the Open University was CoSy. FirstClass is installed on a Macintosh Quadra at OLA, and can be 'networked' with other 'servers'.

The Open University obtained a 'site licence' for the use of CoSy, which cost £1,359 (US$2,038) per annum. With hardware, modems, manuals, etc., the total capital cost for installing FirstClass Server at the Open Learning Agency was about US$6,750 (C$9,000) in 1994.

Technical support

Both the UKOU and the OLA recognised the need to provide on-going technical support to students and tutors. The UKOU provided such a service for all its computing courses, so the marginal cost for the extra work associated with student requests for help on the computer communications aspects of DT200 was estimated at £1,000 (C$2,000). In the first year at OLA, with 10 courses using computer conferencing, one person was assigned full-time to provide student and tutor assistance, at a cost of approximately C$30,000 (US$22,500). This figure includes this person's contribution to training of central and tutorial staff.

Student-related costs

Hardware costs

A critical factor is whether students already have a suitable computer and modem, either at work or at home. For DT200, the university recommended an IBM-PC-compatible standard, which at that time cost around

£780 (US$1,170), including printer. Rumble (1989) included the full cost of rental or purchase by students in his calculations (even for those who already had their own computer before enrolling in the course).

Suitable modems were £84 (US$126) a unit. The Open University loaned each student a modem. This was a major cost of £160,000 (US$240,000) for the university, although the cost of the modems could be amortised over a number of years since the modems were returned by students when they had completed their course. In addition, the total cost of storage, packaging, mailing, and returning 1,400 modems was £10,600 (US$15,900) (mainly recurrent).

At the OLA, FirstClass can work with both Macintosh and IBM machines. OLA expects students to provide their own computer and modems.

Software

The Open University developed its own communications software for students, to facilitate dialing-in and logging-on procedures. In addition, the Open University developed its own student and tutor manual for CoSy, and audio cassette/print material for training students in the installation and use of CoSy. With the additional cost of six microcomputers for software development, these production costs came to almost £90,000 (US$135,000), including staff time. These costs would be amortised over the life of the software (probably six years). This would work out at approximately £10.70 (US$16) per student. In addition there are direct costs for the discs that contained the software (27 pence each/US¢40) and a licence fee to CoSy based on the number of users. These costs (recurrent) totalled approximately £1,000 (US$1,500).

The main advantage of FirstClass is that it is much more user-friendly than the early version of CoSy used on DT200. FirstClass also has an excellent user's manual, and front-end software already developed, so OLA has been able to avoid the large development cost that was necessary at the UKOU. Student software is C$2 (US$1.50) each for a pack of 500, and the manuals cost C$10 (US$7.50) each. Thus the cost of setting up a student with software and a manual at OLA is C$12 (US$9), half the cost of the OU student software, even allowing for amortisation over six years for the OU software.

Telephone line costs

In the United Kingdom, the Open University made use of a public high-speed data network. In 1988 there were 17 dial-up nodes in major cities around the UK. Students living close to the local nodes could call in at local call rates and be connected to the university's central computer. This enabled 54 per cent of students to access the network at local call rates.

Students were responsible for paying their own telephone costs. Rumble (1989) calculated the average line cost per student to be £1.95 (US$2.92) per hour.

The DT200 course team anticipated that students would be on-line for an average of 10 hours throughout the course (20 minutes a week). In fact they averaged 9 hours 15 minutes (with very large individual variations). This gives an average cost of £17.84 (US$26.76) per student for the course.

Until a careful cost analysis is done of the various options, it is difficult to know what the actual long-distance charges will be for OLA students. OLA is experimenting with the use of 1–800 numbers (which charge the cost to the agency).

Tutor-related costs

Tuition costs

The most difficult cost to assess is that for academic time. This will depend on the design of the course and the role of the tutor or instructor.

On DT200, the 65 tutors were using computer conferencing to supplement other media on the course. The tutors were paid £17.33 (US$26.29) an hour for eight hours of CMC tutoring on the course. This covered reading and preparing messages and responses. They were also paid a total of £14.16 (US$21.24) per student completing CMC-related assignments. Each tutor would have roughly 20 students. The tuition costs for CMC-related activities totalled £152.80 per tutor, equivalent to £1 (US$1.50) per student study hour. However, tutors actually spent an average of 20 hours on-line, equal to an hourly rate of £6.93 (US$10.39) and 38 pence (US¢57) per student study hour. It can be seen that tutors put in much more time on-line than the course team were expecting, or at least paying for.

If computer conferencing is being used as the main medium of instruction, the instructor could be an academic employed full-time at a university or college, with a computer and access to public E-mail as part of their office work environment. The course could be offered to either students on-campus or off-campus. As well as the computer conferencing element, there would probably be set readings, plus some face-to-face and/or telephone contact. The instructor is likely to be spending at least 12 hours a week on such a course, equivalent to US$2,250 in salary costs for a one-term course of 13 weeks. This would include assignment marking, as well as being available at set times of the week for telephone contact by students.

Hardware and software costs

The Open University covered the cost of the loan of a computer and modem to tutors (£150/US$225/per annum per tutor or a total of £9,750/

US$14,625). Tutors' software costs were negligible. OLA will similarly cover the tutor hardware and software costs. The annualised cost of supplying and maintaining individual work-stations at the Open Learning Agency is approximately C$1,000(US$750) per employee per annum.

Telephone costs

There was also an allowance of £1.47 (US$2.20) per hour for telephone line charges for tutors at the UKOU. In fact, the actual cost averaged £2.63 an hour for tutors (13 pence per student study hour). Tutors were on-line for 20 hours, so the total cost was £52.60 (US$78.90) per tutor. OLA will also cover tutor telephone costs for CMC.

Tutor training

One of the few costs not covered by Rumble was the cost of tutor training. The DT200 course team organised a series of one-day, face-to-face training workshops for tutors, which included instruction on both the technical aspects and instructional methods of CMC. The OLA estimates that with travel, accommodation and daily fee, it will cost approximately C$700 (US$525) per tutor to be trained.

Summary

Table 10.2 summarises these costs. First of all, there is a great deal of similarity in many of the costs between the UKOU and OLA, despite the difference in time and context. Coming into the field six years later, start-up costs are less for OLA, because of the improvements in user-friendliness and the availability of 'off-the-shelf' microcomputer-based central software. The cost of student hardware is a major item for many students in both organisations. This is not a problem if students already have access to a suitable computer. If they do not, however, obtaining one is a large investment, especially in terms of cost per study hour. OLA also needs to find a way to keep down long distance charges. New developments, especially 'off-the-shelf' software, have helped reduce student software and manual costs since 1988.

New scenarios

Using the experience and data from both the UKOU and OLA cases, it is possible to develop a realistic, if hypothetical, cost scenario that enables comparison to be made with other technologies.

University P in the USA offers a number of courses via computer conferencing, both for on-campus and off-campus students. Half the students taking CMC courses are registered as on-campus; 25 per cent of

Table 10.2 Comparison between computer conferencing costs at the UK OU and the OLA

	UKOU		OLA	
	Total DT200 US$	Cost per student study hour US$	Total per course US$	Cost per student study hour US$
Start-up costs				
Research and planning	>350,000?	n/a	>75,000?	n/a
Central hardware/software	112,500?	n/a	15,000	n/a
Annual recurrent				
Central software	2,038	0.16	0	0
Technical support	1,500	0.12	2,250	0.24
Student hardware	199,485	15.81	146,250	15.81
Student software	135,000	10.69	9,018	0.97
Student phone costs	36,904	2.92	?	?
Tuition fees	7,191	0.57	6,937	0.75?
Tutor hardware costs	14,625	0.37	11,250	0.55?
Tutor telephone costs	25,350	0.55	?	?
Tutor training	34,125	3.28	26,250	3.28

Note: n/a = not applicable (fixed costs)
 ? = costs unknown or rough estimates

students are registered as off-campus, but live within a local telephone calling rate to one of the university's five campuses; the other 25 per cent are off-campus, and would be subject to long-distance charges. The campuses are linked by a private wide-area network, with a local server at each campus site. The CMC traffic on the internal network is treated as a zero marginal cost. To maintain comparability with the costing of other technologies, course life/amortisation of fixed costs is assumed to be eight years, although realistically equipment and software replacement/up-grading is likely to occur in a shorter time period.

Academic time: 13 weeks at 12 hours a week = $3,000 = $19 per hour

5 servers: $100,000

Multiplex modem + 4 standard modems: $22,000

Technical support: $30,000 for every 10 courses/1000 students

Student hardware: students both on- and off-campus are expected to provide their own hardware; the university provides 'ports' for on-campus students to plug into the network. In calculating the hardware costs to a student, it is assumed that the cost will be $300 a year, or $100 per one-term course.

Student software: the university provides the appropriate communication software to students: = $2 per student (software is returned/destroyed at the end of the course).

Student phone costs: students are expected to spend 12 hours a week reading/responding to messages/assignments, etc. Because of the ability to up-load and down-load in bulk, students are allowed a maximum of one hour a week actually on-line; they are charged for anything more at a flat rate. The university charges a flat fee for all students on these courses, and through a 1–800 number covers the cost of the long distance charges. For the 25 per cent of students who incur long distance charges for the university, this works out at $20 a week per student; this results in an additional $5 per student (i.e. all students) per week of the course ($45, per term course) on the course fee.

Instructor hardware and software costs: all faculty are also linked to the network through their local (and often their own home) work-stations. However, this network and campus hardware had already been installed for administrative purposes, so is treated as a zero marginal cost. Instructors (faculty) will be either on a local area network, or using free local calling, so there are no tutor line costs.

Instructor training: each instructor receives a one-day workshop: cost

Table 10.3 Total costs: computer conferencing in a dual-mode institution (over eight years)

	1,000 students (125 students per year x 8) $	5,000 students (625 students per year x 8) $	10,000 students (1,250 students per year x 8) $
Institutional			
Instructors	6	31	63
Fees/salaries	432,000	2,232,000	4,536,000
Training	960	4,960	11,340
Servers	122,000	122,000	122,000
Technical support	144,000	744,000	1,512,000
Sub-total	698,960	3,102,960	6,181,340
Student			
Hardware	300,000	1,500,000	3,000,000
Telephone	135,000	675,000	1,350,000
Sub-total	435,000	2,175,000	4,350,000
Total (8 years)	1,133,960	5,277,960	10,531,340
Total (1 year)	141,745	659,745	1,316,417
Cost per study hour	2.42	2.26	2.25
	(£1.61)	(£1.51)	(£1.50)

Note: 39 weeks: 3 × 13-week terms, 12 hours per week = 468 hours on-line

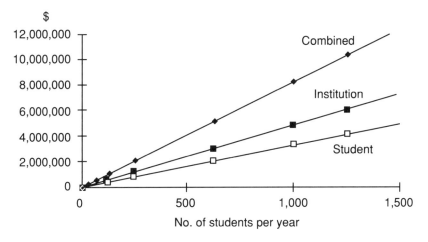

Figure 10.1 Total cost: computer conferencing (over eight years)

$160 per instructor, amortised over 8 years = $20 per year; instructor: student ratio = 20 (necessary to maintain interactivity).

In this model, costs are split between two areas: those costs paid by the institution; and those costs paid directly by the students. A much higher proportion of instructional costs has been placed on the students than in a traditional teaching environment. This raises a number of equity and access issues. It is not a problem if the courses are directed at professionals working in business or computer-based industries; it is an issue if the aim of the course is to widen access to knowledge and skills in the area of information technology.

In this model, total costs rise directly with student numbers (see Figure 10.1). There is relatively little front-end investment in these courses, and if interactivity, a major feature of CMC, is to be effective, the number of instructors increases with the number of students. Instructors are the main cost with this technology.

Figure 10.2 shows the graph for cost per student study hour. Fixed costs quickly average out at around 125 students a year, and settle down at around a cost per hour (all costs) of $2.25 for larger numbers of students, of which $1.33 is paid by the institution.

A CMC-based course is likely to have a relatively low development cost, compared with a print-based course, but costs increase in proportion to the number of students, if levels of interactivity are to be maintained. Computer conferencing is a relatively low-cost medium, especially for courses with low numbers of students, even if institutions cover the cost of hardware and telephone charges for students.

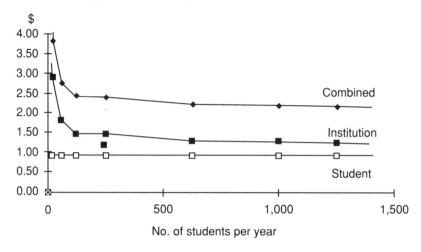

Figure 10.2 Cost per student study hour: computer conferencing (over eight years)

ORGANISATIONAL ISSUES

Legal and ethical issues, and the issue of control

The control of what flows across the networks, both internally and externally, is an important issue for institutions to consider. Computer conferencing may appear an intimate, almost private medium to users, but in fact
it is just as public a medium as television, and subject to the same laws of
defamation, privacy, and copyright.

In addition to the legal aspects, individuals have a right to be treated
courteously. It is necessary then for institutions to establish both written
policies, and codes of ethics, that are clearly communicated to users (staff,
tutors and students), which should include punishments (such as removal of
ID, or expulsion from the course) and the conditions for which these
punishments will apply. Mason (1993, pp. 34–36) provides good examples. Students need to know that they are agreeing to follow such guidelines on conduct when they enrol in a course. This means that with very
few exceptions computer conferences need a moderator with authority.

However, apart from such guidelines that would apply to any form of
public communication, institutions should avoid exercising control over the
content of conferences, especially if the students are adults. For instance,
students should be allowed to set up their own conferences, if they wish,
without a staff moderator, although one of the students may need to be
identified as the 'official' moderator. Abuse of long-distance charges by
students can be avoided by setting time or cash limits; any use over that

limit is paid for by the student. (Some systems can limit access or extent of use for any individual account.)

Cultural change in the computer department

The introduction of low-cost microcomputers requires a major change in the organisational culture of professional computing departments, with more emphasis on service to local users and the support of 'off-the-shelf' software, and less on development and central control. Computer-mediated communications require yet another shift in culture, with an even more increased emphasis on networking, and even less central control over the use of the technology. There are genuine concerns about the impact of networking on an institution's telephone costs, but these are more controllable than traditional phone costs, which vary according to distance and time.

Computer-mediated communication requires a whole new range of skills and expertise within most computing departments, and providing high-quality service to relatively naive, remote users can be an interesting challenge for traditional computing departments.

Resource re-allocation

A major organisational issue for a traditional single mode distance teaching institution is to establish a means by which resources can be re-allocated from established technologies/budgets, such as print or face-to-face tutorials, to computer conferencing. If, for instance, computer conferencing is to be used as the primary instructional technology, course development costs will be far less, but annual recurrent costs will be higher.

Clearly some form of cost–benefit analysis needs to be done, taking into account the total cost of the course over a period of years, the numbers of students, and the volume of activity, rather than looking at computer conferencing as just an extra cost for existing courses, or as a cheap way to start up a new course.

Despite these organisational challenges, the technology behind computer-mediated communication is relatively simple, low-cost and robust. Provided mind-sets are changed to accommodate a more collaborative and learner-centred approach to learning, organisational issues should not be a major obstacle to the implementation of CMC.

NOVELTY

There is still a strong novelty value associated with CMC, although the technology has been around since the early 1980s. There is also a good deal of hype associated with this technology. While the language that goes with it, such as 'global networks', 'virtual classrooms', and 'paradigm shifts' can push the right buttons with politicians and funders, it can also provoke strong negative reactions from other people (including myself).

At its heart, computer conferencing is just another means to provide academic discourse, debate, discussion, and friendly communication, in a convenient form for people who are scattered in time and place. For these reasons, it can be an appealing technology to both traditionalists and modernists.

SPEED

This is a major benefit of CMC. Once the communications system is in place and the main outline of a course has been decided, teaching can start relatively quickly. It is easy to up-date material, and to bring in experts from outside to respond to latest developments or events.

CONCLUSIONS

Computer-mediated communication is being used both by conventional campus-based institutions and by dedicated distance teaching univer-trsities. Indeed, CMC is blurring the distinction between on-campus and distance students. The technology is relatively simple, robust and cheap to install and use. Student access to computers, especially in North America, is rapidly increasing, and is already at a level where for many courses access to a computer is not a barrier.

Computer conferencing has been the main form of computer-mediated teaching to date, but the increase in accessibility to the Internet and its services provides an opportunity for the development of new curricular models based on the use of remote data-bases.

Computer conferencing has several strong instructional features. It is a highly interactive medium, allowing for equal access and participation by all learners, and in particular allows mature learners to bring their own experience and expertise to the learning process. It is good for developing academic discourse, for collaborative learning, and for knowledge building. Its weaknesses are that without skilful moderation and design, students can be passive or non-participants, and the quality of interaction can be poor.

Computer-mediated communication is relatively low cost, especially for courses with low numbers of students. It seems that in some circumstances, for instance courses with less than 50 students a year, it would be cheaper for an institution to provide students with computers, on a loan basis, for a course built around computer-mediated communication, than to provide a more traditional distance education course. However, as student numbers increase, so do the total costs of using CMC.

This technology arouses great enthusiasm among some educators and many students. However, it is not a technology that suits all types of teaching, courses or learners. It is usually best used in conjunction with other technologies, particularly where there is a need for information transmission as well as discussion. Its strength as a teaching medium will grow considerably when the technology improves to the point where it can integrate multimedia inter-personal communications with remote multimedia databases.

COMPUTERS AS TEACHERS – OR COMPUTERS AS TOOLS?

Finally, developments in multimedia that give teachers and learners the tools to re-construct and personalise knowledge, the development of computer-mediated communications, and the eventual integration of multi-media with electronic networks, suggest that the essential function of computers in education is moving away from the notion of the computer as substitute teacher towards that of a 'true' technology, a set of tools to be used by teachers and learners, to facilitate the task of learning and understanding.

Computers are more likely to become 'transparent' or 'invisible' in the learning process, as significant to the learner as the electricity that carries the power to a refrigerator: essential for its operation, but independent of the function that the refrigerator performs. Nevertheless, this does not mean that computers will become less important in open and distance learning; quite the contrary. They could in fact revolutionise the organisation and structure of education, so much so that the term 'distance education' itself will be rendered meaningless. This will be discussed further in Chapter 11.

11 Technology and the future of education

PLUS ÇA CHANGE. . . .?

'If you don't know where you're going, any road will do.'
(The White Rabbit, in *Alice in Wonderland*, Lewis Carroll)

The prevalent forms and methods of education and training today are little changed from those of 200 years ago. Children and young adults are taught in groups, within institutions called schools, colleges and universities, with instruction provided by teachers face-to-face. To date, while many examples of successful applications can be cited, educational technology has had a marginal impact on education and training. Where computers or television have been integrated into the classroom, it is mainly an 'add-on' activity or teacher's aid.

The one and important exception to this generalisation has been distance education. Even in distance education, the 'core' technologies (print, audio, and television), have been used primarily for one-way delivery, and distance education itself remains a marginal, if increasingly significant, activity in education and training.

Nevertheless, despite all the false promise of technology in the past, technological developments already available or in the pipeline have the potential to revolutionise both conventional and distance education and training as we know it, far more so than the technologies commonly used to date.

TECHNOLOGICAL DEVELOPMENTS

Within the next 10 years, we will see the following important technological developments so commonplace that they will be found in the majority of homes in developed countries:

- integration of television, telecommunications and computers, through digitisation and compression techniques;
- reduced costs and more flexible uses/applications of telecommunications, through developments such as ISDN/ fibre-optics/cellular radio;

- miniaturisation (tiny cameras, microphones, small, high-resolution display screens);
- increased portability, through use of radio communications and miniaturisation;
- increased processing power, through new micro-chip development and advanced software techniques;
- more powerful and user-friendly command and software tools, making it much easier for users to create and communicate their own materials.

These developments, already available at a price or currently under development, will result in a single, integrated entertainment–communications–learning 'box' in each home. A wide range of applications will be accessed through this multi-purpose box, including 'on-demand' films, television programmes, music, home shopping, banking and financial services, and education and training.

Multimedia in education has been seen by many primarily as an extension of computer-based learning. Certainly 'stand-alone' computer-based learning will become even more powerful as artificial intelligence and virtual reality develop. However, while 'stand-alone' applications of multimedia will continue to be important, a much more significant development will be the application of high-speed multimedia networks for educational purposes.

These developments will arrive with astonishing speed and will be available on a mass scale by the year 2000. For instance, in April 1994, Stentor, an alliance of Canadian telephone companies, announced an $8 billion, 10-year initiative, called BEACON, that will bring broadband, multimedia services to 80 per cent–90 per cent of all homes and businesses in Canada by the year 2004. These developments are being driven mainly by the entertainment industry, but the significance for education is the promise of low-cost, mass-produced technology in every home and office, in the form of a black-box or computer that will give access to and interaction with the information highway.

The implications for education and training are immense. Learning can be independent of time and place, and available at all stages of a person's life. The learning context will be technologically rich. Learners will have access not only to a wide range of media, but also to a wide range of sources of education.

The challenge for educators is how to utilise this power, so that education and training meet the needs of individuals and society at large.

THE CONTEXT OF EDUCATION AND TRAINING IN THE TWENTY-FIRST CENTURY

The way educational technology has been developing somewhat resembles the frenetic activities of the White Rabbit in *Alice in Wonderland*; because it does not seem to know where it is going, any road will do. Educational technology applications though should be driven by our vision of education and training in the 21st century. That vision should take into account the potential of technology, but the vision should be driven by the needs of individuals and society at large, rather than by technological development per se. What technology *can* do – or what technology suppliers may suggest we do – may not be what we *want* it to do.

I believe that the increased and intelligent use of technology for education and training is fundamental for the continuing economic development and survival of the leading developed countries such as Canada, USA, Britain, Australia and Sweden.

The needs of the workforce are rapidly changing. In 1993, 78 per cent of all jobs in the USA were in service industries, and the trend to even more service-based jobs is likely to continue (*The Economist*, 1994). Microsoft's annual revenues are greater than Sony's and Honda's combined, but they employ 100 times fewer workers. Most new jobs are being created in Canada by companies with less than 20 workers; indeed, the trend to both self-employment and working from home is likely to grow. Many of the new jobs will be on a part-time or contract basis, with at least two-thirds of the new jobs going to women, and a majority of new jobs will be relatively low-paid (Statistics Canada, 1992).

Furthermore, work will continue to change dynamically. Someone leaving school today will need to be re-trained at least five times in their working life. Nearly half the new jobs created will require graduates or people with the equivalent of 17 years full-time education (Canadian Labour Market Productivity Centre, 1989).

The traditional picture of work as a lifetime commitment to a particular trade or institution, with a secure pension at the end, will apply to an increasingly smaller proportion of the population. A very small proportion of the youngsters leaving school will find employment as unskilled or semi-skilled workers in the traditional manufacturing or resource-based industries; the majority of those already unemployed, and a good proportion of those already working in large companies or in manufacturing or primary-resource industries, will need to be re-trained in the next few years, as manufacturing companies increasingly move to automation to reduce labour costs, to compete with the economies of emerging nations such as the 'economic dragons' of South East Asia.

Many labour markets in industrial, developed countries are showing the following employment trends:

From	resource-based	to	knowledge-based
From	manufacturing	to	services
From	large companies	to	small companies
From	full-time/full year	to	part-time/contract
From	employed	to	self-employed

From	low, specific skill-levels	to	generic, high-skill levels
From	brawn	to	brains
From	men	to	women
From	factory/office	to	home/in transit

The most significant development is that many of the new jobs will require a much higher level of skill than the jobs they are replacing, especially in manufacturing and resource-based industries, traditionally the source of relatively high-wage, low-skill employment. People will retain existing jobs only if they are retrained to higher standards. Even for the majority of new jobs that will be low-paid and require generally lower skill levels, training or re-training will be necessary, especially in basic skills, just in order to keep the job.

The wealth of nations will depend increasingly on knowlege-based, high-tech industries, in areas such as bio-technology, health, environmental products and services, tourism and hospitality, telecommunications, computer software and software applications, financial services, and entertainment (film, television, games). Furthermore, these are highly competitive, global industries. Keeping even a few months ahead of the competition, in terms of innovation and knowledge, is critical to survival, as is the quality of product and service. This means that education and training, not just in the pre-work years, but throughout a lifetime, are essential elements of a successful workforce.

At the same time, and not surprisingly, demand for education and training is increasing. This increased demand is coming from two sources. The first is from young people continuing into post-secondary education. This demand will continue to increase slightly in most developed countries (between 2 per cent to 5 per cent per annum for another 10 years at least) as more and more young people realise the importance of further education for their future prosperity. Because this pressure is obvious and politically sensitive, some governments, especially in North America, are concentrating their efforts on improving the school system and the transition from school to work. While this is essential, the workforce in most developed countries is replenished by no more than 2 per cent–3 per cent each year from those entering the workforce from schools and universities. The vast majority of those who need to up-grade and re-train are already in the workforce.

However, if every worker currently in the workforce was sent back to college for three months training every five years (a very conservative estimate of the average amount of job-based training required), the post-secondary education system in Canada, already one of the most comprehensive in the world, would have to increase by more than 50 per cent. Even if taxpayers were willing to create more colleges and universities, this would be an inappropriate response for most of this target group, who are working, have families, and cannot afford or do not want to be full-time students.

The requirements of this new market for learning are very different from those of the youngsters the system has traditionally served. Work and learning will be inseparable. Most learning at work will be informal and lifelong. Much of the learning in the workforce will be initiated by individuals as part and parcel of their working and leisure lives. It will be informal (i.e. not leading to any formal qualification), self-directed, and piece-meal (broken into small chunks of learning, some as small as a few minutes a day, some several hours in length). It will be driven as much by short-term needs as by any conscious plan of study. Thus it will not be determined by some institutional-based curriculum planner, but by the task at hand (Weimer, 1992).

With respect to the skills needed in the workforce, these have been well defined by the Conference Board of Canada (1991):

- good communication skills (reading/writing/speaking/listening);
- ability to learn independently;
- social skills: ethics; positive attitudes; responsibility;
- teamwork;
- ability to adapt to changing circumstances;
- thinking skills: problem-solving; critical/logical/numerical;
- knowledge navigation: where to get/how to process information.

Thus, learning as a lifelong process will be essential and will need to increase substantially, due to:

- the rapid change in occupational profiles (more 'different' jobs created each year);
- overall increases in the skills requirement of all jobs;
- rapid technological change impacting on the workplace;
- an inadequate supply of young people through the school system to meet the increasing demand for highly skilled labour in many countries;
- a large pool of unemployed without the skills needed for the new jobs;
- changes in the age distribution, affecting willingness to pay via taxation for conventional education by the 'baby boomers', now their children are grown up (the 'California syndrome').

Most developed countries are increasingly recognising that they are facing an educational and training crisis, in terms of numbers, if they are to survive in the new, high-tech, global economic environment. The skill base is not adequate and cannot be provided through traditional routes alone. Nor are there the resources through public sector funding to address these needs by traditional means.

NEW APPROACHES TO LEARNING AND TEACHING

Once learning moves beyond the recall of facts, principles or correct procedures, and into the area of creativity, problem-solving, analysis, or evaluation (the very skills needed in the workplace in a knowledge-based economy – see Conference Board of Canada, 1991), learners need inter-personal communication, the opportunity to question, challenge and discuss. I see learning as an individual quest for meaning and relevance. Learning is as much a social as an individual activity. However, for someone working in a small company, and particularly in leading-edge technologies, the nearest person with similar interests and expertise may be somewhere on the other side of the country, or even the world.

Because knowledge is expanding so rapidly, even specialist researchers have a hard time keeping up with developments in their field. Teachers then will increasingly be advisors, managers and facilitators of learning, rather than providers of information. Access to information will be primarily through telecommunications. The teachers' role will concentrate more on developing skills, and in particular skills of navigating knowledge sources, and skills of processing and analysing information. People with subject expertise will often not be professional teachers, but those working at the leading edge of technological development, in both the public and private sector. These subject experts though can still be drawn upon, as mentors, for education and training.

It is possible to develop a set of curriculum models which reflect a variety of ways in which technology could be used for instructional purposes (Table 11.1).

Most learning will probably require a mix of these models, since learning requires a mix of individual study and two-way communication with other learners and teachers. It is possible to flesh out some new curriculum models that exploit the potential of the new technologies.

The global classroom

Teles (1993) has argued that new technologies can be used to better prepare people for the information age, through the development of curricula that not only deal with issues arising from the information society, but also use technologies in such a way that they develop the skills needed within such a society. Thus courses could be constructed using different subject specialists from around the globe, available for discussion and questioning by learners; the course, by using different sources, could ensure that gender, multi-cultural and ethnic issues are not just 'dealt with', but are reflected in the teaching itself. Learners would also be drawn from a wide geographical area; they would be encouraged to define more precisely their own learning needs, to work in small groups, to seek out sources of information they need, and to communicate their learning to other groups on the course.

Table 11.1 Different models for the applications of technology for learning

Curriculum model	Technology	Role of teacher	'Most appropriate' applications	Issue
The real classroom (technologically-enriched) *Current practice*	Work-stations/telecommunications	In control	Social development; (e.g. social behaviour; friendships); how to use technology	Add-on cost
The remote classroom *USA today*	Classrooms linked by telecommunications technology	In control/source of knowledge	New research/up-dating; small numbers of students	Low front-end costs; quick/easy
The remote data-base *Internet today* *Multimedia in future*	Interactive information banks	Guide/helps process information	Knowledge navigation skills	Copyright; access; ownership
Networking (individual and group) *Computer conferencing today* *Video conferencing in future*	Work-stations linked by telecommunications	No role/guide/in control	Exchange of information/professional development/community action/problem-solving/needs definition	Low cost
The box as teacher *CAI/multimedia now* *Virtual reality in future*	Work-stations with stand-alone/down-loaded instructional software	Designer of materials/trouble-shooter	Basic knowledge/skills that do not change quickly; mass markets/high value training	High front-end cost
The learning machine *Ten years away*	Work-station with AI-enhanced software/linked to remote data-bases	None	Adapts to learners' needs/learning style; cognitive/motor skills development; knowledge access/management	Can it be done? Should it be done?

They would do this by using the communications tools of the information society.

Just-in-time training in the workplace

It is not difficult to build a convincing portrait of learning at the workplace. We can envisage a television animation artist, called Wayne, probably working from home, needing information on a certain technique or approach, or advice on how best to create a certain effect. From previous experience and contacts, or on the advice of a colleague, he has the name of someone half-way across the country (Sue). From his work-station, Wayne calls Sue, talks about the problem, and Wayne loads up some software which he 'shares' with Sue via the network. Sue looks at what Wayne has done, makes some comments, puts up some new software, and demonstrates a process that creates the effect Wayne was looking for. Wayne asks a few questions, tries a couple of things on-line while Sue watches and comments, downloads the new software, then thanks her for her help.

Sue and Wayne are both registered with an educational institution that has been set up to enable the exchange of commercially sensitive material and software for learning purposes. Sue is working at a set rate for consultancy, which is automatically debited from Wayne's account by the educational institution, and transferred to Sue's account. The exchange of software is automatically recorded, and the institution electronically recovers these costs from Wayne's account and forwards them to the software company. Wayne's work-station has automatically displayed the cost per minute of consulting Sue, and the cost of rights for downloading the software. Wayne now not only has the software he needs, but also can contact Sue (on a chargeable basis) any time he has a problem with the software. The learning context has been established. Note it is fragmented, on demand, and commercial.

Resource-based tutoring for accreditation

This model is aimed at students seeking accreditation within a particular subject area who already have a good foundation, but who are working towards a more advanced level of study and a personally relevant area of expertise. In this model, the learner is put in touch with a tutor with specialist expertise who can guide the learner to sources of information and pre-prepared multimedia learning materials relevant to their interests. The tutor helps the learner navigate remote databases, or institutional libraries, which contain the multimedia instructional materials needed by the learner, sets and evaluates relevant learning tasks such as project work, and puts the learner in contact with other learners and experts with similar interests. This model is not very different from learner-centred teaching practised in British primary schools, except that it operates at a distance via telecommunications.

These are just three examples; many more could be developed for different target groups. The essential point though is that in order to meet future education and training needs, we need to develop new approaches to teaching and learning in ways that allow us to tap into the full power of new technology.

ORGANISATIONAL IMPLICATIONS

Designing new systems

While there will still be a need for educational institutions, their form and operation will need to change.

- Communications allow learners to access knowledge from a variety of locations, including the home and the workplace, as well as from the educational 'campus'.
- Educational institutions do not have to be rooted in time and place; they can be electronic, accessible from anywhere, and available at all times.
- Institutions should be a mix of physical campus and remote access; this requires careful definition of the different educational purposes of physical and electronic access.
- Electronic access to learning would be used to widen access to groups whose family or work commitments prevent them from attending at a specific place and a specific time.
- Electronic access would also enable more people to access education for the same cost, because the costs of providing physical space (classrooms, car-parking) would not increase proportionate to the numbers; this would also protect the environment, by reducing the need for commuting.
- Face-to-face group teaching of 20-30 learners or more should be used selectively, for well-defined purposes that cannot be met through technology.

Learners will interact with their desk-top or portable work-stations in a variety of ways, determined by the nature of the learning task, and their preferred style of learning. These preferred styles will vary considerably, both within a single person, depending on the task, and, for the same task, between different individuals.

The learning context will need to encompass the following:

- working alone, interacting with learning material (which may be available locally or remotely);
- working collaboratively (and in an equal relationship) with fellow students or workers at different remote sites, either synchronously or asynchronously: both these modes are likely to be multimedia;

- as an 'apprentice' or 'student', working with a more experienced worker, supervisor, or instructor;
- as an instructor, supervisor or more experienced colleague for other less experienced colleagues.

The same people may find themselves in each of these roles within a single working day. Learners will also need to be able to work from home, or from a work-site, or while in transit. They will need the following facilities or tools:

- access to information (searching, downloading) from multiple sources in multiple formats;
- selection, storage and re-ordering/re-creation of information;
- direct communication with instructors, colleagues, and other learners;
- incorporation of accessed/re-worked material into work documents or assignments;
- sharing and manipulation of information/documents/projects with others;
- accessing, combining, creating and transmitting audio, video, text, and data as necessary.

If we take these as design requirements, there is then a need to build systems that support this form of learning, both for formal and informal learning. I give my own personal 'vision' of how such a system could provide the kind of educational experiences I would like to see. This is summarised in Figure 11.1.

The work-station

The work-station of the future will be a multi-purpose machine, probably in modular form, including input (voice, pen, keyboard, gestures) and display

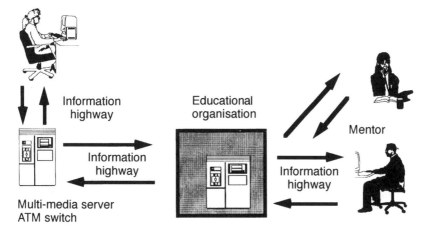

Figure 11.1 An educational multimedia network

(screen, sound, printer) devices, telecommunications, computing and television. It will be at least in part portable.

Key features will be the interface between the user, the tools available to the learner within the work-station, and a range of services, both educational and non-educational, that can be accessed remotely via the work-station.

The interface

Design work has already begun on building interfaces for the information highway. The Virtual Interactive Environment for Workgroups (VIEW) is one such system currently in the initial stages of development in Canada by MPR Teltech, the Open Learning Agency, Simon Fraser University, Science World (British Columbia), the British Columbia Educational Technology Centre, and Stentor. The VIEW system will provide tools for creating and using 'multimedia conferences', and for enabling users to engage in individual and collaborative group activities using information from diverse sources and in a variety of media formats, operating either in synchronous or asynchronous modes (Teles and Laks, 1993).

In essence, when learners switch on their work-station, there is a window with a choice of services. One of the choices (others may be films, home shopping, financial services, messages, etc.) will be education and training. When the learner chooses education and training, VIEW will provide a new window, with a choice of educational services, and a range of software tools to facilitate the learning and communication process. Thus learners will be able to search, access and download information from a variety of sources in a variety of media formats.

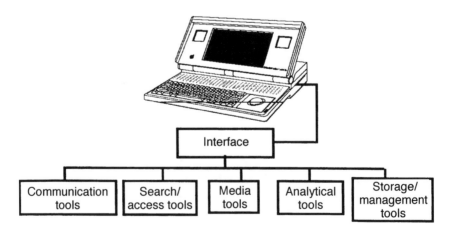

Figure 11.2 A multimedia network interface

The tools

A critical element are the software tools available in the work-station. As well as tools for communication, management and storage of information, there will also be tools that assist in searching, accessing and compressing information, in analysing accessed data for relevance, in 'grouping' appropriate types of information, and tools for importing different types of media-based information, editing, and exporting them. These tools will need to be intuitively simple to use.

New educational institutions

What will make or break such a system will be the creation of new organisational structures for educational institutions to provide the administrative and educational support for lifelong learners.

Roles for 'electronic' educational institutions

The critical roles of an 'electronic' educational institution built to meet the learning needs of the twenty-first century will be as follows:

- to provide information on education and training needs and opportunities, from a wide variety of sources;
- to provide quality control;
- to provide accreditation, through independent assessment of learning;
- to develop coherent curricula, where appropriate;
- to provide a service that will make the use of communications to import and export multimedia learning materials easy and user-friendly;
- to network learners and instructors, and to provide 'gateways' to other networks and education and training providers;
- to create high-quality educational multimedia materials in an easily accessible form;
- to conduct research into education and training needs;
- to apply new technologies, as they develop, to education and training, and to evaluate their use.

Note though that many of the instructors or tutors that are used will not 'belong' or work for the educational institution; many will be independent contractors, or working full-time in a knowledge-based industry, or working for another educational institution.

Nor will learners necessarily be 'registered' with that institution, in the sense of taking all or any courses. The institution is primarily a facilitator of learning. In the example of Sue and Wayne, all the educational institution may do is invoice, and collect and deliver payment, regarding fees and royalties, to and from Sue and Wayne, to the owners of the software, and possibly to the telecommunication carrier (plus a service charge).

In other cases, it may offer a full programme to groups of students with its own instructors and multimedia materials, leading to its own credential. In others, it will be like a multimedia reference library, with learners just accessing the information they need. It will be a mix of a public and commercial organisation, collecting fees for many of its services, where this is appropriate.

The internal multimedia network infrastructure

The heart of this service is the internal multimedia network infrastructure, that allows the institution to access, create and deliver educational multimedia services in a variety of formats and a variety of modes. The Open Learning Agency is developing an integrated information management approach that will include both administrative and instructional systems, based on a multimedia relational data-base (see Figure 11.3).

Basically, learning materials can be accessed and/or created in any format (video, audio, text, graphics, or any combination), and stored digitally. Course designers can access this material electronically, re-edit and re-create learning materials, store them, and export this learning material in a variety of formats (print, CD-ROM, or down-loaded to local work-stations), depending on the learners' needs.

This ability to deliver in a variety of formats will be essential over the next 10 years, because of the variable rate at which different individuals and 'markets' will have access to technology. Low-income single-parents may still need materials delivered by printed text and broadcast TV, because they cannot afford a computer, while the business corporation needs – and will pay for – multimedia delivered to the desk-top. Also, while the trend to mass and low-cost access to the information highway will widen the range of delivery options even to the relatively poor, it will not roll out evenly over the next 10 years. Urban and suburban areas are likely to be connected first to wideband networks.

The networked multimedia relational data-base will allow for the tracking of materials and services, the on-line payment of fees and charges for services, and student or client record-keeping (including grades and credentials), as well as providing management information on finances and learner activities. This infrastructure is connected through the information highway to multimedia servers or switches.

This vision for a system is not a utopia, nor even many years away. The wideband highways are at this moment being constructed, and should be in place within 10 years. Multimedia switches, using ATM technology, are now being built. Interfaces to the information highway, and software tools to facilitate multimedia learning, are being designed. The software for handling multimedia communications is being developed by companies such as Oracle.

However, the most difficult part of the system to put in place will be an

Educational Institution
production / brokering / management

Output

Input

**Interactive multimedia
network infrastructure**

Output

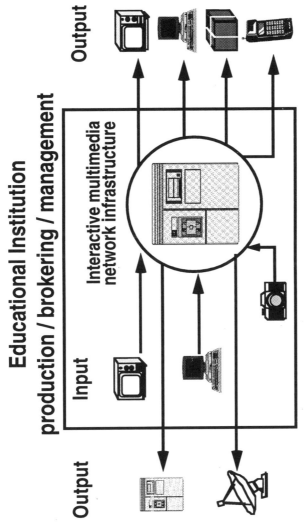

Figure 11.3 The internal multimedia relational data-base

appropriate educational infrastructure to support the kind of learning needed in the twenty-first century. The provision of appropriate education and training services to run on the information highway is critical; there is no automatic guarantee that people will use the information highway to an extent that justifies the cost of investment, if services are not provided that meet people's needs.

IMPLICATIONS FOR LEARNING

Mixed-mode learning

While schools, colleges and universities will still have reason to provide campus-based learning to groups of learners over set terms or semesters, for social and for some instructional reasons, a great deal of learning will take place outside of this context. Full-time students are *already* a minority in Canadian universities and colleges (British Columbia Ministry of Skills, Training and Labour, 1994).

Even with full-time students, it will be difficult to categorise them as either 'campus-based' or 'distance education' students within a few years. They will be accessing information and communicating with their instructors, other students, and other subject experts outside their own institution, through multimedia telecommunications, from home and the workplace.

Furthermore, multimedia telecommunications will allow them to do this whenever they want, in small chunks as well as in whole courses or programmes of study, thus making learning more flexible and accessible, to all ages of learners, and not just young people in the formal system. Learners will also have a much wider choice of sources of learning, being able to access expertise from anywhere in the world.

Hello, technology; goodbye, distance education?

The impact of technological change will be just as great on traditional distance education institutions, particularly single mode institutions, such as the British Open University, as on more conventional institutions. Indeed, modern two-way communications technologies enable conventional campus-based institutions to position themselves better, since they can offer not only highly interactive education·at a distance, but can also provide the on-campus facilities, such as laboratories and occasional opportunities for personal interaction, that are so difficult and costly for single-mode distance teaching institutions to provide.

This does not mean the large, autonomous, single-mode open universities will disappear quickly. They are still the most cost-effective means of providing standard mass education for large numbers. For countries such as India, China, and Indonesia, where most people do not yet have access to telephones or computers, single mode institutions that rely on the one-way mass media of print, television and radio will still have great value.

However, as countries develop economically, to the current status of those such as Singapore, Hong Kong, South Korea and Malaysia, with rapid penetration of telephones and computers into homes and businesses, they too will need to develop educational institutions that make use of two-way, interactive technologies, as they switch to an information-based economy.

Instructional strategies

As important as the context of learning will be the approaches to learning and instruction:

- multimedia telecommunications will allow learners and subject experts to engage in dialogue, questioning, and exploration of a wide range of alternative approaches, as well as the sharing and joint working of multimedia documents;
- programmes and instruction can be tailored to the needs of each individual;
- multimedia telecommunications can also encourage collaborative approaches to learning;
- learning will often occur without the direct intervention of a formal instructor, through the use of peers and people working in a job who have expertise;
- most important of all, as they learn through multimedia telecommunications, people will use the same tools and develop the same skills that will be an essential part of their work and leisure activities.

It is clear that the current approach of 'adding-on' technology to existing institutional structures not only fails to exploit fully the educational potential of technology, but actually increases the cost of education. In short, we need to examine very carefully the purpose and function of educational institutions in the twenty-first century, and use electronic technologies to build new institutional models to meet new educational needs.

DEFINING THE LIMITS OF TECHNOLOGY

To do this means being aware of the limits as well as the potential of technology. In particular, we need to define very carefully those areas where we do not *want* to use technology, even if we could. For instance, do we want children to learn social skills primarily through machines, or through direct interaction with other children? Do we want to develop machines to a level of sophistication that allow teachers to be replaced? Is efficiency the only criterion? Difficult questions need to be answered about the qualitative differences between face-to-face and mediated social interaction.

We need to understand far better than we do the social roles of education, and how these can best be met. I suspect that there will always need to be a balance between face-to-face contact at a local level, inter-personal contact through telecommunications, and interaction between an individual and a piece of technology, whether it be as 'primitive' as a book or as sophisticated as an intelligent talking computer. What we need to discover are the principles that determine this balance, and this means a lot more research into the social as well as the cognitive aspects of learning.

Lastly, we need to discriminate between the needs of different sectors of the educational world. Young children need the social context that schools provide, the opportunity to mix with children from different social and ethnic backgrounds, the opportunity to learn social skills in a safe, friendly but controlled environment. The younger the child, the greater the need for security, a rich social context, and the direct responsibility of a professional with a deep understanding of children's development, with the training to enable children to develop the social and ethical skills needed to live harmoniously in society.

In such an environment, technology can and should play a relatively minor role, enhancing the learning environment, and providing young people with the first steps towards technological mastery, but essentially subsidiary and minor to the other needs just described. Thus while computers and electronic networks will become increasingly available to young children as they grow up, they will still be primarily background tools within an essential face-to-face environment. For me, it would be a disastrous mistake, socially and educationally, to try to replace teachers with technology for children up to the age of 16 or so.

As they become older, and enter secondary or high school, there should be more opportunity for access to information through technology, more opportunity to develop the basic skills needed in a highly technological society, and more opportunity for mediated communication with young people of other cultures. Nevertheless, until towards the end of adolescence, the social context of schools and colleges will still be critical, because of the need for young people to mix with other young people of their own age, and also the need for some degree of direct adult control and guidance. Thus technology will increasingly provide the means through which adolescents access knowledge, but within an institutional framework that provides security and social and personal contact between young people and teachers.

It is at the post-secondary level where the greatest changes in institutional organisation are needed. As the full-time student studying consistently for three to four years to obtain a bachelor's degree becomes a minority in the post-secondary system, and more and more enrolments come from young students studying part-time as they work their way through college or university, or from mature students returning for further post-graduate education, or accessing post-secondary education for the first time while working and with families, so must post-secondary institutions provide greater flexibility and a wider range of ways to deliver services.

It is at this level where institutions need the greatest mix of provision. Some students will need or want to be on a campus, full-time, as much for social as educational reasons. They may not yet be ready for independent, self-directed study, and may still need the discipline and guidance of an institutional framework. Other students, while studying partly on campus, will need to access some learning and services off-campus, because of work or family commitments. Other students will be studying primarily off-campus, but will need to access facilities – such as laboratories, or summer schools – for specific purposes. Other students will need or want to study entirely off-campus. Furthermore, the more dependent they are on an institutional environment, the more important it becomes for the institution to help students develop independence and lifelong learning skills. The more students need to be independent of an institutional campus, the greater the value of educational technology.

Lastly, there are the increasingly important and growing numbers of mature learners who need to learn formally or informally in the work-place. Providing support for this group is an essential component for economic growth and development. This is the area where technological applications can be of most value.

POLICY MAKING: GOVERNMENTS AND INSTITUTIONS

What steps can be taken to develop an educational system adapted to the needs of the twenty-first century, and which fully exploits new technologies in a humanistic manner?

Teacher training

The major barrier to innovation, the use of technology, and alternative delivery methods within existing educational institutions is not lack of resources, although greater investment would help, nor lack of will or recognition of the need for change by their managements, nor even an ideological or philosophical objection by most teachers to the use of technology or to doing things differently. The major barrier is fear: most teachers do not feel comfortable with the technology, but most important of all, they do not know how to use it effectively.

The problem is not so much one of knowing how to use a particular technology, but the lack of an appropriate conceptual framework to guide the use of technology. Put simply, this means that many people with the responsibility to teach have not been given an appropriate instructional framework on which to base their practice.

At least most school teachers have a foundation in educational theory and practice. They have some knowledge of how children learn, and of different approaches to teaching. They understand what learning objectives are, how different levels of learning require different instructional approaches, and how children differ in the way they approach learning. This provides a basis for curriculum development, classroom organisation, children's group work, and the way they as teachers interact with the children individually and as a group.

In the post-secondary system, few with responsibility for teaching have such an instructional background. They are appointed because of their knowledge and expertise within a particular subject discipline, and/or their research performance. What they know of teaching has come primarily from their experience as students. Many become excellent teachers, through a deep understanding of their subject matter, and of what it requires for students to become experts in that subject area. Others have become good teachers through trial and error. Many others though with responsibility for instruction in colleges and universities never become proficient teachers. They copy the methods that were used to teach them. While this may have been acceptable in a stable education system, where one generation could learn in the same way as previous generations, this is not an adequate strategy for a society undergoing rapid change.

Thus it is essential, in order to use technology appropriately in education and training, to have a good grounding in educational theory and teaching practice. However, on its own, this is not enough. In addition to this basic knowledge, teachers must have some understanding of instructional design and the different, unique instructional characteristics of different technologies. However, even most people trained as school teachers do not have this element in their training. In a country such as Canada, for instance, there are only one or two institutions which provide any training whatsoever on the use of technology in education, as part of a regular baccalaureate or post-doctoral course of study. In the Open Learning Agency, most of our staff have to be trained in-house, or learn from experience on the job; there is nowhere for them to go in Western Canada to get these skills.

This is not rocket science. We would not expect general practitioners to be effective with training in science but not in skills of diagnosis and treatment. We would not expect pilots to fly an aeroplane with just a knowledge of aerodynamics. It is not surprising then that there is fear and resistance from educators to the use of technology.

Two things governments could do to foster more effective use of technology in education is to require, as a condition of appointment to any permanent or tenure track appointment in schools, colleges or universities, qualifications in instructional design and the use of educational technology; and they could establish, as a priority for funding, centres of excellence for education and training in these areas. Unless adequate re-training of teachers is made available, change and innovation in educational institutions will remain on the periphery.

The need for a system approach

Governments could also improve the cost-effectiveness of technology applications by taking a *system approach* to the development of educational communications. The more networks are shared, the greater the economies of scale. This means that all educational sectors – schools, colleges, institutes, universities, and even private training organisations – should, wherever possible, be on common networks and operating to common standards. Indeed, this should not be limited just to education, but should also include other government agencies, such as highways, health, and government administrative services.

Unfortunately, current practice in most countries is almost the opposite. Individual institutions are given autonomy to make their own decisions about equipment purchase and network developments. Telecommunications carriers and equipment suppliers therefore pick off individual institutions one by one, and sell them isolated services (compressed video conferencing in one institution, audio-graphics in another, analogue two-way television in a third). This means that often there is no inter-connectivity between institutions or services. Students in one location or educational institution cannot be linked to students or tutors in other institutions or locations. Each institution ratches up a number of different telecommunications costs (telephone, fax, data, video) independently, the sum of which comes to many millions of dollars or pounds. Governments miss the opportunity to buy services as a single client, through competitive bidding.

Governments, in consultation with carriers and educational institutions, need to develop policies for educational applications of telecommunications, to provide equity of access, common standards, a unified network strategy that includes all telecommunications services (voice, data, fax, video, etc.), and inter-connections both between institutions and with the external world (e.g. with the Internet). A unified network strategy needs to be accompanied by a detailed analysis of teaching and administrative applications required by institutions in order to determine likely traffic volumes, before appropriate technological decisions can be made. Lastly, governments need to act as large corporate clients, buying services *en bloc* from telecommunications companies through a competitive tendering process.

Volume of traffic is critical. Few individual institutions have been able to generate sufficient traffic to justify dedicated wide-band systems. On-demand services (i.e. services that allow educational organisations to pay for just the bandwidth used, rather than flat-rate charging) has obvious economic advantages for individual educational users. An alternative strategy to 'on-demand' services is to buy out from common carriers a dedicated, government-funded network that is shared between all educational (or all government) services. This has been done in Norway, and is the basis for the Supernet proposal in the USA, and the Canarie project in Canada. Governments either need to establish units within government which develop such policies or practices, or 'arms-length' organisations that can act as independent consultants to government.

Lastly, governments, who fund and regulate public educational institutions, need to promote radical innovation and change much more seriously than they have to date. Existing institutions, such as schools, colleges, and above all universities are extremely conservative, and slow to change. Governments usually put aside tiny sums of money, less than 1 per cent–2 per cent of operating funds, for innovation and change in education and training, while at the same time spending huge sums of money on capital investment, such as new buildings, that replicate or add to the stock of conventional education. This needs to be compared with investment in the telecommunications and computer industries for new products and services, which is often 10 per cent–15 per cent of revenues.

There are increasingly strident calls from the business sector and from right-wing politicians for radical reforms or even the replacement of the public education sector by technology (see for instance Perelman, 1992). Technological developments make it increasingly easier for private sector institutions to by-pass the public education system, and meet education and training needs that are not being addressed adequately by the public sector institutions. We are seeing private, technology-based high schools being created, and private corporate-based 'universities' being established, such as the Microsoft University, or the Novell diploma, that are increasingly being recognised as industry standards for training, promotion and job placement.

However, there will still be the need in the twenty-first century for the independence and academic freedom of the universities, for basic research that has no immediate direct application, but which advances knowledge and understanding and eventually leads to new commercial products, that asks questions and provides research that challenges power and privilege in society. We need public institutions that help develop social and ethical skills, as well as vocational skills, that provide a safe haven for the abused or handicapped child, that provide a richer cultural environment for young people which would be beyond the capability of their own family or social context. It would be a terrible tragedy if these institutions are destroyed by their own inability to adapt to the other changing needs of the twenty-first century. Technology is not the answer on its own; but it does have the potential to allow institutions to change and adapt from within, while retaining the essential components of a liberal education system.

A QUESTION OF CHOICE

A number of choices lie ahead:

1 *An extension of the status-quo*: technology as an add-on to current institutions; marginalised, unequal in provision; elitist: 70 per cent of the population cut off from technology and knowledge. This is not really an option – the system is already cracking, and it would be economic and social madness to continue down this road.
2 *Knowledge in a box or through a tap*: an increasingly centralised, impersonal education system, machine-driven, with knowledge treated as property and owned by large multi-national companies. This is a real possibility, and will be the predominant paradigm, if left to market forces.
3 *A networked society*: one with equal access to knowledge and information and humanistic applications of technology; communities and individuals in charge of their learning environments; government, educators and the private sector working in partnership; an education and training system delivering the skills and knowledge needed for a free and prosperous society in the twenty-first century.

The last option requires tough political decisions, regarding access to and regulation of telecommunications networks, copyright law, investment in educational materials and communications facilities, system planning and, above all, radical reform of public educational institutions.

Existing educational institutions were created to meet the needs of a society that is fast disappearing. We need new educational organisations that can exploit the new technologies to meet the needs of the twenty-first century. Economic development will depend as much on the success of creating and supporting such organisations, as on establishing the technological infrastructure. It is critical to get this right because those countries that harness the power of multimedia communications for education and training purposes will be the economic powerhouses of the twenty-first century.

Bibliography

Agency for International Development (1990) *Interactive Radio Instruction*, Newton, MA.: Education Development Centre.

Ahrens, S., Burt, G. and Gallagher, M. (1975) *M231: Analysis*, Milton Keynes: The Open University Institute of Educational Technology.

Bacsich, P. (1990) 'Electronic publishing in distance teaching universities' in Bates, A. (ed.) *Media and Technology in European Distance Education*, Heerlen: European Association of Distance Teaching Universities.

Baldwin, L. (1993) *Enabling Technical Professionals and Managers to Share Premier Educational Resources Globally via Telecommunications*, Fort Collins, CO: National Technological University.

Bates, A. W. (1975) *Student Use of Open University Broadcasting*, Milton Keynes: The Open University Institute of Educational Technology.

Bates, A. W. (1981) 'Some unique educational characteristics of television and some implications for teaching or learning' *Journal of Educational Television* Vol. 7, No. 3.

Bates, A. W. (1983) 'CYCLOPS: Where Now?' *Media in Education and Development* Vol. 16, No. 2.

Bates, A. W. (1984) *Broadcasting in Education*, London: Constable.

Bates, A. W. (1992) *Cost-Benefit Analysis of the Open Learning Agency's Activities: Part 2 Outputs and Expenditures by Functional Areas*, Burnaby, BC: The Open Learning Agency.

Bates, A. W. (1994) *Costing Distance Education Technologies* Burnaby, BC: The Open Learning Agency.

Bates, A. W. (1995) 'Research and development in distance education' in Lockwood, F. (ed.) *Open and Distance Learning Today*, London: Routledge.

Bates, A. W. and Gallagher, M. (1987) 'Improving the educational effectiveness of television case-studies and documentaries' in Boyd-Barrett, O. and Braham, P. (eds) *Media, Knowledge and Power*, London: Croom Helm.

Bates, A. W., Berrigan, F., Brown, D., Durbridge, N., Gallagher, M., Grundin, H., Lockwood, V. and Rodwell, S. (1981) *Radio: the Forgotten Medium?*, Milton Keynes: The Open University Institute of Educational Technology.

Beijderwellen, W. (1990) 'Interactive video in geology at the open university of the Netherlands' in Bates, A. W. (ed.) *Media and Technology in European Distance Education*, Heerlen: European Association of Distance Teaching Universities.

Black, D. (1992) *Lifelong Learners: An Overview of Distance Students at the Open Learning Agency, 1990–91*, Burnaby, BC: The Open Learning Agency.

Black, D. and Harasim, L. (1993) *The ISDN Distance Learning Trial: Evaluation of Phase 1* Burnaby, BC: The Open Learning Agency.

Black, D., Bischoff, P. and Bates, A. (1994) *Further Information on Open Learning Agency Distance Education Students*, Burnaby, BC: The Open Learning Agency.

Bloom, B. (ed.) (1956) *Taxonomy of Educational Objectives: The Classification of Educational Goals*, Handbook 1, *Cognitive Domain* New York: McKay.

Brey, R. (1991) *US Postsecondary Distance Learning Programs in the 1990s*, Washington, DC: Instructional Telecommunications Consortium/American Association of Community and Junior Colleges.

British Columbia Ministry of Skills, Training and Labour (1994) *Key Facts on Post-Secondary Education in British Columbia*, Victoria, BC: Ministry of Skills, Training and Labour.

Brown, D. (1980) 'New students and radio at the Open University' *Educational Broadcasting International*, Vol. 13, No. 1.

Brown, S. (1983) *The 1982 Video-Cassette Loan Service: a Report on the First Year of Operation*, Milton Keynes: The Open University Institute of Educational Technology.

Bruner, J. (1966) *Towards a Theory of Instruction*, Cambridge, MA.: Harvard University Press.

Burge, L. (1987) *Listening to Learn*, Toronto: OISE/CJRT-FM Open College.

Butcher, P., Laurillard, D. and Williams, K. (1989) 'Computer assisted learning numeracy software from the Open University Technology Foundation course', in Bates, A. W. (ed.) *Media and Technology in European Distance Education*, Heerlen: European Association of Distance Teaching Universities.

Canadian Labour Market Productivity Centre (1989) 'The linkages between education and training and Canada's economic performance' *Quarterly Labour Market and Productivity Review* Winter.

Castro, A. (1988) *Critical reflections on the introduction of computer-mediated communication into a distance-teaching institution*, Milton Keynes: The Open University Institute of Educational Technology.

Clark, R. (1983) 'Reconsidering research on learning from media' *Review of Educational Research*, Vol. 53, No. 4.

Conference Board of Canada (1991) *Employability Skills Profile: The Critical Skills Required of the Canadian Workforce*, Ottawa: The Conference Board of Canada.

Conklin, J. (1993) *Managing Diversity Video-conference: Cost–Benefit Analysis of Decentralized vs Centralized Delivery Approaches*, Burnaby, BC: Open Learning Agency.

Conway, C. (1991) *Computer Use, Attitudes, and Ownership among AU students: Implications for Computer-Mediated Course Delivery*, Athabasca, Alta: Athabasca University.

de Vries, F. and Huisman, W. (1989) 'Educational computer simulations at the Open University of the Netherlands' in Bates, A. W. (ed.) *Media and Technology in European Distance Education*, Heerlen: European Association of Distance Teaching Universities.

Durbridge, N. (1981) *The Use of Audio-Cassettes* in Bates, A. et al. (1981) *Radio: the Forgotten Medium?*, Milton Keynes: The Open University Institute of Educational Technology.

Durbridge, N. (1982) *EM235: Developing Mathematical Thinking*, Milton Keynes: The Open University Institute of Educational Technology.

Durbridge, N. (1983) *Design implications of audio and video cassettes*, Milton Keynes: Open University Institute of Educational Technology.

Durbridge, N. (1985) *Integrating television and audio-cassettes*, Milton Keynes: Open University Institute of Educational Technology.

Economist, The (1994) 'Schools brief: the manufacturing myth' Vol. 330, No. 7855 (March 19–25).

Employment Department, 1991 *How to Profit from Open Learning: Company Evidence*, Sheffield: Learning Technologies Unit.

Environics Research Group (1994) *National Survey of Post-Secondary Students' Preferences for Educational Material*, Toronto: Canadian Book Publishers' Council.

Friesen, V. (1991) *A Critique of Computer-Managed Instruction in the Light of Key Principles of Adult Education*, Burnaby, BC: Simon Fraser University, M.A. (Education) Thesis.

Fuenzalida, E. (1992) *Alfabetización y Postalfabetizatión por radio*, Madrid: Editorial Popular.

Gallagher, M. (1977) *Broadcasting and the Open University Student, 1976*, Milton Keynes: The Open University Institute of Educational Technology.

Garrison, D. R. (1989) *Understanding Distance Education: A Framework for the Future*, London: Routledge.

Gagné, R. (1985) *The Conditions of Learning and Theory of Instruction*, 4th edition, New York: Holt, Rinehart and Winston.

Godwin, M. (1994) 'Nine principles for making virtual communities work' *Wired* 2.06 (June).

Greenfield, P. (1984) *Mind and Media*, Cambridge, MA.: Harvard University Press.

Grundin, H. (1978) *The effect of transmission times on students' use of OU broadcasts*, Milton Keynes: The Open University Institute of Educational Technology.

────── (1980) *OU broadcasting times: a study of viewing and listening opportunities in 1978–79 and in the future*, Milton Keynes: The Open University Institute of Educational Technology.

────── (1981) *Open University Broadcasting Times and their Impact on Students' Viewing/Listening*, Milton Keynes: The Open University Institute of Educational Technology.

────── (1983) *Audio-visual media in the OU: Results of a survey of 93 courses*, Milton Keynes: The Open University Institute of Educational Technology.

────── (1984) *Audio-visual media in the OU: results of a survey of 93 courses*, Milton Keynes: The Open University Institute of Educational Technology.

────── (1985) *Report of the 1984 AV Media Survey*, Milton Keynes: The Open University Institute of Educational Technology.

Harasim, L. (1989) 'Online education: a new domain' in Mason, R. and Kaye, A. (eds) *Mindweave: Communication, Computers and Distance Education*, Oxford: Pergamon.

Harasim, L. (1990) (ed.) *On-Line Education: Perspectives on a New Environment*, New York: Praeger.

Harris, D. (1987) *Openness and Closure in Distance Education*, London: Falmer.

Hawkridge, D. and Robinson, J. (1982) *Organizing Educational Broadcasting*, London: Croom Helm.

Hezel Associates (1993) *Educational Telecomunications; The State-By-State Analysis*, Syracuse, NY: Hezel Associates.

Holmberg, B. (1983) 'Guided didactic conversation in distance education', in Sewart, D., Keegan, D., and Holmberg, B. (eds) *Distance Education: International Perspectives*, Croom Helm, London.

────── (1990) 'A paradigm shift in distance education? Mythology in the making' *International Council for Distance Education Bulletin* Vol. 22.

IBA (1988) *Annual Report* London: Independent Broadcasting Authority.

Iser, W. (1978) *The Act of Reading*, London: Routledge & Kegan Paul.

Johnson-Lenz, P. and Johnson-Lenz, T. (1993) 'Writing and wholeness: online islands of safety' in Mason, R. *Computer Conferencing: the Last Word*, Victoria, BC: Beach Holme.

Kaufman, D. (1989) in Sweet, R. (ed.) *Post-Secondary Distance Education in Canada: Policies, Practices and Priorities*, Athabasca: Athabasca University/ Canadian Society for Studies in Education.

Kirkwood, A. (1987) *Access to Micro-computing Equipment for Study Purposes – Undergraduate Students in 1986*, Milton Keynes: Open University Institute of Educational Technology.

Kirkwood, A. and Crooks, B. (1990) 'Video-cassettes by design' in Bates, A. (ed.) *Media and Technology in European Distance Education*, Netherlands: European Association of Distance Teaching Universities.

Latchem, C., Mitchell, I. and Atkinson, R. (1993) 'Videoconferencing networks and applications in Australian higher education' in Davies, G. and Samways, B. (eds) *Teleteaching*, Amsterdam: North Holland.

Laurillard, D. (1993) *Re-thinking University Teaching*, London: Routledge.

Loftus, G. and Loftus, L. (1983) *The Mind at Play*, New York: Basic Books.

Lorentsen, A. (1989) *Presentation and Analysis of 'Project Computer-Aided Distance Teaching': A Project at Jutland Open University*, Aalborg: Aalborg University, Department of Language and Intercultural Studies.

McConnell, D. and Sharples, M. (1983) 'Distance Teaching by CYCLOPS' *British Journal of Educational Technology*, Vol.14, No.2.

Malone, T. (1980) *What Makes Things Fun to Learn?*, Palo Alto, CA: Xerox.

Marland, P. et al. (1990) 'Distance learners' interaction with texts while studying' *Distance Education* Vol. 11, No.1.

Marton, F. and Säljö, R. (1976) 'On qualitative differences in learning I: outcome and process' *British Journal of Educational Psychology* Vol. 46.

Mason, R. (1989) 'An evaluation of CoSy on an Open University course' in Mason, R. and Kaye, A. (eds) *Mindweave: Communication, Computers and Distance Education*, Oxford: Pergamon.

Mason, R. (1993) 'The textuality of computer networking' in Mason, R. (ed.) *Computer Conferencing: the Last Word*, Victoria, BC: Beach Holme.

Mason, R. (1994) *Using Communications Media in Open and Flexible Learning*, London: Kogan Page.

Mason, R. and Kaye, A. (1989) *Mindweave: Communication, Computers and Distance Education*, Oxford: Pergamon.

Meed, J. (1974) *Classification of Radio Broadcasts; Format and Technique*, Milton Keynes: Open University Institute of Educational Technology.

Moore, M. and Thompson, M. (1990) *The Effects of Distance Education: A Summary of the Literature*, University Park, PA: American Centre for the Study of Distance Education.

Muzio, J. (1989) 'E-mail and electronic transfer of data files for a distance education course' in Mason, R. and Kaye, A. (eds) *Mindweave: Communication, Computers and Distance Education*, Oxford: Pergamon.

National Technological University (1992) *Annual Report, 1991–92*, Fort Collins, CO: National Technological University.

Nipper, S. (1989) 'Third generation distance learning and computer conferencing' in Mason, R. and Kaye, A. *Mindweave: Communication, Computers and Distance Education*, Oxford: Pergamon.

Northern Telecom (1991) *Distance Learning Using Digital Fibre Optics*, Richardson, TX: Northern Telecom Education Systems.

Olson, D. and Bruner, J. (1974) 'Learning through experience and learning through media' *Media and Symbols: The Forms of Expression*, Chicago: University of Chicago Press (The 73rd NSSE Yearbook).

Open University (1982) *Tutoring by Telephone: A Handbook*, Milton Keynes: Open University Press.

Open University (1988) *Delivery Technologies*, Milton Keynes: Open University Visiting Committee VCO(88)20.

Paivio, A. (1980) 'Imagery as a private audio-visual aid', *Instructional Science*, Vol. 9, No. 4.

Perelman, L. (1992) *School's Out*, New York: William Morrow.

Peters, O. (1983) 'Distance teaching and industrial production: a comparative interpretation in outline' in Sewart, D., Keegan, D., and Holmberg, B. (eds) *Distance Education: International Perspectives*, London: Croom Helm.

Piaget, J. (1970) *Science of Education and the Psychology of the Child*, London: Longmans.

Portway, P. and Lane, C. (1992) *Technical Guide to Teleconferencing and Distance Learning*, Applied Business Communications.

Postman, N. (1982) *The Disappearance of Childhood*, London: W.H. Allen.

Press, D. (1993) 'Desperately seeking connection', in Mason, R. (ed.) *Computer Conferencing: the Last Word*, Victoria, BC: Beach Holme.

Reiser, R. and Gagné, R. (1983) *Selecting Media for Instruction*, Englewood Cliffs, NJ: Educational Technology Publications.

Rekkedal, T. (1978) *Undervisning av Brevskoleelever*, Oslo: NKI-skolen.

Rekkedal, T. (1990) 'Recruitment and study barriers in the electronic college', in Paulsen, M. and Rekkedal, T. (eds) *The Electronic College: Selected Articles from the EKKO Project*, Bekkestua: NKI.

Riel, M. (1993) 'Global education through learning circles' in Harasim, L. (ed.) *Global Networks: Computers and International Education*, Cambridge, MA: The MIT Press.

Robinson, B. (1984) 'Telephone teaching' in Bates, A.W. (ed.) *The Role of Technology in Distance Education*, London: Croom Helm.

Robinson, B. (1990) 'Telephone teaching and audio-conferencing at the British Open University' in Bates, A,W. (ed.) *Media and Technology in European Distance Education*, Heerlen: European Association of Distance Teaching Universities.

Robinson, J. (1982) *Learning Over the Air*, London: BBC.

Rogers, C. (1969) *Freedom to Learn*, Columbus, OH: Charles E. Merrill Publishing Co.

Romiszowski, A. (1988) *The Selection and Use of Instructional Media*, New York: Kogan Page.

Rubin, J. (1989) 'Training technology in retail' in Tucker, R. (ed.) *Interactive Media: The Human Issues*, London: Kogan Page.

Rumble, G. (1986) *The Planning and Management of Distance Education*, London: Croom Helm.

Rumble, G. (1989) 'On-line costs: interactivity at a price' in Mason, R. and Kaye, A. *Mindweave: Communication, Computers and Distance Education*, Oxford: Pergamon.

Salomon, G. (1983) *Using television as a unique teaching resource*, Milton Keynes: The Open University Institute of Educational Technology.

Schlecter, T. (1988) 'An examination of the research evidence for computer-based instruction' in Hartson, R. and Hix, D. (eds) *Advances in Human–Computer Interactions, Volume 2*, Norwood, New Jersey: Ablex Publishing Corporation.

Schlecter, T. (1990) 'The relative instructional efficiency of small-group computer-based training' *Journal of Educational Computing Research* Vol. 6, No. 3, 329–41.

Schramm, W. (1972) *Quality in Instructional Television*, Honolulu, HI: University Press of Hawaii.

Schramm, W. (1977) *Big Media, Little Media*, Beverley Hills, CA: Sage.

Schwartz, E. (1994) 'Interrupt-driven' *Wired* 2.06 (June).

SCN (1992) *Saskatchewan Communication Network Annual Report, 1991–92*, Regina: SCN.

Self, J. (1989) 'The case for formalizing student models (and Intelligent Tutoring Systems generally) *4th International Conference on Artificial Intelligence*, Amsterdam.

Skinner, B. (1968) *The Technology of Teaching*, New York: Appleton-Century-Croft.

Søby, M. (1990) 'Traversing distances in education: the PortaCOM experiment', in Bates, A.W. (ed.) *Media and Technology in European Distance Education*, Netherlands: European Association of Distance Teaching Universities.

Sparkes, J. (1984) 'Pedagogic differences between media' in Bates, A. (ed.) *The Role of Technology in Distance Education*, London: Croom Helm.

Stahmer, A. and Green, L. (1993) *Analysing Costs/Benefits of Training Technologies: Some Guidelines*, Toronto: The Training Technology Monitor.

Statistics Canada (1992) *Labour Force Survey*, Ottawa: Ministry of Industry, Science and Technology.

Statistics Canada (1993) *Household Facilities by Income and Other Characteristics*, Ottawa: Ministry of Industry, Science and Technology.

Stone, H. (1992) *Use of Videoconferencing at Rennselaer Polytechnic Institute*, Washington, DC: United States Distance Learning Association Conference.

Teles, L. (1993) 'Cognitive apprenticeship in global networks' in Harasim, L. (ed.) *Global Networks*, Cambridge, MA: MIT Press.

Teles, L. and Laks, A. (1993) *Virtual Interactive Environments for Workgroups: A Broadband Educational Application*, Burnaby, BC: The Open Learning Agency.

Trenaman, J. (1967) *Communication and Comprehension*, London: Longmans.

UNESCO (1986) *Statistical Yearbook*, 1986 Paris: UNESCO.

van der Brande, L. (1993) *Flexible and Distance Learning*, New York: John Wiley.

van Meurs, C. and Bouhuijs, P. (1989) 'Tele-education: An experiment on home computing at the Dutch Open University' *Open Learning* Vol. 4, No.1.

Verduin, J. and Clark, T. (1991) *Distance Education: The Foundations of Effective Practice*, San Francisco: Jossey-Bass.

Vernon, P. (1950) 'The intelligibility of broadcast talks' *BBC Quarterly*, Vol. 5.

Wagner, L. (1982) *The Economics of Educational Media*, London: Macmillan.

Weimer, B. (1992) 'Assumptions about university–industry relationships in continuing professional education: a re-assessment', *European Journal of Education* Vol. 27, No. 4.

Wells, R. (1992) *Computer-mediated Communication for Distance Education: An International Review of Design, Teaching and Institutional Issues*, University Park, PA: American Centre for the Study of Distance Education, Pennsylvania State University.

Winograd, T. and Flores, F. (1986) *Understanding Computers and Cognition*, Norwood, NJ: Ablex Publishing Corporation.

Name index

Subject index